Compliments of

AIM

INVESTMENTS

The Winner's Circle®
Asset Allocation Strategies from America's **Best** Financial Advisors

Foreword by Gene L. Needles, Jr.,
President & CEO, AIM Distributors, Inc.

R.J. Shook

HORIZON
Publishers Group

Library of Congress Cataloguing-in-Publication Data
Shook, R.J. (Robert James)
    The Winner's Circle: Asset Allocation Strategies from America's Best
Financial Advisors / R.J. Shook
    p. cm.
    ISBN 0-9721622-9-1
1. Financial Advisors—United States. 2. Investing.
I. Shook, Robert J.,   II. Title
338.7—dc21   2007

This publication is designed to provide accurate and authoritative information to the subject matter covered. It is sold with the understanding that neither the publisher nor the author is engaged in rendering legal, accounting, or other professional services. If legal advice or other expert assistance is required, the services of a competent professional person should be sought. The views expressed by these advisors may not represent the views expressed by their companies.

—From a Declaration of Principles Jointly Adopted by a Committee of the American Bar Association and a Committee of Publishers and Associations

The Winner's Circle® is a registered trademark of The Winner's Circle, LLC.

ISBN 0-9721622-9-1

Published by

HORIZON
Horizon Publishers Group
Printed in the United States

10 9 8 7 6 5 4 3 2

To the loves of my life—
Elisabeth, Jacob, Jamie-Brooke and Jeremy

CONTENTS

APPENDICES

ACKNOWLEDGMENTS

Hundreds of people contribute to the success of The Winner's Circle Organization and this book, and I appreciate all of their hard work, dedication, and passion for our mission of promoting best practices in the industry and the value of advice to investors. The *Winner's Circle* simply wouldn't exist without the tremendous support from the entire industry, ranging from the industry leaders that serve on our advisory board and home office support, to the *Winner's Circle* financial advisors that are dedicated to giving back to our industry.

Special gratitude is also due to the members of The Winner's Circle Organization who took the time to contribute to this book. These financial advisors need not seek publicity. Their dedication to clients keeps them busy enough. However, they are dedicated to giving back to the industry to help raise standards.

Other industry professionals have contributed countless hours toward the *Winner's Circle*, to whom I am very appreciative: Jim Wiggins, Andrea Slattery, Erica Platt, Greg Tevis, Katrina Clay, Tracy Story, Jan Weith, Paul Lockwood, Kimberly Lemmon, Laura Norman, Andrea Dagnelli, Michelle Creeden, Gerty Simon, Lisa Palmer, Kandis Bates, Nicole Walters, Jana Hunter, Doug Fecci, Anne Jeffres, Joanne Caruso, Latoya Henry, and Jeannette Weaver.

Like the advisors in this book, I rely on a world-class team to help with the editing, writing, and administration. This includes my incredibly reliable writer, Jordan Gruber; Marty Hester, who orchestrated this project and is a vital member of the Winner's Circle team; editor Claire Zuckermann; Debbie Watts; and Brian Boucher for cover design. And importantly, my world-class agent Al Zuckerman and other professionals at Horizon Publishers Group.

FOREWORD

By Gene L. Needles, Jr.
President and CEO
AIM Distributors, Inc.

It's been more than six years since the tech bubble burst. And though the Dow subsequently passed 11,000, investors are still eyeing the markets with extreme caution. Ironically, experts largely agree that investor behavior is as much to blame as other factors for the market blowup in 1999–2000.

Emotion-based investment decisions, a herd mentality, and the so-called "recency bias" (a tendency to focus on recent market movement and project it onto future conditions) are just a few of the elements that led investors to "irrational exuberance" in 1999 over dot.com and other tech companies. That painful lesson begs a couple of questions: What did we learn? What would investors have done differently if they had known then what they know now?

I'm certain that those who didn't have a financial advisor in 1999 would go right out and get one if they could relive the past, and I hope the first thing they would discuss with that advisor is asset allocation, that is, putting together an appropriately diversified investment portfolio reflecting the needs, goals, and risk tolerance of the client. Asset allocation is one of the best tools available to help advisors manage investors' expectations about their finances—especially when emotions begin to dictate investment decisions.

The advisors profiled in this book not only understand and believe in the importance of asset allocation, they know how to practice it. In these pages, you'll find methods used by top-notch advisors that you can apply to working with your own clients, tips and advice from leaders in the field on how to use asset allocation to manage clients' portfolios—and expectations—through good markets and bad.

The approaches and techniques described in this book vary, but whether they are building a portfolio from scratch or using turnkey asset allocation products, *Winner's Circle* advisors have one thing in common: First they make the effort to know their clients, not only their baseline information such as risk tolerance and time horizon, but who they are fundamentally—their hopes, fears, and dreams.

They take the time to understand who their clients are as people so that they can better understand who they are as investors—and then they help their clients to understand themselves as well.

The *Winner's Circle* advisors know that only an increased level of knowledge will result in a truly appropriate asset allocation for any given client. And only through appropriate asset allocation can investors avoid repeating mistakes and stay focused on their long-term goals.

Shakespeare said, "What is past is prologue." I believe *Winner's Circle* advisors would disagree. These talented investment professionals understand that history doesn't have to repeat itself. If you apply lessons learned in the past to your current business practice and educate the clients who entrust you with their financial well-being, then—armed with experience and knowledge—you can help them build a well-diversified portfolio that's appropriate for their individual needs and goals.

I encourage you to read what these men and women have to say about their approach to asset allocation and consider how you might incorporate their winning strategies into your own practice. I have no doubt both you and your clients will benefit.

ABOUT GENE L. NEEDLES, JR.

Gene Needles serves as director, chairman, president, and chief executive officer of AIM Distributors, Inc. as well as director and executive vice president of AIM Management Group Inc. and director of AIM Global Holdings, Inc. and AIM Global Ventures Co.

Mr. Needles joined AIM in 1982 and has nearly a quarter of a century of investment industry experience. Prior to AIM, he was a wholesaler for both Putnam Investments and State Street Research, as well as a retail broker in Chicago and Cedar Rapids, Iowa. In addition to his experience in financial services, Mr. Needles also managed a district congressional office for Congressman Berkley Bedell. A native of Chicago, Mr. Needles now resides in Houston, Texas, where AIM is headquartered.

AIM was founded in 1976 and entered the mutual fund market with the first high-yield bond offering. In the subsequent 30 years, AIM expanded beyond mutual funds and now offers products that include not only traditional mutual funds, but college savings products, separately managed accounts, retirement products, offshore funds, cash products, structured products, and, most recently, exchange-traded funds.

INTRODUCTION

By R.J. Shook
Founder, The Winner's Circle Organization

I have a burning passion not only to identify America's outstanding financial advisors, but to learn everything I can from them and share that knowledge with the industry. It's good for the advisors and it's good for the firms. Most importantly, it's good for the clients.

To satisfy this passion, over a decade ago I began to compile lists of outstanding advisors—based on both quantitative and qualitative data—something that had not been done before. The ultimate result has been four *Winner's Circle* books to date, as well as *The Winner's Circle Organization* itself, which is dedicated to identifying and honoring America's outstanding financial advisors while promoting the highest levels of integrity, ethics, and professionalism.

I've been extremely privileged to speak with hundreds of these top advisors, as well as their clients and management. Throughout these conversations, one topic and one skill—or perhaps I should say, one art and science—has continually come up as having great importance: *asset allocation.* As the pragmatic wing of Modern Portfolio Theory (MPT), which was essentially invented by Harry Markowitz and his peers starting in 1952, asset allocation is a systematic way of diversifying our portfolios and spreading our investments among a wide variety of asset classes that are not perfectly correlated with one another That is, as some asset classes perform poorly, others perform well and vice versa. Asset allocation thereby enables us to most efficiently manage the trade-off between risk and reward. Put differently, when an entire portfolio—and not just the individual stocks, bonds, and other investments that make it up—is considered, we can invest so that for any given level of risk we can maximize likely return, or so that for any desired level of return, we can minimize the likely risk. (The "likely" part comes in here because an ideal asset allocation mix can be determined only retrospectively, and, as we all know far too well, past performance does not guarantee future results.)

In a world of random walks and efficient market pricing, where a general consensus has arisen that consistently picking stocks or timing the market is either impossible, extremely difficult, or simply the province of the very best money managers, the importance of asset allocation stands out in even greater relief. Why? Because *asset allocation really works*, both theoretically—there is an especially sweet *aha!* that often strikes individuals the first time they really "get" the core mathematical truth behind asset allocation and what's been called the "efficient frontier"—and practically. Yes, criticisms of asset allocation can be made, but even the critics admit that it is about the best thing going in the financial investment world, an actual silver bullet of sorts that can be deployed in a wide variety of ways by advisors to reliably serve the highest needs, goals, objectives, and dreams of their clients.

ASSET ALLOCATION AND THE TECH BUBBLE

Unfortunately, the lessons delivered by the steady accumulation of wealth that can result from consistently practicing asset allocation (including, for example, regular rebalancing to bring portfolios back to the desired optimal mix) were overlooked or ignored by many investors *and their advisors* during the dot.com bubble and subsequent crash (see Chapter 12, Stories & Lessons: The Tech Bubble, 9/11, and Beyond). Far too many advisors were—and still are—just pitching and trading their favorite stocks and other products. Time and again they end up losing their clients' money, hurting those who entrusted them with so very much. Given what we know about asset allocation and the importance of truly serving the long-term interests of clients, this makes little sense and borders on the shameful.

Admittedly, a top-flight manager must have many skills and character traits to thrive and survive in today's world, *it's a simple, indisputable truth that no advisor worth his or her salt can afford to lack a basic knowledge of asset allocation and related subjects.* These include MPT, the efficient frontier, portfolio construction, rebalancing, the variety of asset classes and new investment opportunities to consider, strategic versus tactical asset allocation, and, most importantly, the various technical investment and behavioral finance factors that go into choosing or constructing a portfolio that is uniquely tailored to the individual needs, risk tolerance, and life goals of each client.

This last point is a critical one and is well worth repeating: Virtually every advisor I've spoken with said that the *individual relationship* he or she had with each client was at the core of their practice, in particular when it comes to asset allocation. When done right, it is always custom-tailored (even when that means picking the right "lifestyle" fund or "fund of funds," or the right mix of such funds for less affluent clients). Those clients who (with the help of their advisors) stuck with sensible asset allocations all the way through the recent tech bubble and bust suffered far, far less than those who chased "hot" tech stocks and related investments.

There is another good reason why every financial advisor should master asset allocation. In a recent survey of *Winner's Circle* advisors who serve affluent clients, one of the top reasons these advisors were winning new business was their asset allocation expertise and the overall investment perspective that they offer clients. In fact, many advisors told me that after their personal relationship, what their clients valued most was their asset allocation strategy (in fact, the two go hand in hand). Without this expertise, advisors are well positioned to lose business, especially in the high-net-worth arena.

A DIVERSITY OF BEST PRACTICES AND THINKING

This book is written for both financial advisors and interested and savvy investors. (But let me be up front here: Because of the skill required and the many emotional issues and factors that come into play, I advise everyone to work with a reputable advisor, preferably one who shares the same characteristics as *The Winner's Circle* advisors we study. It's just too hard to keep your own emotions in check when things go wrong, and that's one of the times when an advisor can make a huge difference. Even when things look bleak, or when a particular asset class is underperforming, a good advisor can help you hold steady to your overall asset allocation and prevent you from turning a small setback into a major series of losses. Moreover, as Richard Bernstein, Merrill Lynch's Chief U.S. Strategist and Chief Quantitative Analyst, astutely points out in his book *Navigate the Noise* (Wiley, 2001), "It is virtually impossible to assess your own risk tolerance. Very few people can objectively critique themselves, and the psychological aspect to investing should never be ignored." Despite my own background in research and as an advisor, I wouldn't dream of not working with a top-flight advisor when my own investment portfolio—and therefore my family's future—is at stake. So, go it alone if you must, but it's not something I would recommend to anybody.)

Whether you are an advisor or an investor, this book represents an opportunity to gain both practical knowledge and theoretical insight from some of the best advisors in America. As with other books in *The Winner's Circle* series, we therefore focus on the advisors themselves: their ideas, their thinking, their stories, their successes and failures, and what they think is especially important for others to know. Bottom line: No one should have to reinvent the wheel and suffer setbacks. I like to see advisors learn from the best so they can become the best, as they focus on doing a great job for their clients.

Just as there are a wide variety of successful advisory business models, there are many ways to practice asset allocation successfully. A wide range of *Winner's Circle* advisors have been interviewed for this book, from those who have just a few dozen extremely wealthy clients to those who practice asset allocation on behalf of up to thousands of relatively modest retail clients, and from those whose specialty is individual portfolio management to those who are primarily institutional consultants. Ideas from such widely divergent advisory practices will make you more likely to *find practical wisdom that resonates with your own practice and the needs of your clients.* In any case, you'll undoubtedly benefit from hearing what such a wide range of fantastically successful practitioners have to say on this subject.

So please, whether you read this book straight through (which I recommend) or whether you go right to the chapters that interest you the most, make sure to pick and choose the techniques, tactics, and strategies that resonate most strongly with you, the ones that feel really right for you and your clients. It's a little like asset allocation itself: By listening to the advice of a variety of advisors on a wide range of subjects, you can maximize your knowledge while minimizing your risk of following a strategy that will hurt you or your clients!

Then, it's your job to test what is offered here in the crucible of your own day-to-day investment practice. Thinking about asset allocation won't do any good, but actually practicing the collected wisdom here in a disciplined manner can make all the difference. Asset allocation is here to stay, and, on behalf of *The Winner's Circle,* I invite you to drink deeply from the wisdom and strategies gathered here as you expand the limits of just how good a financial advisor and investment practitioner you can be.

R.J. Shook
Founder & President
The Winner's Circle Organization

CHAPTER 1: ASSET ALLOCATION: AN OVERVIEW

These days, when a client asks a competent and trustworthy financial advisor to help with investing his or her life savings, a number of things tend to happen almost automatically. For example, it almost goes without saying that the advisor will begin by learning about the client's life situation in some depth, especially the client's financial and life goals, time horizon, risk tolerance, and more.

Then, with a deep-in-the-bones knowledge that greater returns can be achieved only by taking on greater risk (and that the consistent picking of stocks or timing of the market is extremely difficult or perhaps even impossible), the advisor *will propose to the client a portfolio that includes more than just one or two stocks or bonds*. In fact, it's well understood today that in most cases, a sensible portfolio should include a balance of investments from several different types or "classes" of assets. Further, within those asset classes, there may very well be a diversity of specific investment vehicles—stocks that are unlike each other, bonds that are unlike each other, alternative investments that are unlike each other—so that no one type or class of investment, and no one type of industry or even country, is overly represented. In this way, if things go poorly for a particular industry, country, or class of assets, the client's overall portfolio won't be too terribly hurt. In fact, some of the assets can be expected to perform well while others are doing poorly.

The importance of having a sensible asset allocation may be well understood today, but this wasn't always the case. Despite the age-old wisdom of "not putting all one's eggs in one basket," it was not uncommon as recently as 25 years ago for individuals, and to a lesser extent, institutions, to be invested in a much more concentrated way, and therefore be vulnerable to much greater loss. Consider, for example, the situation in this country just before the Panic of 1893 (which led to what was then the worst financial crisis ever faced by the United States). With railroads constituting a large percentage of the capitalization of the entire U.S. stock market, imagine the number of individuals and institutions that must have had all or nearly all of their money invested in the railroads and associated companies that calamitously failed.

Unfortunately, we still see this type of overconcentration today. For example, the successful corporate executive who receives company stock as part of his or her compensation and who does not sell any of that stock and diversify his or her holdings may face a similar situation. Similarly, individuals who get caught up in a "hot" sector, such as large-cap technology and communications stocks in the late 1990s, will sometimes—despite the advice of their advisors—put all or nearly all of their assets into this one basket. (Some of the lessons learned from the tech bubble will be covered in detail in Chapter 12.)

While once a new concept, asset allocation, and the economic theory that gave rise to it—Modern Portfolio Theory or "MPT"—are now the gold standard by which financial advisors are judged. John Mauldin, in *Bull's Eye Investing* (Wiley, 2004), writes that "Modern Portfolio Theory has become the sine qua non, the gold standard of investing ... There are hundreds of studies that illustrate the superiority of portfolios constructed with MPT." Burton G. Malkiel echoes this sentiment in his classic *A Random Walk Down Wall Street* (Norton, 2003): "One insight—modern portfolio theory—is so basic that it is now widely followed on the Street." Malkiel further adds that MPT "has revolutionized the investment thinking of professionals." But where did MPT and asset allocation come from in the first place?

THE ORIGINS OF MODERN PORTFOLIO THEORY AND ASSET ALLOCATION

As described in Appendix B, "A Brief History of Asset Allocation," in 1952, at the age of 25, Harry Markowitz came up with then revolutionary insights. Markowitz realized *first that investors must focus on their entire portfolio, not just on the individual stocks and other assets within it, and second that investors must focus not only on the possible rewards of investing, but on the risks of investing as well.* By equating risk with volatility, by measuring volatility through the mathematical concept of standard deviation and by seeing how different assets in a portfolio related to each other through the mathematical concept of covariance and a simple-to-understand graph known as the "efficient frontier," Markowitz laid the necessary groundwork for what would become the modern practice of asset allocation. Markowitz would later win the Nobel Prize in economics for his contribution.

Modern Portfolio Theory spread slowly at first and remained primarily in the province of academia through the 1960s. In the 1970s asset allocation came into practical use in certain institutional investment settings. By the late 1970s and early 1980s, asset allocation was being deployed for the benefit of ultrahigh-net-worth clients. In part, this increasing usage was facilitated by the wider availability of computers capable of retrospectively reconstructing the efficient frontier and making future predictions as to portfolios with the best risk/return trade-off.

While MPT and asset allocation had been increasingly taught in undergraduate finance courses, business schools, and industry training programs, it was a 1986 study by Gary Brinson that brought asset allocation widespread attention. The study, which examined the performance of 91 pension funds over at least 40 quarters, purported to show that 90 percent of the return variability between funds was attributable not to stock picking or stock timing, but simply to the asset allocation that was used. While this study has been questioned (see Appendix B), its basic premise—that asset allocation is by and large a considerably more important and reliable factor than stock picking or stock timing—remains unquestioned.

Today, asset allocation is nearly universally accepted throughout the financial services industry and the investment community generally. (Asset allocation is, of course, not without its critics, as discussed in Chapter 11.) As Stephen J. Huxley and J. Brent Burns write in their book *Asset Dedication* (McGraw-Hill, 2005), "Asset allocation became the dominant paradigm of investment strategy in the late 1980s ... and asset allocation remains the preeminent model used throughout the investment industry today." It would be hard to dispute the assertion that virtually all financial advisors at every level of expertise are, or should be, familiar with its basics. There is somewhat less agreement, however, about exactly what asset allocation is, the meaning of some of the underlying terms, and precisely how one should go about it.

THE VARIETIES OF ASSET ALLOCATION

Consider the term "asset allocation" itself. On the one hand, "asset allocation" can refer to the way that the investments in a portfolio are set or allocated into different asset classes at any given time. (After they are set, they will typically be "rebalanced" on some regular or irregular schedule, a topic covered in detail in Chapter 8.) On the other hand, "asset allocation" can refer to the action or activity of allocating assets. "What does the asset allocation of your portfolio look like?" is an example of the first usage. "How do advisors in your firm typically perform asset allocation?" is an example of the second. Finally, "asset allocation" can be thought as an entire approach or school of thought on how to best satisfy the investment needs of individuals and institutions, especially with respect to balancing risk and return.

Asset allocation can also have distinctly different technical meanings. David M. Darst, Chief Investment Strategist of Morgan Stanley's Global Wealth Management Group, in his extraordinary volume *The Art of Asset Allocation* (McGraw-Hill, 2003), lists four different fundamental meanings of asset allocation:

- Blending underlying characteristics of various asset classes to produce a stronger composite than any single element
- Recognizing and balancing trade-offs including time horizon, capital-preservation goals, and expected sources of return
- Setting minimum and maximum constraints to ensure sufficient representation, but not overconcentration
- Diversifying asset classes to align portfolio and personal risk/reward profiles and to be compensated for bearing nondiversifiable volatility

Darst also points out that "asset allocation" may mean different things to professional investors and individual investors. Taking this a step further, the way "asset allocation" is understood and practiced by institutional investors and their advisors, by high-net-worth investors and their advisors, and by retail investors and their advisors, may be significantly different. Institutional investors, for example, may be more likely to make use of cutting-edge computerized statistical programs (such as mean-variance optimization programs) to analyze various portfolio possibilities and make choices in concert with an institution's long-term goals and investment horizon; high-net-worth investors may receive a great deal of individualized attention from their advisors, who, having determined their risk tolerance vis-à-vis their financial needs and other goals, may recommend a certain portfolio to them based on asset allocation principles (trying to place them on Markowitz's efficient frontier, the line of optimal risk/return); and retail clients may find that their needs are best served by answering a questionnaire that helps place them into one of a few investor categories (conservative, moderate, aggressive) and then being placed into just a few investments or a "fund of funds" or "lifestyle fund" that satisfies their needs.

There will, of course, be many blendings of these different "types" of asset allocation by different advisors to fit the needs of individual clients. The point, however, is that depending on the economic starting point of the investor (institutions are generally very different from high-net-worth investors, who in turn are very different from middle-class investors), "asset allocation" may refer to a substantially different set of activities, resulting in quite different outcomes. For example, Chapter 8 will cover the critical activity of rebalancing, whereby the assets within a portfolio are reallocated from their existing mix by selling some assets and buying others. Rebalancing can be undertaken strategically, tactically, or in an ad hoc manner, and according to very different timetables (as often as weekly and as infrequently as yearly or biyearly), resulting in widely differing portfolios and rates of real return.

Significantly, there is also disagreement as to some of the underlying *definitions of terms* that come into use with respect to asset allocation. Chief among these is the term "asset class" or just "class." Jim Hansberger (Smith Barney, Atlanta, Georgia) states that "despite all the hullabaloo, there are basically only four asset classes: private and public equities (stock), fixed income (bonds, mortgages, credit structures, etc.), commodities, and currencies. That's it. Everything else falls as a subsector." Others argue that there are many more asset classes, especially when asset class subcategories are included. Darst (McGraw-Hill, 2003), for example, gives the following breakdown of asset classes and asset class subcategories:

- *Equity:* U.S. equity; non-U.S. equity; emerging markets equity
- *Fixed-Income:* U.S. fixed income; high yield; non-U.S. fixed income; emerging markets debt; convertible securities; inflation-indexed bonds
- *Alternative Assets:* private equity; commodities; real estate; hedge funds; gold; art
- *Cash* (and cash equivalents)

Then, of course, within most of these asset class subcategories, there is a further breakdown. For example, Darst states that U.S. equity can be further broken down into large-cap, mid-cap, small-cap, micro-cap, growth, value, core, preferred stock, master limited partnerships, and options and futures.

The point here isn't to try to arrive at a definitive description of what the "true" set of asset classes and subclasses are, but rather to illustrate that different advisors and investors may see asset classes in very different ways. Ultimately, there is no single "right" answer to such definitional quandaries, and this book will attempt to steer clear of purposefully or unconsciously choosing one side over the other.

Instead, the advisors whose wit and wisdom constitute the bulk of this book will be allowed to speak in their own voices, using their own terms, with context making their meaning clear.

THE BOTTOM LINE: IT REALLY WORKS

Why does asset allocation hold such a prominent place in the minds of most advisors, fund managers, and savvy investors? Simply, because it really works. The unassailable core truth of asset allocation begins with the common sense notion of "not putting all one's eggs in one basket." It is then not too hard to demonstrate to almost anyone how, in the context of an investment portfolio, adding relatively uncorrelated investments can lower risk without substantially diminishing (and in some cases, actually increasing) return. Similarly, the efficient frontier—where Harry Markowitz was able to visually demonstrate optimal risk/return trade-off combinations (at least retrospectively) on a straightforward graph—is intuitively graspable and makes simple sense. In his book *Straight Talk on Investing* (Wiley, 2002), Jack Brennan, Chairman and CEO of The Vanguard Group, sums up the benefits of asset allocation:

> If you hold a portfolio that's balanced across the asset classes and diversified within those asset classes, you'll avoid the risk that goes with pinning all your hopes on one company's stocks or bonds. Your balanced, well-diversified portfolio will be less volatile than one that has concentrated holdings ... If you have a portfolio that's better equipped to ride out the ups and downs in the markets, you're likely to sleep easier at night. This isn't just academic theory. It's a real-life strategy that works.

If Brennan is right, we would expect asset allocation to hold a central place in the hearts and minds of America's best financial advisors. This is exactly what the research interviews conducted for this book have shown. Jon Goldstein (Smith Barney, Menlo Park, California), who specializes in family office services for ultrahigh-net-worth clients, needs only a few words to say it: "Asset allocation is the very foundation of what we do." Tim Kneen (Citigroup Institutional Consulting, Englewood, Colorado), who in addition to advising his own ultrahigh-net-worth clients serves as an institutional portfolio management consultant, frames it in military terms: "Ever since I can remember, I knew that asset allocation was what you had to be able to win if you were going to win the war."

Louis Chiavacci (Merrill Lynch, Coral Gables, Florida), who also specialized in ultrahigh-net-worth clients, explains why asset allocation is *de rigueur:* "Asset allocation is one of the few free lunches in the financial world. It works if done smartly. It is the reduction of risk without necessarily any loss of return and perhaps even an incremental return over a comparable nondiversified portfolio." Meg Green (Royal Alliance, North Miami Beach, Florida), who has a mixture of high-net-worth and retail clients, makes the point with a food metaphor: "Just like you can't learn about the restaurant business and food preparation without knowing that there's bread, you can't learn about investing without knowing about asset allocation. Basically, asset allocation comes with the territory: You never put too many eggs in one basket."

If we can talk about asset allocation in cooking terms, is it fair to say that there are as many ways to undertake asset allocation as there are ways to cook a nutritious, delicious, and cost-effective meal? While certain elements of asset allocation are scientific and frequently recur, other elements are much more subtle, more intuitive than rational, and uniquely dependent on the circumstances of the client at hand. In other words, asset allocation is truly as much an art as it is a science.

THE ART AND SCIENCE OF ASSET ALLOCATION

Asset allocation is a skill, a practice, an art, and a science. The "science" part mainly concerns mathematical models, the understanding of risk and volatility, notions such as optimal trade-offs of risk and return along Markowitz's efficient frontier, and sophisticated spreadsheets and modeling programs that help advisors construct appropriate portfolios in a more automated and efficient fashion. But the "science" of asset allocation and MPT can take us only so far.

It is in the skill, the practice, and the art of asset allocation that the rubber really meets the road. For example, moving beyond questionnaires, how does an advisor efficiently and accurately determine his or her client's risk tolerance? How well must an advisor know a client before making such a determination? How much experience does an advisor need to have before he can know, in his heart of hearts, that he has accurately assessed his client's risk tolerance vis-à-vis the client's needs, goals, and dreams?

And what about the actual construction of a portfolio? How much of this can be done mechanically, relying on home office recommendations and computer programs, and how much of it comes down to the advisor's gut feelings and wisdom? How does an advisor know when to override his or her intellectual assumptions and follow a strong gut feeling instead? When should an advisor stick to tried-and-true asset classes, and when should an advisor feel comfortable in choosing an alternative investment that offers much promise but also an unknown amount of risk? How many classes of assets should be included, and, within those classes, how many subclasses? How favorably should hedge funds, index funds, turnkey asset allocation funds, or alternative investments (of many different types) be treated?

What about rebalancing? How often, really, should an advisor recommend that clients rebalance their portfolios? What if there is a sudden change in interest rates, a natural disaster, or another national emergency? How can an advisor know when more rapid, tactical readjustments of a portfolio are called for and when to stick with what initially seemed a very sensible asset allocation?

Similarly, consider the best way to bring a client fully on-board with the asset allocation process. How deeply does an advisor want to go into the mathematics of asset allocation with a client? Is it important that a client understand risk, variance, and correlation? Does a client benefit from understanding the efficient frontier? How much difference does the client's level of sophistication make with respect to how much an advisor needs to convey in order to get his or her full cooperation?

These and many other questions ultimately depend on the instincts, wisdom, experience, and individual style of the advisor in concert with the needs, desires, experience, resources, and sophistication of the individual client. More than anything else, the art of asset allocation boils down to the advisor's ability to tailor what he or she knows how to do to his or her client. The rest of this book will examine how the science and the art of asset allocation are practiced by some of the very best advisors in America. Reading about how these *Winner's Circle* advisors go about asset allocation will shed a good deal of light on your own practice of asset allocation.

CHAPTER 2: THE BENEFITS OF ASSET ALLOCATION AND IS IT FOR EVERYONE?

T he previous chapter's overview of asset allocation briefly mentions many of its benefits. This chapter will review these benefits objectively, and also look at them from the subjective perspective of some of the best financial advisors in America. By placing a special emphasis on how the advisors see their clients benefiting from asset allocation, we begin to sense why they hold it in such high regard. This chapter will also consider whether asset allocation benefits all kinds of clients equally, that is, whether it is equally suitable for all kinds of investors, or whether there might be certain types for whom it is less appropriate.

THE BENEFITS OF ASSET ALLOCATION

There are at least eight major benefits from having a portfolio that is consciously constructed according to the principles of asset allocation:

1. Risk/reward trade-offs of individual investments can be seen in the context of the entire investment portfolio.

2. Risk/reward trade-offs of entire portfolios can be tailored to the individual needs of clients and (within limits) can be predicted and maximized.

3. During disastrous downturns, capital is preserved and losses are minimized.

4. With capital preserved and losses minimized, the power of compounding returns can continue to have maximum effect

5. With liquidity needs taken into account, clients are more likely to remain calm, stay fully invested during downturns, and avoid disastrous timing mistakes .

6. Widely diversified clients are more likely to capture some of the upside of sudden gains or major upswings in any asset class, market sector, or national economy.

7. Rebalancing guarantees a discipline of "selling high and buying low" and maintains risk tolerance at an acceptable level.

8. Clients (and their advisors) sleep better at night

Let's consider each of these in turn.

Risk/reward trade-offs of individual investments can be seen only in the context of the entire portfolio.

Modern portfolio theory and asset allocation begin with the notion that the trade-off between risk and return can be properly evaluated only in the context of an investor's entire portfolio. In other words, investment portfolios must be looked at holistically or synergistically, because the whole of a portfolio is more than the sum of its parts. To approximate the likely real risk and real return of a portfolio, the past and likely future relationships and interactions of all of its investments must be taken into account.

When constructing a portfolio, it is important to consider the totality of a client's financial situation. Jim Hansberger (Smith Barney) reminds us that many individuals and families (and even institutions) are more diversified than we realize: "Keep in mind that the vast majority of investors of any real size automatically have their own diversification. They own some kind of real estate, either personal or investment, or both. Many have their own businesses, or they are executives or work in a large company and therefore have 401K plans and stock options or stock ownership. So, it's never automatically dependent upon the advisor to create diversification without first gathering all the information on the total assets. Most people have more diversification than may be apparent." Financial advisors who construct customized asset allocation strategies for clients should therefore take all assets, including personal real estate and 401Ks, into account.

Risk/reward trade-offs of entire portfolios can be tailored to the individual needs of clients and (within limits) can be predicted and maximized.

This is the real "payoff," as it were, that has made asset allocation the dominant modern investment methodology. Simply, portfolios constructed using asset allocation can (in theory) maximize the client's likely risk/return trade-off. If a portfolio lies as close as possible to the efficient frontier (See Chapter 1 and Appendix B), then for any given level of return a minimum level of risk (defined as volatility) is likely to have been taken, and, for any given level of risk, a maximum real return is likely to have been generated. Mark Curtis (Smith Barney, Palo Alto, California), who advises a broad range of wealthy clients from high- and ultrahigh-net-worth individuals and families to

Silicon Valley corporations, foundations, and endowments, puts this core goal of asset allocation in slightly different terms: "It's to earn an expected rate of return with as high a probability as possible, or another way of saying it is to earn an expected rate of return, a hoped for rate of return, with as little risk as possible."

Once a client's risk tolerance and investment objectives are known, it becomes possible to put together the best possible portfolio for them. Joe Jacques (Jacques Financial, Rockville, Maryland), an advisor with many retail as well as affluent clients, points right to the bottom line: "Via a proper asset allocation formulation, we are trying to consistently beat the market and add value to the portfolio." Mark Sear (Merrill Lynch, Los Angeles, California), who advises ultrahigh-net-worth clients and endowments, also emphasizes the idea of positive returns for clients: "For every year we've been here, we've never lost money for a diversified client. Even in the worst year, we made money. That's our goal—always have positive returns. We realize that we are not dealing with institutional accounts, we are dealing with individuals and they don't like to lose money, period. So what we learned was that it was better to have diversified portfolios to generate positive returns every year. If stocks go up, that doesn't necessarily mean bonds are going to go up. If you insert commodities and hedge funds into the mix, now you've broadened that portfolio to include more asset classes, and we can have positive returns no matter what happens to the market. If you are a wealthy individual and you just want to basically have a great life and you always have positive returns, and you average 2 or 3 percent better than inflation, you are done."

It's important to remember, however, that while existing data makes it possible to pinpoint the efficient frontier retrospectively, it can never be known ahead of time. While an advisor can help put together a diversified portfolio that is in theory best suited to the needs, goals, and risk tolerance of a client, it is just a theoretical foray until time has passed and actual real returns are determined (taking into account any fees, commissions, tax consequences, and so on). Put differently, asset allocation gives advisors a powerful predictive tool, but there are no guarantees that it will produce the "correct" or best possible real-world result.

In fact, one of the criticisms of asset allocation (see Chapter 11) is that picking asset classes is probably also nearly impossible as stock picking and therefore asset allocation is fundamentally flawed. There are two responses to this. First, asset classes as a whole tend to

be more predictable than individual stocks, bonds, or other investments. Second, as the studies conducted by Gary Brinson have
shown, asset allocation explains more of the return variability
between different professional fund managers than any other factor
(see Appendix B). Even if asset allocation isn't perfect, it is a very
powerful tool that, unlike stock picking or stock timing, is within
our control and can be regularly deployed and individually tailored
to the benefit of a wide range of clients and investors.

> *During disastrous downturns, capital is preserved and
> losses are minimized.*

This is a return to the common sense notion of not putting all of
one's eggs in one basket. Louis Chiavacci (Merrill Lynch) points out
that asset allocation helps to avoid big mistakes and that "over time,
if we avoid the big mistakes, that puts us ahead of 95 percent of our
competitors." Simply, in a portfolio that is properly asset allocated,
the effects of disastrous downturns in any one type of investment,
sector, or national economy will be minimized. The greater the lack
of correlation between the assets classes in a substantially diversified
portfolio, the more protected the portfolio will be in case of a
dramatic downturn.

Martin Halbfinger (UBS, New York, New York), who advises
high-net-worth and ultrahigh-net-worth clients, as well as corporations and endowments, is clear about the value of needs-driven
diversification: "I think the most important benefit of an asset allocation model (and appropriate rebalancing) is that you catch yourself before you get overly weighted in an asset class, which in my
mind could be the absolute worst thing you could ever do from a
financial point of view. So, it keeps you honest in making sure that
your dollars truly are diversified. The key is to really have your allocation modeled for risk tolerance while taking into account investment objectives."

Some people have argued that as we move into the twenty-first
century, all asset classes are becoming more positively correlated
with each other—for example, some data does indicate that U.S. and
international stocks seem to be moving more and more in step with
each other—and that in a worldwide recession or depression, even a
well asset allocated portfolio will suffer tremendously. Nonetheless,
both history and common sense make clear that even if we are considering the most basic of all asset allocation splits—that between
equity (stocks) and fixed income (bonds)—in a major downturn
results will vary greatly depending on how the assets in a portfolio

are allocated. So even if it is true that some asset classes are becoming more closely correlated, thereby yielding somewhat less value from a proper asset allocation, this is a relatively minor factor.

In short, just as capital was preserved for those clients who were properly asset allocated throughout the entirety (and especially at the end!) of the tech bubble, asset allocation is likely to continue to preserve the capital and core wealth of clients no matter what the next major economic and investment downturn looks like. Jim Hansberger (Smith Barney) is clear about the importance of asset allocation for his high-net-worth clients: "It's made a huge difference, mainly because of consistency of performance and comfort levels. Once somebody has made his money—serious money—it is absolutely necessary for him to be educated and to have a comfort level that he can preserve that capital. Still grow it, but first and foremost preserve it. You do that through consistency of performance, and you don't get consistency of performance with only one or two asset classes."

John Rafal (Essex Financial, Essex, Connecticut), who works with everyone from medium-sized to large individual investors as well as corporations, foundations, and endowments, sums it up this way: "Once you've created wealth and you don't want to lose it, my job is to not lose it for you and to make sure it's there when you need it for different events in your life." Mark Sear (Merrill Lynch) also feels strongly about high-net-worth families that entrust themselves to him. "I have one family that owned a four-generation-old family business, and then the kids started running it. A couple of years later they sold it. Think about how bad they would feel if their father's father's father created this business, and it was run by every generation, and then they blew all the money. So you just can't let that happen."

With capital preserved and losses minimized, the power of compounding returns can continue to have maximum effect.

For a client whose portfolio is well asset allocated, the power of compounding has more chance to work. As John Bowen and Daniel Goldie state in *The Prudent Investor's Guide to Beating Wall Street at Its Own Game* (McGraw-Hill, 1998), "[W]hen two portfolios have the same arithmetic average return, the portfolio with smaller up and down swings in value (less volatility) has a greater compound return. By building a portfolio with asset classes that do not move together, you can significantly reduce its overall volatility.

Consequently, your prospects for a greater compound rate of return over time are improved." The importance of this point should be readily apparent to all advisors and investors who understand the "magic" of compound interest.

For Jon Goldstein (Smith Barney), this factor made a big difference to his clients' portfolios after the tech bubble collapsed: "It's easy to show mathematically that if you don't have these big drawdowns, there's more money there to compound when the market recovers. And our clientele was really rewarded for that during the bear market because our managers were so defensively oriented. They didn't have drawdowns anywhere close to what the S&P and the NASDAQ did. And because of that, portfolios recovered very quickly."

With liquidity needs taken into account, clients are more likely to remain calm, stay fully invested during downturns, and avoid disastrous timing mistakes.

Perhaps the worst mistake investors make is to panic and sell at exactly the wrong time, just when a downturn has bottomed out and a sustained rally is about to begin. One of the reasons stock timing works for very few investors is that they end up being not fully invested during the relatively few days or periods in any up-cycle when the market makes major advances. With the risk/reward trade-offs of an entire portfolio taken into account and tailored to an individual client who understands the likely benefits of the asset allocation approach, and with capital preserved during downturns and the power of compounding continuing to work in their favor, clients are much less likely to panic and make horrific timing mistakes. John Rafal (Essex Financial) states it as a simple formula: "The bottom line is, asset allocation in theory leads to diversification, which in theory leads to safety, which in theory leads to a better result."

Clients are also far less likely to panic and make disastrous timing mistakes if their lifestyle and liquidity needs are well considered and provided for during portfolio construction. As discussed in Chapters 6 and 7, many of *The Winner's Circle* advisors interviewed for this book begin by discovering what a client's true liquidity needs are, making sure that they are addressed with appropriate investments regardless of what happens in the various markets, and only then allocating the rest of the portfolio to nonrevenue-producing assets. They do this because they know that if clients run out of cash, or if their lifestyle is threatened, or if their goals (especially family goals such as housing, child education, health care, etc.) are jeopardized, they will be subjected to enormous stresses and be tempted to make very bad timing mistakes. As Jon Goldstein (Smith Barney) says, "When things are bad, they are bad everywhere. In crisis, there is nowhere to hide. So true asset allocation and the way to protect it goes back to what we start with, which is liquidity planning. The only way to keep a cool head is knowing you don't have to leave in a panic."

It is critical for the advisor to explain to clients, ahead of time, that there will necessarily be times when at least some of their portfolio is underperforming (see Chapter 5) and that there may even be times when their entire portfolio seems to be heading downward. It is at these times that the willingness of the client to trust his or her advisor comes into play so that disastrous timing mistakes are not made. If an advisor expects his or her clients to remain steadfast, these clients must have been properly prepared, and the advisor must remain clearheaded and resolute even during panic-laden days, weeks, or months. Joe Jacques (Jacques Financial) emphasizes the importance of this approach: "I think educating your clients to make sure they don't panic and get out of the market is critical, because the people who try to time the market are usually the big losers."

Mark Curtis (Smith Barney) frames the issue here with respect to time: "As an investor, time is your ally. My experience is that investors typically make money, while speculators don't always make money. What's the difference between a speculator and an investor? It's time frame. So if you know that one has a very high likelihood of succeeding versus the other and that the difference fundamentally between the two is time frame, then what you want to do is to extend your time horizon. Ideally you want an asset allocation that buys you as much time as possible and, by doing so, increases your probability of success."

Widely diversified clients are more likely to capture at least some of the upside of sudden gains or major upswings in any asset class, market sector, or national economy.

The three previous benefits described focused on minimizing the effects of disastrous downturns in any single asset class or market sector. The converse is also true: broadly diversified clients are more likely to benefit when things improve. Suppose 15 percent of a well diversified portfolio is invested in international stocks. If there is a tremendous upward movement in an international sector, then at least some of that upside movement will be captured. Or suppose a specific technology sector has a startling breakthrough, e.g., nanotechnology or applied physics stumbles upon an energy break-through on the order of the discovery of electricity. A properly diversified portfolio, while perhaps not heavily invested in that particular company or technology sector, would still capture a reasonably significant percentage of the positive market effects that would follow from such a discovery.

> *Rebalancing guarantees a discipline of "selling high and buying low" and maintains desired risk tolerance at an acceptable level.*

Rebalancing (discussed in detail in Chapter 8) is a critical part of asset allocation. Done in a sensible and regular manner (not too frequently, not too infrequently), encourages clients to do the opposite of what they might normally do. Most clients, left to their own devices, will want to hold onto their best performing assets and get rid of those that are currently underperforming. Because rebalancing brings a diversified portfolio back into alignment with a predetermined desired asset allocation, it "forces" the client to sell some investments from better performing asset classes and buy some from underperforming asset classes. In a manner akin to dollar cost averaging, clients on average end up purchasing assets when they are cheap and selling them when they have appreciated. Of course, there are risks here as well. Clients may end up missing some of the additional upward movement in an asset class. But this risk has to be seen in the context of the overall benefits delivered by asset allocation.

Hank McClarty (Gratus Capital Management, Atlanta, Georgia), who focuses mainly on ultrahigh-net-worth clients, also sees rebalancing as critical to maintaining risk tolerance. He explains it to his clients in this way: "Suppose in a bull market you set up an asset allocation strategy with 30 percent in equities, and that's your risk tolerance, which is fairly conservative, and then it goes unmonitored from that point forward. At the top of the market, if left unmanaged, you could be looking at an allocation of 92 percent in equities, just by nature of the compounding over those previous strong years when it's been left unmanaged. Suddenly, you enter into one of the worst market downturns in market history, like the one we had in the early 2000s with a 92 percent equity portfolio, although you had said previously your risk tolerance dictated a 30 percent allocation. The point is, while asset allocation to maximize return is important, asset allocation to maintain your risk tolerance is far more critical."

Clients (and their advisors) sleep better at night.

Consider the totality of the benefits of asset allocation. An individually tailored asset allocation helps a client better than any other known approach to obtain the greatest possible return with the least possible risk. It is extremely effective in preserving capital during times of substantial downturns in particular asset classes, market sectors, or national economies. It helps clients to avoid disastrous timing mistakes while also ensuring that they will capture at least some of the upside during substantial rallies. It enforces a kind of "sell high, buy low" discipline that is otherwise often difficult to maintain.

Given all of these benefits, it is not surprising that several of the advisors interviewed for this book pointed out that asset allocation helps their clients and themselves sleep better. As Meg Green (Royal Alliance) says, "It's part of reasonableness. Asset allocation really made its way when people realized that they had some responsibility for the risks that they were taking. And for people who are in the financial services industry, they had to realize at one time or another that there were risks in not doing appropriate asset allocation." Given the state of modern investment knowledge, any advisor or client who chooses not to take advantage of asset allocation is certainly more likely to suffer anxiety and sleepless nights.

John Rafal (Essex Financial) states that in some ways asset allocation is actually more valuable for advisors than for clients: "I don't think many clients intellectually embrace the concept. I think it's much more helpful as a concept for advisors, for whom it's advisable to have a policy and a framework. When I work with an endowment I say to the investment committee, 'We have to have an investment policy statement to protect you in case things go badly. We have to have an agreed-upon policy that, in effect, tells the world why we did what we did. And that will also tell the people who come after you why we did what we did. And how we did it and how we went about it.' Well, if you are an advisor, it's tremendous when you have a client who says to you, 'This is what we did and I agreed to it.' "

IS ASSET ALLOCATION SUITABLE FOR ALL INVESTORS?

Asset allocation, for the reasons just spelled out, has become the dominant modern investment methodology. But is it the right approach for everyone? Or are there some clients and investors who might gain only marginally from following asset allocation, or who might be better off taking an entirely different approach to investing?

Three main objections have been raised to the idea that every investor and every advisor on behalf of every client should pursue asset allocation. Each objection will be examined in turn. At the end of this chapter, a simple graphic will be presented that sums up the suitability of asset allocation for different types of investors and clients.

Objection 1: The time horizon of asset allocation is most suitable for institutions, not individuals.

Many academic writers and several of the advisors interviewed for this book have pointed out that asset allocation works best with a decades-long time frame in mind, while most individuals have far shorter time frames. The claim here is that asset allocation is equivalent to a "buy and hold strategy," and that while it may be true that time is the ally of the investor, individual investors have shorter time frames and greater liquidity needs than would be necessary to take advantage of the long-term gains that come from holding investments.

Jim Hansberger (Smith Barney) amplifies this point, as he reminds us that institutions have access to opportunities that ordinary investors do not, and in many cases also have a superior tax status: "Very importantly, let's not forget that modern portfolio theory in its finest form is mostly applied at the institutional level. It's mostly applied with tax-free accounts, extremely long-term accounts, accounts that do not need a great deal of liquidity. They may only need to meet the 5 percent foundation payout or whatever it takes to run the endowment. Major institutions and endowments also have access to all sorts of managers because they can meet higher minimums. So, applying modern portfolio theory in its finest form at Yale is very different from applying it to a $25- or $50-million, high-net-worth investor. It's very different."

The response here is that individual investors benefit just as much as institutions from a reduction in volatility and conscious management of the risk/reward trade-off provided by sensible asset allocation. Moreover, as individuals continue to live longer and longer, and tend to drastically underestimate how long the retirement phase of their lives may last, extended time frames and their benefits will come into play more and more. Similarly, high-net-worth and ultrahigh-net-worth clients often have intergenerational family needs and philanthropic considerations that extend the time frame through which asset allocation will need to work. In sum, while asset allocation may be most suitable for institutions, which can take advantage of very long time frames, tax advantages, and unique investment opportunities, noninstitutional investors will also experience substantial benefits.

Sanford Katz (UBS, San Francisco, California), with a strong institutional background and a current client base consisting of mainly ultrahigh-net-worth families, makes this point in a different way by drawing a telling analogy to one very particular type of institution—the Wall Street Firm: "If you look at the best firms on Wall Street and the way they manage their own proprietary risk, there's a tremendous amount of modeling and correlation understanding that they spend time on, so that if a global meltdown occurs, they may not know exactly where they are going to stand, but they have a pretty good idea of whether it's going wipe out their capital. And why should it be any different for an individual? If anything, it's more important!"

Objection 2: Asset allocation works to preserve capital and make steady long-term gains, but is not suitable to creating new wealth through concentration and risk taking.

The claim here is that while asset allocation may preserve capital and enable the steady, long-term accumulation of wealth, a portfolio diversified through asset allocation will never make anyone rich in the short term. Mark Sear (Merrill Lynch) makes this point in a vigorous and comprehensive manner:

> Asset allocation doesn't make you money. Money is not made through diversification. It's *protected* through diversification. It's *made* by taking a bet. It's made by quitting your job and going and buying a solar panel manufacturer and growing it into the world's biggest solar power company and having this become the world's next energy. And you get to be rich. That's how capitalism works and that's how wealth is created.
>
> I think it's a mistake for people, with a couple of hundred thousand dollars, who are looking to really grow that money, to asset allocate broadly. Because if you asset allocate broadly, you have an expected return of somewhere, after taxes, between 6 to 8 percent. Well, if you are really trying to grow your money at 20 percent a year, asset allocation is not going to work for you.
>
> I think that people really need to get an understanding of what they want to do. Let me use two examples. If you had $10 million from the sale of the family business and you came to me and said, "Hey, I really want to grow this principal in excess of inflation

and I want to save for my children and I want to make sure I can do this," and you really didn't want to lose the money, then you are a prime candidate for diversification and asset allocation. Because then my job is to find you the highest rate of return with the lowest amount of risk that gives you the cash flow that you need in the times you need it. And there is an optimal solution to that, given historical returns. I can calculate that mathematically.

If on the other hand you came to me with a quarter million dollar and said, "Look, I'm making a lot of money in my job. I'm a lawyer. And I really want to take this $250,000 and look for ways to make money. This is the money I really want to grow. I've got an IRA that's invested prudently in the S&P 500 and I've got my job and I've got a bunch of real estate assets providing income, and this is the money that I want to have grow." For that person asset allocation doesn't make sense, because that person should be looking for ways to really make money.

That's not the type of investor I would work with. But if I were in that business and wanted to fashion myself as somebody who was more of an idea-generation guy, my pitch wouldn't be asset allocation. It would be more like, "I have great ideas and here's why I am able to come up with them. I'm thinking outside the box. I come up with ideas and try to make people money." If you are looking for somebody to help make you money on the coolest idea of the day, I wouldn't go to an asset allocator. I would go to the guy who spends all of his time looking at charts and trading with hedge funds and that's all he does. He's the guy who can't sleep at night because he's coming up with good ideas. He's looking on the Internet at 2 o'clock in the morning, trying to find the next great thing to call his clients about. That's a different guy than me, but they are out there.

I think that advisors should either be really good at ideas, or they should really be good at asset allocation. You should only participate in one area. Don't come to me if you are trying to make a $100,000 become a million in two years. I'm just not that guy. But there are guys like that out there. And they shouldn't be doing asset allocation. You can only focus on one thing. It's hard.

Richard Bernstein, Merrill Lynch's Chief U.S. Investment Strategist and Chief Quantitative Strategist, makes this same point in *Navigate the Noise* (Wiley, 2001): "Diversification is a risk-reduction tool, not a return-enhancement tool. If you want to sleep at night, then you diversify. If you want higher returns, then strap on your seatbelt. History has shown that it is extremely rare to achieve very high returns *and* sleep at night."

Objection 3: Asset Allocation is appropriate for institutions or affluent clients, but not for retail or middle-class clients.

Is asset allocation appropriate for the small investor—the retail or middle-class investor who has on the order of thousands, tens of thousands, or at most hundreds of thousands of dollars to invest—as opposed to the millions, tens of millions, hundreds of millions, or more that is in the hands of high-net-worth, ultrahigh-net-worth, and ultra-ultrahigh-net-worth clients or institutional investors? At first, it may seem that asset allocation is more suitable for the wealthy, since they have a wider range of investment opportunities and choices, can afford superior advisors and advice, and often have a longer time frame and less chance of becoming illiquid. Somewhat surprisingly, a number of the advisors interviewed for this book had strong opinions in the opposite direction. That is, they felt that asset allocation was just as important, or perhaps even more important, to the average investor.

Sanford Katz (UBS) focuses on the importance of asset allocation for the smaller investor in the context of wealth and life energy: "In my opinion, asset allocation is important for everybody. I think that if anything, it's incrementally more important for people with lower tolerance of illiquidity and lower wealth levels. Primarily because principal preservation is crucial, and the nature of life—what it costs to live and where you are at a certain point in life—is the biggest variable of all. All wealth creation is about personal energy to a large degree, unless you win the lottery or get lucky. Think of the person who spent 20 years to generate $500,000 in life savings. If that's lost, what is the real cost of replacing it? It's the same amount of personal energy and work over a very long period of time. The importance of asset allocation goes hand in hand with the importance of wealth preservation and the unknowns in life from inflation, illness, or anything else. It's therefore disproportionately important to investors with lower net worth."

Several advisors focused on the practical effect of a small investor following or not following an asset allocation strategy. Jon Goldstein (Smith Barney) puts it simply: "It gives the average person a leg up if they do it versus if they don't do it. Because otherwise they just chase performance, and that ends badly." Ron Carson (Linsco/Private Ledger, Omaha, Nebraska), who works with clients at all levels of wealth, makes a very similar point after citing a recent study: "The typical investor has averaged about 3 percent return versus the indices at 12 percent over the time period studied. The reason is, most people don't have the staying power needed during a downturn. With asset allocation, they do. So they get to enjoy the benefits of their asset classes while they are in favor without really experiencing or feeling the total volatility of the individual asset classes. Asset allocation gives people the staying power for the long term." Finally, Jim McCabe (Wells Fargo Investments, Beverly Hills, California), who works with affluent and ultrahigh-net-worth clients as well as foundations and endowments, points out that despite the full-time financial news media blitz that we are all subjected to, there are many investors who nonetheless do not regularly watch their investments. "For those people," he says, "asset allocation is even more important. If you are going to look at your portfolio only once a year, and only because you get your 401K statement and have to make elections, you really need to understand the process."

Mark Sear (Merrill Lynch) starts with a more philosophical tone that serves as a preview for the discussion on wealth management in Chapter 3 and ends up concluding that asset allocation is relevant for individuals at all levels of wealth. "Money is not a goal in and of itself. Think about what that means for you and what your real goals are. That's the goal, and you are managing toward this liability or toward this goal. And then your asset allocation needs to reflect the reality of your current net worth, which you are going to save or inherit, or whatever cash flows you anticipate versus that goal in the future. Your allocation should be oriented toward getting there with as little risk as possible, not toward making as much money as possible. This holds for people at all levels of wealth, it really does. For the retail client and all the way up to the ultra-ultrahigh-net-worth client, it's absolutely applicable." After pointing out (as he did earlier in this chapter) that asset allocation is not for those who want to rapidly make very high returns on their investment, Mark runs through how an average investor—who is truly willing to accurately assess his or her current situation—can take advantage of asset allocation:

> I think it's very applicable to retail investors if that's what they want. So, for somebody who's saving for retirement and is 35, they should have a very good investment advisor sit down with them and say, "Look, you are earning X, you are spending Y, the difference is Z. If I take that difference and redeploy it at $6\frac{1}{2}$ percent for 40 years, here's how much money you'd have. Is that enough? Oh, it's not enough. Okay. So we've either got to grow it faster, which means take more risk, or you've got to spend less or earn more. What's it going to be?" That should happen every day. It doesn't, but it should, because it's absolutely critical for

that person who needs that money to rely on, to be there. What typically happens is that a person who really needs diversification and a good plan comes in and the advisor says, "Oh yes, well I'm really in the energy sector right now. Let's buy these five energy stocks." And it works for six months. And then they end up losing all their money and they are unhappy. So it's clearly good for retail investors as well. But only for those who want to put a strategy together and think about the entirety of what they're trying to do and make sure that they grow at a rate that's reasonable. If you are going to be half in bonds that are yielding 4 percent, and you are going to be half in stocks, and let's make the assumption that stocks return 10 percent, then your expected return is 7. Plus you throw a little cash in there and it brings it down to 6, pretax. After tax, it's $4\frac{1}{2}$. Just make sure that you are playing with the right numbers and you can see what it's going to be worth. That's where an asset allocation strategy comes in. And that's really good for the retail investor.

THE PYRAMID OF SUITABILITY

Notwithstanding the enthusiasm some of our interviewed advisors hold for the practice of asset allocation by middle-class investors, is there still something to the notion, as Jon Goldstein (Smith Barney) put it, that in most cases asset allocation has "to be watered down a bit so it has more application"? In other words, given the nature of asset allocation, doesn't it still work best for the very wealthy and for institutions? The following simple graphic, "The Pyramid of Suitability," helps to show that asset allocation is suitable to almost all large institutions and extremely wealthy individuals and families, and somewhat less so down the line to middle-class investors.

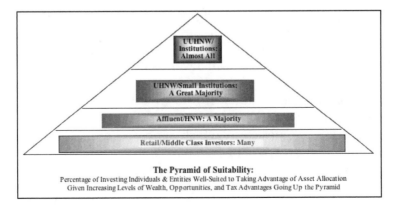

The Pyramid of Suitability:
Percentage of Investing Individuals & Entities Well-Suited to Taking Advantage of Asset Allocation Given Increasing Levels of Wealth, Opportunities, and Tax Advantages Going Up the Pyramid

The Pyramid is not drawn to scale, and it only very roughly groups the entire universe of potential investors into four classes: Retail and Middle-Class Investors; Affluent/High-Net-Worth Investors; Ultrahigh-Net-Worth Investors and Small Institutions; and Ultra-Ultrahigh-Net-Worth Investors and Institutions generally. Throughout this chapter, the following distinctions have been drawn as to what type of investor will benefit the most from asset allocation:

- Those who want to preserve capital and safely grow it, including those who always strive for positive returns, but not those who wish to "strike it rich" or make enormous returns on their investments

- Those who can take advantage of a longer time frame and who will not be prematurely forced out of their asset allocations by liquidity needs or personal disposition in times of downturn

- Those who, by virtue of their wealth or status, have greater access to more opportunities (e.g., opportunities for "qualified investors only," opportunities to invest with private money managers or in private funds with substantial minimums, and opportunities to work with top advisors who handle only substantial portfolios)

- Those who by virtue of their status, such as nonprofit institutions, have tax advantages

Putting all of these factors together and starting at the bottom, the Pyramid indicates that many middle-class and retail investors will benefit from asset allocation. Asset allocation won't be appropriate for those who seek the highest possible returns on their investments, as Mark Sear (Merrill Lynch) has so clearly pointed out, nor will it be suitable for those who have very short time frames and pressing needs for cash. Moreover, the opportunities for middle-class investors may be relatively limited compared to those who are wealthier. That is, certain types of private funds, commodities situations, and other investments will not be available to such individuals, and they may have to work hard to find a competent advisor to work with who will accept their level of investment. On the other hand, such investors may be perfectly well suited to turnkey asset allocation funds (see Chapter 10), to investing in index funds or ETFs (see Chapter 9), and to taking advantage of online sites, such as www.Financial Engines.com, which embrace an asset allocation strategy and offer a variety of online tools to the interested investor. (In the vast majority of cases, however, even these individuals will be better off working with a good investment advisor, for reasons stated in the Introduction to this book.)

Moving up the Pyramid, we come to affluent and high-net-worth individuals (and families). While some of these individuals may find asset allocation inappropriate because they wish to greatly increase their investments or perhaps do not have the liquidity, assets, or the disposition to take maximum advantage of asset allocation's time frame, it's still fair to guess that a majority of these investors are well suited to asset allocation. Moving further up the Pyramid, we come to the realm of ultrahigh-net-worth individuals and families, and small institutions. Applying the same analysis, given the greater liquidity and overall asset base of these investors and the tax advantages accruing to many institutions, a great majority here are well suited to asset allocation.

Finally, at the top of the pyramid, in the realm of ultra-ultrahigh-net-worth clients and large institutions (including corporations), asset allocation is applicable in almost all situations. Those with the most wealth have the most to preserve and grow, and no other investment methodology has proven to be as critical to these functions as asset allocation. If it were possible to thoroughly survey those ultra-ultrahigh-net-worth investors and the institutions that make up the top rung of the Pyramid, it is very likely that almost all of them, to one degree or another, are already taking advantage of the principles of asset allocation.

In sum, while no studies or empirical data directly back up the conclusions drawn from the Pyramid of Suitability, it seems reasonable to state that for most investors, be they individuals, families, or institutions of some kind (for-profit or nonprofit; corporations; endowments; pension funds; and so on), asset allocation is indeed a valuable and appropriate approach to investing. There will always be exceptions, of course, but as we move up the Pyramid we can confidently state that asset allocation comes closer and closer to meriting universal application.

CHAPTER 3: WEALTH MANAGEMENT AND INDIVIDUAL TAILORING

T he "wealth management" approach to providing comprehensive financial- and life-planning–related services has gained great popularity in recent years. This is more than just a buzzword, because a financial advisor who follows the wealth management approach can easily be distinguished from one who does not. The wealth manager focuses not on the sale of products or particular investment vehicles, but rather on the genuine overall needs of each client. Wealth managers are comprehensive in their approach: They look at all of a client's goals, needs, and dreams, and they take care to examine fully the broad range of a client's financial holdings, including real estate, retirement accounts, and even the likelihood of inheritances. Just as asset allocation calls for reviewing the risk/reward trade-off of an entire portfolio, wealth managers are holistic and synergistic in their approach. They look at how all of these financial, legal, and other wealth-related holdings work together as an integrated system, and they are very aware that changes in any of these areas can substantially affect the others.

Wealth management goes hand in hand with asset allocation. To properly asset allocate on behalf of a client, an advisor must delve deeply into his or her financial situation and psychological situation, for only the latter will reveal the client's risk tolerance, overall disposition, and ability to stick with a plan and ride out short-term losses. Financial advisors who take the wealth management approach—and that includes virtually every one of the top advisors interviewed for this book—will do their best to uncover everything relevant to a client's overall wealth, and will consider how all of the factors on the table relate to each other.

The practice of Louis Chiavacci (Merrill Lynch) illustrates this kind of in-depth, comprehensive, and holistic approach to working with clients: "In essence, our practice is made up of about 60 to 70 families. We divide these families into clients and customers; clients are the ones who rely on us for comprehensive wealth management services. What's wealth management? Asset management is one part; it includes manager selection, investment policy, and an overall general investment strategy and how it is implemented. Under asset management, we include review of trusts, review of family limited partnerships, and review of wills, pension plans, and employee benefit plans. We then integrate all that information and analysis with the asset management aspects so that the client has an integrated wealth management strategy. For example, if they have a charitable remainder trust in a foundation and a family limited partnership in individual accounts, we want to be using the proper asset location for the proper part of the strategy. If we have a tax-inefficient asset class that we want to use such as high-yield bonds, we would allocate that to their IRA account."

While wealth management services per se may in some cases may be available only to affluent clients—those who have accumulated sufficient wealth to manage and who can afford the fees associated with a higher level of service—the general lessons of wealth management are applicable to investors at every level of the wealth spectrum. The middle-class investor who cannot necessarily afford a top advisor who follows a wealth management approach can still address his or her own situation from the comprehensive and integrative perspective that wealth management brings. It should be noted that while many of the advisors who were interviewed for this book have "minimums"—that is, they will not work with potential clients who have less than a certain amount of investable assets and will instead usually make an appropriate referral on their behalf— others have no minimums and find a way to bring wealth management to anyone who comes to them.

John Rafal (Essex Financial) explains how he manages to welcome all comers: "It's a question of knowledge, independence, and service. Service means quarterly meetings, and service means Internet access, and service means returning your phone calls. Maybe you are better suited to handle phone calls of the people who have $10 million, and a member of your team is more focused on the clients who have $200,000. I try to be the advisor primarily responsible for the largest clients of the office, and I delegate primary responsibility for service to the smaller clients to others. But I have no minimums, and I don't turn anybody away. We just figure out a way to get things done, and that works pretty well."

Meg Green (Royal Alliance), with a total of 500 clients and a team of 11 people, also finds a way to serve the individual needs of all her clients, especially when they need her personal attention: "There're 11 of us who work here. We all work on the same portfolios and we are all the same team. If you come into this office you are going to have the same experience, no matter who you work with. So, if you divide up those 500 clients, it's not that much. And this is not a trading house, a practice where I am going to speak to somebody every day. Unless they are needy, in which case I am going to be talking to them morning, noon, and night for that week or two. It depends on what's going on in their lives."

With a wealth management approach—an approach that really focuses on "what's going on in their lives"—clients are served at the highest possible level, and advisors end up feeling very good about their profession. As Sanford Katz (UBS) puts it, "I think that as the wealth management paradigm really takes hold on all levels, it just becomes obvious that it's the way to go. It's not about selling products to people. It's about really helping them have better lives." It also gives clients a single point of contact for all their financial needs and thereby simplifies their lives. It's something everyone wants." As John Rafal states: "Embracing the wealth management paradigm: That's where the business is going. People really want things simplified, but they don't want them simplified at the cost of working with people who aren't good at what they do. To the degree that they can have it all in one place, they really want that."

COMMUNICATION AND DETERMINING A CLIENT'S NEEDS

Probably the most important lesson that can be derived from the wealth management approach is that every single investor is a unique individual (or entity) with a very different set of needs and goals, as well as a unique financial and legal situation. While some individuals might look roughly similar at first glance, advisors who practice asset allocation in the context of wealth management know that there are always unique circumstances and motivations that apply to the client before them. Their job is to determine what these factors are so that an overall solution (including but not limited to asset allocation) can be tailored to that client. In this way the full spectrum of the client's needs can truly be served. Anything less would be tantamount to a disservice.

Chapter 6 will discuss in detail how the best advisors determine their client's needs, goals, and risk tolerance. Before that step, however, it is crucial to recognize why this is important. Mark Sear (Merrill Lynch) frames the issue in terms of a new client: "You have made some major money, and you don't want to lose it. And you need certain things. You are going to start a new business in five years. Or you are going to fund an endowment. You tell me what you need, and my job is to find a way to give it to you with a high probability of having it occur." Advisors must find a way to have clients tell them what they need. Otherwise, it is impossible to asset allocate properly.

Martin Halbfinger (UBS) is very clear about the client's individual needs being the driving factor:

> You have to create a model that brings to the table the same trait you've brought to the table in every part of this business—integrity. That means you have to start with the needs of the client, first and foremost. I believe everything in an asset allocation model comes from that. Anybody can say, as they do, that in the mid-'90s you should have been heavier in bonds. But that may mean very different things to different families of different needs and different structures. Whatever the topic is, including asset allocation, you must first be led by what the client's needs and objectives are. The model will flow from that, and then the asset allocation percentages are really just tweaking. An asset allocation model would never be the same model for any two families. Nor should it be. And if it is, we are in the wrong business.

Jim McCabe (Wells Fargo Investments) makes the same point with respect to a new client:

> We have a client who just sold a business and is starting another business. He's a very good businessman, and he wants his liquid assets, roughly $15 million, to be his safety net. The growth for his family and his future is in the new business. They don't need any growth in the liquid portfolio; they are satisfied if the portfolio provides a 4 percent after-tax return. If everything else goes to hell in a handbasket, these funds are there for them. Others would not be similarly satisfied. For example, foundations typically have higher investment goals, because they have 5 percent payouts, costs of 1 percent, and they want to keep pace with inflation. Therefore, they typically want returns of at least inflation plus 6 percent. Finally, there are trusts with both income and remainder beneficiaries. There is no one strategy that fits the needs of all trust beneficiaries. We cannot use a cookie cutter.

Meg Green sums up the importance of knowing and understanding a client's individual needs: "You have to have the understanding of who your client is. *I think that the biggest mistake that people make is that they don't know who their client is. And they don't understand what their client can and cannot tolerate."* Given the obvious importance of this kind of understanding, Meg describes how advisors who are oriented toward selling products can move away from understanding and meeting their clients' needs: "You are at a brokerage firm. You are under the gun. You have to make X amount of sales. Otherwise, you are going to lose your chair, your desk, and your phone. I think this kind of pressure takes a lot of people into a different vein."

Martin Halbfinger starts with the premise that although his clients may be extremely sophisticated, the experience, perspective, and patience that he and his team bring provide a very valuable function: "I think that our clients in general are extremely sophisticated in what they do for a living. When something is looking frothy or something is looking very cheap, we would never give it an equal weighting in a portfolio. We would simply begin the process of allocating money to the cheap asset while reducing outlays to the expensive asset class. So, I think our job is to bring a comprehensive picture to the client of asset classes they should consider and those that they should begin reducing."

The ultimate criterion for Martin, however, is how a proposed asset allocation relates to a family's overall needs: "Our most important job is always to relate the asset allocation model to the family's needs. The client has got to come first in everything that we do. That's how we serve the pubic in the way they should be served."

A Comprehensive and Coherent Plan

Both the asset allocation and the overall wealth management plan created for a client must be comprehensive and coherent. Sanford Katz describes his experience with the typical client who has been very successful in business but does not have a great deal of experience in investing: "A client is often very tempted to say, 'Well, I know what companies or industries I like,' or 'I have knowledge and I know when something is cheap and when it's not.' And they will tend to go out and cherry-pick individual securities, whether it's a company or they've read a story on Russian debt markets, whatever it may be. In a haphazard way, they will slap together a portfolio that may not be well thought out. *The point I make to them is that it's sort of like building a house without a master plan.* If you start putting up a wall, and later on you are building off of that wall and the foundation doesn't match it, you now have a potpourri of things. Some of these may have been good selections, but how do they work together? Clients often lack an understanding or appreciation of this concept."

As previously mentioned, one key to creating a comprehensive and coherent plan is to make sure that all of a client's resources are known to the advisor, including assets that are being managed by other advisors. Ron Carson (Linsco/Private Ledger) makes sure his team carefully addresses this potential problem:

> We've got a wealth management system that really looks not only at all the assets they have with us, but at all the assets that they have in other places. And we get daily downloads. People love account aggregation today. So when we have our meeting, I'll do a rebalance with them, especially if they are paying for comprehensive financial planning. We'll rebalance their assets here, but also their 401K. Even if they are working with another advisor, we'll actually give them written recommendations for rebalancing those assets. If the other advisor is not cooperating and the client wants them to, they often end up transferring the assets. It becomes too difficult otherwise. If we are going to approach this with discipline and the client wants to work with two or three advisors, then we are going to have to have a point person who is in charge of their entire asset allocation.

Without this type of coordination, says Ron, "the client might as well not be paying any of us."

It can take a lot of time to work through all of the implications of a client's situation, especially if it is rather haphazard to begin with. Louis Chiavacci relates the fairly complex story of a client and how her various needs, both financial and psychological, had to be balanced in order to reach a comprehensive and coherent solution over an extended period of time:

> Recently we had a case where a very high-net-worth individual had completely lost control of her financial situation. She had done some reasonably sophisticated estate planning, but between the estate planning and her really not having a financial advisor—but rather a broker who had been selling her things— she really was, in her words, 'a mess.' We are now probably about halfway through reorienting her financial life. We had a very good follow-up meeting with her yesterday, and our next phase is to take on the children's trust accounts. We did not try to take on too much at once for fear of overwhelming her, her assistant, and the team. So first, we got her family partnership almost completely in order. Now we've got her trusts completely

in order, and the next time we get together, we will begin to tackle the children's trusts.

In this case, the client had two concentrated stock positions plus some exchange fund exposure, plus three or four money managers that were predominantly U.S. large-cap stock oriented, plus margin debt. And this is a person who considers herself risk averse! So here she was, on margin with concentrated positions, and where she thought she was diversified with these money managers, she really just had overlapping risk.

We pointed out the obvious: She was paying a lot of fees and receiving no diversification benefit. Even though she had some high-quality managers, there was tremendous overlap. We began by getting her risk level down. And we put a protective strategy in place on one of her concentrated positions. We paid off the margin debt. We terminated several of the money managers. We have started to build out a very high quality, relatively low duration, fixed income component to her portfolio. Most important, we are getting her portfolio close to—it won't be there yet—but close to being in line with her investment objectives. Her investment objectives and her portfolio were not even talking the same language.

While agreeing that the client is probably now closer to the efficient frontier, Louis concludes that "probably more important even than that is she is closer to where we sense her true psychological threshold is for risk versus return."

Once again, it comes down to truly understanding a client's needs, and constructing a coherent and comprehensive plan to meet them. Meg Green frames it this way: "We don't have a one style fits all; it really depends. Taxable account? Nontaxable account? Are they going to need cash flow? Do they need systematic withdrawal? Are they going to be putting money in on a regular basis? Are they sensitive to dividends? Just so many different things will lead us in different directions. *It really depends on the client. It depends on what type of portfolio is appropriate for them.*"

WORKING WITH WEALTHY FAMILIES

Many of *The Winner's Circle* advisors interviewed for this book work with very wealthy families, those who fall into the private bank and family office categories and who qualify as being high-net-worth, ultrahigh-net-worth, and even ultra ultra-high-net-worth. Typically, these advisors work with a relatively small number of such families, which enables them to get to know each family and each of its members intimately. Paul Tramontano (Smith Barney, New York, New York), a senior portfolio manager whose team primarily serves roughly 300 ultrahigh-net-worth families, says, "We are all things to some people. We help folks with their estate planning, with their investment allocation, and with their actual investment placement. We also help them with the liability side of their balance sheet, meaning we will provide loans to buy real estate, finance aircraft, buy businesses or help with any other credit needs a wealthy family may face. We will virtually do anything financially related for the needs of a wealthy family." When asked how he felt about embracing the wealth management paradigm, Paul said, "that's what we've been doing for 20 years, before it was even fashionable."

Martin Halbfinger has discovered in working with wealthy families that their most important goals are to preserve their capital and to prepare for coming generations. "When you think about it," Martin says, "servicing a high-net-worth family today—what wealth management really is all about—is servicing the needs of the wealthy. This covers the gamut from estate planning and preparing for wealth transfer to the next generation to preserving money for this generation. It's not about how to run a portfolio of stocks." Martin goes on to say that the typical wealthy family today "is less interested in making a lot of money by taking a lot of risk. They are interested in preservation of capital first and foremost, with a growth rate attached to that lower risk tolerance, and then preserving money beyond their lifetimes for the next generation."

For Mark Sear (Merrill Lynch), who strongly agrees with the idea of capital preservation and who strives never to deliver negative returns, knowing these families and addressing their wealth management needs rises to the level of a personal mission:

> I've probably got 20 families that I worry about. I worry about them every single day. They are on my computer screen, taped right down the side. Some of them, I'm sure if you asked them, they think I'm a son to them. I know their kids. I vacation with them. I talk to some of them almost every day. I dine with them. I entertain with them. I'll do anything for them.
>
> If I can have between 5 and 12 percent returns every year, that's amazing. And that's what I am trying to do, to go back and say 'No negative returns. You are already rich. I'm not going to be making you rich, you are just not going to lose your money. If

inflation goes up 3 percent and I can average 6 percent, you are always going to be 3 percent richer than you were the year before, as long as you don't spend a super amount of money. So don't worry, you've got enough money to live this lifestyle for the rest of your life.'

To know that I have that kind of relationship with my clients, and that I have a low probability of losing money for them, is spectacular. And when they blow up in a year because they've spent twice as much as they said they would, we say, 'Look, if you are going to spend that much, we've got to change this.' I love that. I love that asset allocation works. It's one of the few things in the investment business that works. You can't guarantee returns, but a good strategy gets your range of outcomes to be much more narrow.

For some people's goals, you can't do it. But I really believe this is achievable. I'm a believer. I'm not a moneymaker—I think I have good ideas, and I think the themes we work on are good, but I'm not about making money. I'm about making sure we get good economics: We charge an appropriate price; we want to make sure we use the most efficient managers; we deliver those managers in an inexpensive fashion; we cut the cost down as much as we can; and we are timely and thematic. This is what we do. At the end of the day, if my clients feel good about and comfortable with the process, that's the best we can do for them.

Ultimately, what wealthy families and clients generally want to know is that their advisor is concerned about them individually. Meg Green puts it this way: "They need the touchy-feely. They need the feeling that they are going to be cared for, that we are going to be watching over them, calling them, making changes when necessary. That we really, really care about whether they meet their goals. I hate to be so lightweight about it, but the truth of the matter is—and I'm proud to say that we are the leading financial planning and investment management firm in our area –that it's just because we are people persons. That's what works for us."

Michael Johnston (Smith Barney, Irvine, California), who works primarily with high-net-worth and ultrahigh-net-worth clients, describes a referral that came into his office in 2002. In their first meeting, the prospect asked why he had lost so much money and was still underperforming the S&P 500, even though he thought he was broadly diversified. Michael reviewed all of equity holdings and a variety of mutual funds overseen by seven financial advisors.

Michael saw that the prospect's largest individual equity holding was in all seven of his portfolios and was also a top ten holding in many of his mutual funds. Michael explained to the prospect that he was overweighted in growth with almost no exposure to other asset classes, and had no protection for when the tech bubble burst. "It's clear," says Michael, "that the high-net-worth segment is interested in one relationship, one trusted individual to keep an eye on all assets. We provide the comprehensive planning and disciplined asset allocation strategies that our 60 families understand and trust."

FINDING THE RIGHT ADVISOR, FINDING THE RIGHT CLIENT

It is well worth repeating that it is crucial for the wealth management style of asset allocation that the client and the advisor be well suited to each other. From the beginning of a possible relationship with a client, Ron Carson (Linsco/Private Ledger) focuses on whether there is a good fit, from both perspectives: "Right up front I tell people, 'You are going to interview us for a relationship. And we are going to interview you, because since we are looking out for the benefit of our existing clients, we only accept a limited number of new clients each year. And we want to make sure we are going to be able to work over the long term together, that we have the same philosophical beliefs about how we should manage your money.'"

Mark Sear (Merrill Lynch) makes the point (previously discussed in Chapter 2) that a client should first make sure that what he or she really wants is someone who takes the asset allocation approach to preserving capital, and, having determined that, the client should make sure that the advisor is indeed an expert in asset allocation: "If I were looking for an advisor today, I would make sure that I really questioned the guy's business model. What exactly does he do for a living? How does he do it? What are the resources he uses? If I were looking for preservation of capital, I wouldn't give my money to some guy who is an idea guy or who has come up with the next greatest widget."

Mark uses a food analogy to illustrate why a firm like his is the best choice for an investor interested in preserving capital. "In California, there's a fast food restaurant that specializes in burgers, and everybody knows that when you're on the road, it's got the best burgers. The difference between eating there and eating at a generic fast food place is focus. I can go to a generic place and get a mediocre salad, a mediocre taco, a mediocre piece of pizza, a mediocre fish burger, or a mediocre hamburger. Or I can go to this one place, and get about the best burger on the market. I think we are a little bit that way. We don't want to be doing everything. We want to do what we do best. So, why are we better at asset allocation? Two reasons: We do more of it, and thus we are better at asking questions and modeling, and we think about it more, and are therefore better than average at picking the right sectors to be in at any given time."

SEVENTY-FIVE PERCENT OF THE BATTLE

This chapter has focused mainly on the importance of embracing the wealth management approach—focusing on clients' needs in a comprehensive, in-depth, and holistic manner—in order to practice asset allocation at the highest possible level. It's a two-way street, however, because without a good asset allocation strategy, it is very difficult to succeed at wealth management.

Rick Blosser (Morgan Stanley, Los Angeles, California), who works with ultrahigh-net-worth clients, holds the following views on asset allocation and wealth management: "Asset allocation has become somewhat of a buzzword in the industry, and I think it's sometimes overused. As I talk to clients about it, occasionally their eyes glaze over. But it's a legitimate practice, and I know it works. The key to asset allocation is not only diversifying risk, but also the interplay between the different asset classes and how risk, including the client's assets versus their risk profile, is reflected in the model."

What's the upside of doing an excellent job at asset allocation? Rick is quite clear about this: "We work very had on asset allocation because *we believe that's 75 percent of the battle in terms of being able to create a comprehensive wealth management strategy.*" Ultimately, then, it's fair to say that without a good asset allocation, a good wealth management strategy cannot be in place, and without following a wealth management approach, an advisor is unlikely to arrive at a truly appropriate, individualized, asset allocation.

CHAPTER 4: DEEPLY UNDERSTANDING YOUR UNIQUE CLIENTS: INVESTOR PSYCHOLOGY AND BEHAVIORAL FINANCE

To fulfill the promise of the wealth management approach described in the last chapter—to arrive at a spot-on, individually tailored asset allocation that truly serves the needs of the client—an advisor needs at least two things. First, an accurate picture of the client's external situation, that is, his existing financial circumstances, including the type, amount, and location of his assets, his tax and legal situation, and other externally determinable and verifiable financial and legal facts and figures. (Some of the best practices for coming up with an accurate external picture will be discussed in Chapter 6.) It may take a good deal of legwork on the part of the advisor and the advisor's team to come up with this accurate external picture, as well as the full cooperation of the client. But, in the end, the relevant information can usually be discovered or determined with a great deal of accuracy.

Second, the advisor must have a deep understanding of the client's *inner* situation—what positively motivates the client (his dreams, goals, hopes, and desires), as well as what motivates him negatively (his fears, concerns, and how averse they are to volatility and risk). It also includes *as accurate as possible an assessment of how this particular client's inner world is structured, that is, what makes him or her tick.* In many cases, what distinguishes ordinary from extraordinary (and extraordinarily successful) advisors is their ability to really get inside the minds and hearts of their clients. Top advisors do this by building strong relationships, by communicating clearly and honestly, and by listening carefully and with full attention to what clients have to say. Additionally, these advisors carefully watch what clients actually do in the outer physical world for clues as to their inner world: Both body language and physical actions—making eye contact or not; sitting up straight versus slouching; arriving on time for meetings or not; returning phone calls or delivering paperwork in a timely manner or not—can give important clues as to a client's inner state, feelings, and intentions.

The best advisors are not only focused on their own clients' inner world, but are also keen observers of human behavior (and specifically, client and investor behavior) generally. The more experience an advisor has in serving clients, the more likely she is to be able to hone in on subtle clues that a client is internally unclear, conflicted, or not being true to his own deepest yearnings. Some charismatic advisors have the capability to create rapport and develop deep insight from the moment they enter the business; in most cases, however, the ability to develop rapport and to understand clients from the inside out is, like most things in life, a skill developed over time through practice, perseverance, and patience.

BEHAVIORAL FINANCE

Some successful advisors take advantage of insights developed in a relatively new academic field known as *behavioral finance*. Most economic theory—including Modern Portfolio Theory and its practical application in asset allocation (see Chapter 1 and Appendix B)—rests on the notion that human beings are rational and always do (or should) act rationally. In fact, the idea that risk is equivalent to mathematical volatility and that individuals want to minimize such risk is at the technical heart of asset allocation.

Human beings, however, do not always act rationally. In his marvelous book *Against the Gods: The Remarkable Story of Risk* (Wiley, 1998), Peter Bernstein writes that the evidence "reveals repeated patterns of irrationality, inconsistency, and incompetence in the ways human beings arrive at decisions and choices faced with uncertainty." Behavioral finance, then, is a field of study that attempts to make sense of anomalous or irrational behavior on the part of individual investors and markets as a whole. Through the use of cognitive psychology, social psychology, and a variety of experimental and empirical methods, behavioral finance has shed some light on why investors (and to some extent advisors) act as they do. As David Darst puts it in *The Art of Asset Allocation* (McGraw Hill, 2003), "[B]ehavioral finance researchers have sought to improve upon the strictly rational decision-making and efficient-markets model of mainstream economics by describing how deeply ingrained human instincts and reflexes can cause individual (and many professional) investors to act in ways that often appear to be erroneous, inconsistent, or even irrational."

"Prospect theory," for example, focuses on why most investors find the loss of an existing dollar to be more painful (roughly twice as painful, according to the researchers!) as the failure to gain an additional dollar. A wide variety of other anomalies have been studied—

the "endowment effect," the "money illusion," "limits to arbitrage," "momentum investing," and so on—and some general principles (for example, that the way investing choices are "framed" or presented to investors makes a substantial difference in what they choose to do) and heuristics (general rules of thumb that investors follow) have been developed. In 2002, the Nobel Prize in Economics was given to David Kahneman of Princeton University for his work in this field and for his pioneering efforts in determining why and how individuals seem to make irrational decisions when faced with uncertainty.

A comprehensive review of behavioral finance and investor psychology is beyond the scope of this book. For the interested reader, Darst's monumental *The Art of Asset Allocation* (McGraw-Hill, 2003) gives a thorough chapter-long overview of these topics. Very helpfully, Darst puts together a list of fourteen "individual investor behavioral characteristics" worth noting, which can be roughly summarized as follows:

- Investors tend to inaccurately estimate time horizons, the importance and impact of taxes, and the effects of annual investment expenses.

- Investors tend to think in nominal terms versus real-return terms, and they tend to underestimate the long-term effects of inflation on purchasing power.

- Investors tend to underestimate their level of portfolio diversification and their ability to tolerate risk or illiquidity.

- Investor tend to ignore asset allocation trade-offs and tend to attach too much significance to short-term results (with portfolios overweighted toward dividends and interest yield).

- Investors tend to assume that returns from their most recent asset class returns will continue unabated and tend to adopt a loss-averse mentality rather than a risk-averse one (i.e., they overweight their portfolios to achieve a less volatile ride at the expense of lower returns).

- Investors tend to experience broad emotional swings and investing moods, from greed and euphoria to panic and fear.

Few advisors are (or need to be) intimately familiar with behavioral finance's theories, experimental studies, anomalies, or heuristics. Instead, successful advisors develop their crucial knowledge of investor psychology and behavior through their overall life experience, through their mentors and teachers, and through interactions with many clients over time. While this chapter will discuss a few of the preceding subjects in some detail, it will mainly provide a small window into the collective wisdom—the experiences, insights, and overall approach—of some of the country's best advisors with respect to deeply understanding, and thereby better serving, their clients. (Note that the crucial topic of assessing and determining a client's risk tolerance will be mainly left to Chapter 6.)

"TREAT ME, NOT MY PORTFOLIO"

Mark Curtis (Smith Barney), consistently ranked by The Winner's Circle Organization as the number two advisor in the nation, approaches his clients from the perspective of a counselor—not just a financial counselor (although he is that too), but as a trusted family advisor. Mark tells us that, "First and foremost, we need to be good counselors; what good is the science of investing if you don't appreciate the importance of listening to and counseling your client? I think that asset allocation is the science that supports the art of counseling. What we do is important to our clients' lives and it's important that we always keep that balance in perspective."

Mark sheds some light on his perspective and approach with a story about a long-term client and family friend:

> My dad passed away a few years ago. His doctor was his close personal friend and client. The doctor is retired and is now my client. I remember once when we were looking at his portfolio, and he asked me a question. I gave him a technical answer about what we know about the capital markets and asset allocation. He looked at me and said, *"That's all well and good. But I'm not asking you to treat my portfolio, I am asking you to treat me."*
>
> He went on to say, "When I was a doctor, and a patient would come in for a physical, I could always look at my computer screen and lab reports and draw conclusions from the tests and the blood work and all the data I had about his health. But I always remembered that I was not treating colds or illnesses, I was treating people. So, when they came to see me I would always ask them how they felt. You learn a lot from a patient by just asking them how they feel and observing them as they answer you. So, let me ask my question again, but this time I am asking you to treat me as an individual, not as a portfolio."

Mark says that this was a significant moment in his career, and that as he has matured as an advisor, he has learned that he is indeed managing his clients' personal objectives and expectations, not just abstract, model portfolios:

> Here's what I thought about when that doctor left that day. I sat there and reflected on what he had said. I thought about what it is that a doctor does. You go to your doctor because you're concerned about your health, the quality of your life, or perhaps a combination of issues. Now think about your expectations of a "good doctor," a doctor who's trying to determine what's bothering you currently and what your future health issues might be. Now, think further about what diminishes the quality of all of our lives ... It's stress and anxiety. Issues surrounding your portfolio or how your money is doing can also affect the quality of your life. Therefore, what we do for a living can potentially affect the quality, and perhaps even the length, of our clients' lives. *We should know our clients' financial goals and objectives, but we should also understand their risk tolerances. It can be difficult to communicate the need to take risk today in order to avoid the potentially greater risk of not achieving one's financial goals in the future.*
>
> As financial advisors we need to communicate the benefits of asset allocation and diversification to mitigate risk. I will tell you that my clients who have allocations that we made for diversification purposes may not have appreciated those allocations when we first made them years ago. But today, with everything going on in the world and the fact that they have seen less volatility and reasonable returns in their portfolios over the past few years, their allocations probably allow them to sleep a little better at night.

Mark gives another example. "Let's take an individual, age 46, who makes $500,000 a year. He's got a portfolio worth $5 million. What should his portfolio look like? We could just look at data related to historical rates of return for various asset classes. We could run various simulations. *We could come up with whatever the model portfolio would be at that given time. But that might not be the right allocation for the individual.* The key is to reach the right allocation for the individual. That's what concerns me. If one just looks at a questionnaire and has never met the client and comes up with a textbook allocation, then more than likely that will be fine. But what if for that 46-year-old client, the 'model' allocation would have caused him sleepless nights and driven him nuts? If at the end of the day it's not what he wants, is it the right portfolio?"

To bring his point home, Mark gives an example of a client, by chance again a doctor:

> Asset allocation is extremely important, but ideally what *you need to employ is an asset allocation that does more than just asset allocate.* I have a recently retired doctor as a client. We began building his portfolio over 23 years ago. Even then we always discussed the primary issue of income and liquidity in retirement. Today we've got about 40 percent of his portfolio allocated in such a way that he can see those needs being met. And we've built in an inflation hedge so that his income goes up every year for the next six to seven years by some incremental amount of 3 or 4 percent. Now because of that, I can show him—and we try to do this with all of our clients as they retire—his projected income for years out. Whatever the number is—30 percent or 40 percent or 60 percent—the remaining money we can put into a diversified portfolio of growth-oriented vehicles. The nice thing about this is that it provides our clients with peace of mind.
>
> *I think about asset allocation—how it works in terms of mitigating risk while achieving your hoped-for rate of return. But there is something else. Asset allocation in a practical sense has to perform more than just that function. It has to address specific needs.* In this case, asset allocation worked in a very practical sense on behalf of our client.

THE LIMITS OF MONEY: WHEN "ENOUGH" IS "ENOUGH"

Part of "treating the whole person," and not just the portfolio, is making sure that clients are familiar with what money can and cannot do for them. Sanford Katz points out that "At the end of the day, this is all about what wealth and money does for you personally. And what I tell most clients—typically people with new money—is that in my opinion, money buys you some security and a lot of convenience, but I think that everybody knows it doesn't necessarily buy you happiness. The responsibility and complexity that wealth brings is usually underestimated."

Mark Curtis once again provides some useful insight here, focusing on making sure that clients know when they have "enough" money:

> There was a money phenomenon in the late '90s when it didn't matter how much net worth someone had, it just wasn't

enough. The metric for how much was enough became how much the guy next to you had or what someone else was earning on their investments.

There's a couple of things that I learned from that time, things that are really more important than asset allocation in some ways. The first is that everybody should have in his mind a goal or a number. When you get to that number—when you are done, so to speak, and you have whatever can be defined as "enough"—then you should be aware of that. What I mean by "enough," is basically that you've got "enough" to support your lifestyle if you choose to no longer work.

We are managing for some goal or goals. The primary goal might be typically defined by a set or "formula" of liabilities. The formula might be a combination of things like college education(s), staying in your home for the rest of your life if you want to, and at what point you can retire and live the life you want to. These are examples of personal future liabilities. You combine them to create your personal liability index and then you create an allocation. The question becomes how can you manage toward achieving that goal—matching your assets with your liabilities—and then try to do it as conservatively as possibly, not as aggressively as possible, but as conservatively as possible. One thing I've learned about how all this works is that you need to help your clients to determine their personal set of liabilities as well as the number when "enough" will be enough. What's important about this is that once you as a client get there, it may have significant ramifications not just on your portfolio, but also for you and your family.

Ironically, sometimes it turns out that what a client at first thinks is "enough" really isn't enough after all. Mark Curtis explains what may at first seem like a contradiction as he recounts advising a client to take more rather than less risk:

> I recently met with a relatively new client who has since become a close personal friend. He has all the money he needs for the rest of his life, and doesn't really need to "make" more money. Now you would think that with what I've said, that I would argue that he should keep it all in T-Bills. "Don't take more risk than you have to" is what I've said. Certainly, this individual doesn't need to take any more risk than T-bills.
>
> When I talk to somebody like this, I want to make sure we are accomplishing all of the goals he has. That's when we started

discussing his financial goals for his daughter as part of his estate plan. We quantified his objectives and started funding her liability needs, so to speak. Then, we discussed his "open" goals. It turns out, as we talked about it, that he has philanthropic goals, so he decided to fund a family foundation. And that money is going into a diversified portfolio of growth-oriented investments.

So, even for this kind of person, there's more to do after he's taken care of his personal financial needs. Now he has the choice to do other things with his money and, to maximize those philanthropic goals, he wants to grow the portfolio. You need to have those kinds of conversations as well with people. It's interesting to note that with ultrahigh-net-worth clients, these conversations are quite common, because more often than not money seems to carry with it is a sense of responsibility."

Mark says that rather then being surprised, clients appreciate it when he brings up these issues. "Ultrahigh-net-worth people—in my experience—are very philanthropic. They understand that there is a responsibility that comes with having wealth, and that since the need goes beyond themselves, it's not right to leave it all in a money market fund. They understand that if their money is working, more good can be done with it."

Sanford Katz brings up a similar issue having to do with suddenly wealthy clients who seem to have reached the "enough is enough" stage, but who may be mistaken. "There are a lot of clients who will walk in the door," Sanford says, "with a bank account full of cash fresh from an acquisition. Particularly when these people have newly created wealth, they will often greatly underestimate their tolerance for risk, and then take more risk than they realize they are taking ... by doing nothing. In other words, they don't realize that the simplest asset allocation, if you can call it that—being overweighted in cash—brings a risk not necessarily of principal loss, but of forgone returns." Once again, it is incumbent upon the advisor to *under*stand, that is, to get *under*neath his or her client's surface position, stand in the client's shoes, and then see, understand, and communicate what the client may be missing.

UNIQUE INDIVIDUALS

An old insurance company TV commercial showed a man expressively celebrating a bowling strike to the accompaniment of the following jingle: "Oh there's nobody else in the whole human race, with your kind of style, and your kind of grace." There are so many similarities among people that there is an understandable tendency to think that they are all deeply alike. While this is true in some ways, in other ways each individual is unique, especially when it comes to their investment situations and overall wealth management needs. Advisors should start with the assumption that each client is unmistakably unique. Despite surface similarities, any particular client may have completely unexpected needs, characteristics, or circumstances—financial, legal, health-related, or otherwise—that may not come to the surface unless the right questions are asked. It is better to hone in on the uniqueness of each client rather than wait for the client proactively to become dissatisfied with some financial result or other aspect of the relationship.

Jim Hansberger (Smith Barney) puts it simply and clearly: "If you believe in behavioral finance, you should automatically believe that every client is different. There is no such thing as one size fits all. It is very much about customization." (Once again, we are back to the core ideas of the wealth management approach, as discussed in the previous chapter.)

Another aspect of individuality is just that: Clients are individuals and, as such, care a great deal about how their portfolios are doing and the preservation of their capital. Clients and advisors can have very different understandings of what counts as an "acceptable" portfolio return. Mark Sear (Merrill Lynch) had to learn this the hard way, as he recalls in a career-changing and even life-altering conversation with a client:

> I wasn't too far into my career, and it was one of those really bad years when the market was down. I got on the phone and very proudly told my client that I was only down 15 percent for him when the market was down much more for that year. I was so proud of myself. And he said, "I just want you to know, I'm not going to fire you on this call. But if you ever do that again, our relationship will end. I came to you to not lose money. And telling me you are down 9 percent less than the market is the most embarrassing thing I've ever heard. I don't know how you sleep at night, losing 15 percent and being proud of yourself. You should go into the washroom and take a long hard look in the mirror. If that's what you are all about, then you are in the wrong business." Well, I knew what he was talking about. My focus then was on outperforming the market. Now my focus is on not losing money. There's a big distinction.

As a result, I realized that my clients are individuals. They are not institutions. They want to know that we've picked good managers and they are doing as well as the index or maybe a little better, but they want to make sure that I'm getting them out of the way of a disaster and I'm picking investment managers who are conservative and safe, and that's what I learned from that conversation. And it's stayed with me since.

The bottom line here? No matter how wealthy, clients are people, and people care very much and in unique ways about how their money is doing.

CONTROLLING ENTREPRENEURIAL FLAIR

There is yet another kind of individuality that advisors must be aware of: the individuality that drives entrepreneurs and successful businessmen and women. Sometimes, the very strength of a client—his or her ability to succeed in business—also makes it difficult for them to get out of an overconcentrated stock position or give overall control of their portfolio over to an advisor. Sanford Katz has experienced this dynamic a number of times and explains it this way:

Suppose someone is acquired as a smaller, private player by a large telecom company or a networking company. He suddenly has this concentrated stock position and assumes that because he understands the technology of the business, he also understands the valuation of the stock, of which he is now holding nearly $100 million. This is the hardest thing to change in terms of client logic. Even if it's not an emotional attachment, it's somehow engrained in their mind that this is something they understand, even if they don't have control or an understanding of concentration risk.

Often these people will be more comfortable holding a concentrated stock position in a company they've gone through a heavy negotiation with and feel strongly about. They are more afraid of things they don't understand, like the diversification process and asset allocation. They are particularly more afraid of things they cannot control, like the markets in general and the way that plays into a diversified portfolio. Mysteriously enough, they will sometimes prefer to hold onto something they think they understand far better than they actually do. It's an illusion we see over and over again.

> *In my opinion, it's very difficult for people who have run business-es—who are used to being in control of the outcome of their invest-ments—to suddenly get comfortable with a more passive approach to asset management on their part.* Now their assets are in companies run by other people, and that's a very hard thing to get used to. So we spend a lot of time educating clients on why it's important to get comfortable with being more passive, being investors with less direct control.

Sanford feels that the successful entrepreneur, in particular, is a tough nut to crack: "You would be amazed at how rationality goes out the window with some of the brightest people on the planet, some of the best entrepreneurs out there. With investing, you need to discipline yourself to think within the box, or at least know the parameters. Successful entrepreneurs become successful by thinking out of the box. It's pretty hard to get them back in the box!" Sanford's final set of reflections on entrepreneurs, on knowing how they really tick, points us in the direction of determining risk tolerance, a subject that will be discussed in great detail in Chapter 6:

> I think there is a certain amount of entrepreneurial machismo, and it's not necessarily gender-related. People who have been suc-cessful creators of wealth through their own effort tend to believe they have a higher level for risk tolerance than they do. I honestly think they are sincere about it. They do, when they are in control. When they are steering the car, they are willing to go faster than when somebody else is driving. That's why I usually assume—and I think eight out of ten times it's the right approach—that an entre-preneur's level of risk tolerance is a couple of notches lower than they think it is. If they say they are a 9 out of 10, they're probably a $7\frac{1}{2}$ or an 8.

Michael Johnston (Smith Barney), who works with many high-net-worth and ultrahigh-net-worth entrepreneurs, feels that clients often tend to miscalculate their own risk tolerance:

> Most of these individuals haven't experienced large amounts of wealth being managed for them. Up until this point, they have felt more in control of their income stream because they were running a company. They feel they know how that money is coming in. Our concern, when we create the asset allocation, is that they not react negatively at the wrong time. When the mar-kets are down, that's usually when the clients are getting nervous about their asset allocation and might sell at the wrong

time. So we compensate for what they think their risk tolerance is and add a little bit of cushion so that when a March of 2003 comes around—we are about to invade Iraq and the markets are down dramatically—we don't have clients calling in and panicking at the worst possible time, right before a 16-month market rally.

GETTING THE MESSAGE ACROSS

On the one hand, clients are unique individuals, each with his or her own set of wealth management needs, circumstances and ways of seeing things. On the other hand, experienced advisors (and, at least in theory, behavioral finance professors!) are often able to recognize suboptimal patterns, mistakes that clients tend to make over and over again because they lack self-understanding or investment knowledge. Given what they know, should advisors try to communicate their understanding of investor psychology and behavioral finance directly to their clients?

Jim McCabe (Wells Fargo Investments) says that he generally does not talk to his clients about behavioral finance. "It's lost on most people. I will recommend specific reading material from time to time. And if they want deeper analysis, we are open, but generally, I think clients quickly lose interest." As with the entrepreneurs discussed previously in this chapter, it's not because of a lack of intelligence. "Our clients are all very intelligent. It's simply that they are often financially inexperienced. Most of our clients have built their business and then have a liquidity event. They are very smart people and know the businesses very well, but they are neither financially experienced nor financially sophisticated."

Kathy Tully (Morgan Stanley, Ontario, California), who works with high-net-worth individuals and endowments, agrees that direct discussions of behavioral finance would generally not be that useful: "Probably if I used that term, their eyes would cross." Instead, Kathy focuses on what she calls "emotional education." Whether the subject at hand is the long-term impact of inflation, the need for growth-oriented assets in a portfolio, or being relaxed about the daily value of one's portfolio, Kathy has found ways of communicating important points to her clients based on understandings that they already have and subject matter that they already relate to:

> Clients understand their values and when their accounts are going up and down. They also understand—when you relate it to the price of bread and the price of a car—that they are paying

for a car what they used to pay for a house. So, to explain why they need growth, it has to be related to something they understand. They can relate to rental properties. They think those are wonderful. I'll ask, "Would you have your rental property appraised every day?" Well, of course they wouldn't. So I'll say, "But then why are you looking in the paper every day to see what your investment account is worth?" Ninety percent of what I do is emotional education.

I'll ask clients, "Do you know what your greatest risk is going to be?" Then I'll say, "Inflation. Not a bad stock market, but inflation." That's a key element in every conversation I have. They forget about inflation, and then I remind them. Home prices are the best examples to use.

When they sign on to be clients, I make them promise me they will live to be 100. Later, they say, "I'm getting old. I'm not going to go back to work to build this portfolio again and then feel safe with CDs." I respond, "But remember, you promised me you were going to live to be 100, so I need to make sure we've got a growth element in the portfolio." So it's a lot of emotional education on the difference between inflation and your actual expected return from anything that gives you growth. There are primarily two things in this world that will give you growth: stocks and real estate. CDs will only give you your money back. Once inflation is counted, it's a negative. They start to relate to that when I throw out the examples of food, cars, houses, and putting their kids through college. If you discuss examples, something that they understand, then they are right on the same train with you.

In many cases, advisors simply focus on explaining core concepts to clients. The "investor psychology" component is taken care of through the act of communicating clearly. For example, instead of discussing behavioral finance, John Rafal (Essex Financial) says that with most of his clients, "We talk about yield versus total return. With yield so low, in order to achieve your income objectives, you have to manage most portfolios for total return. Your payouts will come form a combination of income and growth, not just from income alone. I don't know if you call that behavioral, but it works."

For Hank McClarty (Gratus Capital Management), it's ultimately the well-earned trust of his clients that gives him a leadership position. "I know them like they're members of my family," he says. "They trust me." The question then becomes, "What, exactly, should an advisor tell a client to do, and before that, how much should an advisor communicate to a client about asset allocation?" Conveying the basics of asset allocation—what to communicate, how much to communicate, and how best to do it—will be the subject of the next chapter.

CHAPTER 5: COMMUNICATING ASSET ALLOCATION BASICS TO CLIENTS

If the previous chapter was mainly about advisors plumbing the depths of their clients' minds and hearts, then this chapter is about the opposite: How much of what they think and know about asset allocation should advisors communicate to their clients? How much is necessary, desirable, or wise to attempt to convey?

The wealth management approach described in Chapter 3 embraces a two-way communications model. On the one hand, it is important for advisors to know everything they can about their clients. Some clients are fully cooperative and communicative. Sometimes the advisor has to "pull" the information out of more reclusive clients. Either way, it is only by gaining a full understanding of their clients' inner and outer worlds that advisors can best serve them.

On the other hand, it is also important for advisors to communicate clearly to their clients. For some clients, all that will be necessary will be a thorough understanding of how the advisor works in general, that is, how the advisor gets paid, what the advisor's overall approach to working with clients is, and what the client can generally expect the advisor to do for him or her. For other clients, it may be both necessary and desirable to convey a great deal more, including details about the advisor's approach to portfolio management overall and asset allocation in particular.

Generally speaking, a well educated client is a cooperative client. This does not mean, however, that every client will have the same appetite for details or that every advisor will be equally open to or skilled at communicating those details. Some clients have such great trust in their advisors and so little interest in the details, that it may be a push for the advisor to convey more than the very basics. Other clients will request detailed consultations about asset classes, returns, the efficient frontier, rebalancing, and more.

Part of an advisor's skill set, then, is balancing the advisor's need to communicate with the client's desire and capacity for communication. Over time, many advisors develop a repeatable package of information on asset allocation that can be expanded or summarized to meet a particular client's appetite for information. This chapter will discuss the kinds of information advisors usually communicate to their clients, the ways in which they do so, and the surprisingly wide variety of opinions that different advisors have on how much to communicate.

NOT OVERWHELMING CLIENTS

One strong refrain from our *Winner's Circle* advisors is that *it is important not to overwhelm clients, not to give them more information than they need, and to keep things as simple as possible.* For example, when asked if he uses charts to get across the core mathematical principles of asset allocation, Joe Jacques (Jacques Financial) unhesitatingly replied "No, I don't, because you can overwhelm the client. I think the client wants the basic principles. They want to make sure the advisor knows what he is doing. But they want to eat the hamburger. They are not interested in all the processes of how to get to the hamburger. They don't want to have to learn how to raise the cow and what to feed it. They don't want to understand how it gets slaughtered and processed. They just want to know that somebody knows what he is dealing with and is on top of it. That's how most of my clients are. They are not so interested in the technical aspects of asset allocation. They just want to know that I know them." While he acknowledges that asset allocation has earned a Nobel Prize, Joe adds, "I don't think my clients will make a decision based on that."

Meg Green (Royal Alliance) also says that she rarely uses charts to represent concepts such as the efficient frontier or correlation and points out that there is certainly no need for her to impress anyone. "It doesn't help the situation. I don't have to impress anybody with how intellectual I am. I have to be able to explain to them what they are doing in a manner that they not only understand but are comfortable with. And I think that takes a heck of a lot more talent than starting to talk about theories and grants and charts. People glaze over. You don't always have the time to teach someone everything you know. So I think that the people who come out with very methodical ways of doing things and using efficient frontier charts are trying to be impressive more than they are actually getting the job done. That doesn't mean they won't get the job done. I just find it a lot easier to make it understandable in other ways."

Meg also prefers to refrain from using charts to oversell her clients on the "scientific" nature of MPT and asset allocation. "I don't like to set anybody up for something that's scientific, that's always going to work, because it might not." Meg adds, however, that on occasion she might have "a few people who want a little bit more technical detail, in which case I'm not going to be in that meeting with them. They are going to sit with a couple of members of my team, who will give them every trick in the book if that's what they need."

Although Hank McClarty (Gratus Capital Management) explains a great deal to his clients, he tries to do so using simple charts and is very aware that, at a certain point, he can lose their attention if he is not careful:

> All of our clients come to us by referral. When I sit down with them, they are usually somewhat in a mess, both from the service level of just getting everything organized and taken care of, and then all the way down to the portfolio level. I go through and explain to them the different asset classes and why we are using managed futures and why we are using bonds and why we are using equities and—once we determine their asset allocation—why we are allocating it to certain levels. We show them, on an annual basis going back over the last ten years, how different asset classes have performed.

Jim McCabe (Wells Fargo Investments) has experienced a similar effect: "We are dealing with very smart people who have done very well. But we tend to lose them when we introduce complex mathematical equations. I've seen many eyes glaze over." Instead, of talking and explaining to clients, Jim's main emphasis is on listening: "We can talk all day long about what, in a perfect world, would make sense, but we need to apply it to the client's situation. It's more client driven. It's a lot more listening than talking. We need to listen to determine their experiences, their annual expenses, their fears, their needs, and what their legacy should be." Jim acknowledges that ultimately, "Some people just don't want to know. They say, 'That's why I hired you.' At day's end, they're being intuitive and doing the right thing by hiring an experienced, reputable person from a high quality organization."

Kathy Tully (Morgan Stanley & Co.) similarly relates that her general presentation is "Not real high tech. My clients are either really brilliant at running companies or they are enjoying retirement. They are not doing their own asset allocation or market charting, or they would not need me. They know I love what I do. Their CPAs know I love what I do. That's what helps me get all the business I get. My clients don't want to be the investment expert. They expect that from me." Jim Hansberger (Smith Barney) makes a similar point: "Let's make a distinction here. Money does not equal sophistication as an investor. There's a lot of people with a great deal of money that are not all that sophisticated. And that means that a lot of people are just now getting familiar with how they can invest in private equity or hedge funds. We also are probably only about halfway through relative to people being aware of the consulting approach to equity management." Jim McCabe has a similar take on his clients. When asked if he uses detailed charts to get across MPT and asset allocation, he states that typically he does not. "A select few of my clients are quantitative," he says. "But most are not."

IT DEPENDS ON THE CLIENT

For many advisors, the amount of depth that they go into is very much determined by what the client needs and wants. Paul Tramontano (Smith Barney) is very clear about this: "It depends on the clients and their tolerance for complexity. For some people, I must tell you, we don't even broach it. Their attitude has been, 'You are doing a great job. We love you. Just make sure you take care of it.' And then for other folks, especially the newer folks, we'll be as detailed as they want us to be, and we will show them charts and pictures. It's always easier for some people to look at graphs and pictures to understand how we think about asset allocation. We will show them the efficient frontier, and we will show them how accounts and portfolios have performed versus the indices on simple graphs to illustrate risk and reward. And so, it depends on the person. I am going to see somebody next week who I see once a year; he's brilliant and he likes detail. So we will roll up our sleeves and get into it."

Louis Chiavacci (Merrill Lynch) frames it in terms of "the client's appetite for involvement in the process. If the client really wants to know what's going on and how decisions are made, we will spend quite a bit of time educating him or her. We have put together a variety of educational chapters, if you will, on asset allocation from things as basic as correlation analysis to more sophisticated topics like Monte Carlo simulations." Jim Hansberger also echoes this theme: "It depends on the client, of course. It depends on their level of education." Generally, however, Jim does "talk in detail about asset allocation. We explain the concept of one asset class versus another and probable levels of risk and return. Moving along the risk spectrum, we try to generally assign risk/return levels, but, of course, we have to say that that is based on history. At least, is some guide to the future."

Jon Goldstein (Smith Barney) says that the amount clients want to know has changed over time, and so has the amount he explains. "We used to do it 10 or 12 years ago, and we started boring the heck out of clients. We used to very methodically tell them the whole asset allocation story and they would just say, 'Can you skip to the end and tell me what to do?' So, quite a while ago, they forced us to stop talking about it. We still did all the work; we just wouldn't walk the clients through the whole process. But this has changed. It's become popular to talk about it again. Now we just show them that we are doing the work, and we give them a little bit of a view of the process. They don't want to lose money again, and asset allocation would have protected them a bit more during the bear market."

Mark Sear (Merrill Lynch) has also noticed a difference over time in how much he explains to clients, especially with respect to the mathematical core of asset allocation: "I think we used to more than we do now. We used to go back and show empirically how one could generate higher returns with lower volatility by owning stocks and bonds together. We used to show mathematically that over a period of time you could get about 89 percent of the return of owning stocks only by owning stocks, bonds, and cash and yet having one-fifth of the volatility. Now, I think most people know that. So now we try to talk more about our goal, which is how to generate positive returns in every year."

EXPLAINING IT IN THEIR OWN WAY

Several of the advisors indicated that although they do explain asset allocation to their clients, they do it in their own way. Paul Tramontano focuses on asking his clients questions about their experiences, and works asset allocation into the conversation: "I don't explain it from the top down. What I tell people when they start here is that we are going to ask them more questions about their finances than they have ever been asked before. And we are going to spend as much time as we need to understand what they are doing. At the end of that process, what I generally find is that I know more about people's finances than they do. Sometimes—this has happened a lot over the past five or ten years—people think they are invested one way and, in fact, they are invested completely differently. They think they are diversified, yet they own different mutual funds that are essentially invested in the same things. We've seen this movie before, so I explain more than just our asset allocation strategy. First, I explain the process that I am going through to discover what they are doing. Then I explain to them what they've done in the past, what their portfolios look like now, and what their portfolios should look like in the future."

Sanford Katz (UBS) takes a three-pronged approach, explaining asset allocation to his clients first in logical, then in psychological, and finally in simple overview terms, with a special emphasis on the power of compounding:

> I explain it logically first. Psychologically second. And third, I try to use a very simple 10,000-foot view of the concept that if different parts of a portfolio are moving at different times for different reasons—and they are not correlated or causal to one another (causal, I think, is often the overlooked part of the equation)—that the overall effect through time can be very smoothing on returns.
>
> Also, the way I try to appeal to a client's sense of logic is to suggest that even if absolute returns are compromised slightly in the process, over a five- or ten-year period, you have compounding working for you in a way that it does not with a concentrated or nonasset-allocated type of approach. So what do I mean by that? Well, if somebody, for example, is gunning for 10 to 15 percent returns and says he is moderate in his risk tolerance, and he thinks of himself as a 50/50 stock/bond investor, you need to educate him that a 10 to 15 percent return is probably not achievable except through security selection or particularly good managers. I think you need to convince him that he may be better off shooting for an 8 to 12 percent return, something in that neighborhood, but doing it on a more consistent basis.
>
> If you show clients the math and the power of compounding, without taking any steps backward in returns, the power of compounding suddenly becomes very obvious to them. In other words, a dollar can double in X years at a lower positive compounding rate every year, with no slips. It will probably double faster than, for example, a hedge fund or a particular investment that's up 30 percent one year, down 15 percent the next, then it's up 10 percent, then it's down 20 percent, and so on. For most people it's very hard to visualize the compounding results over a five- or ten-year period. When you show it to them, all of a sudden they don't feel the need to have 15, 20, or 30 percent returns in a given year. Maybe they are willing to give that up for the consistency of compounding at an 8 to 12 percent return.

Notably, Sanford finds that while some clients "get it," there are others who, regardless of how good a job he does, still have trouble accepting the asset allocation approach:

> If I do my job well, and explain it well, and illustrate it well, a light bulb will go off in their heads at a certain point. But there are some people who—even after you think you've made a very effective case—just don't get it. It's their personality. There's something that runs through their blood that is either higher risk or more control oriented than they are willing to admit. They have to have faith in an asset allocation approach, whether you are indexing the global markets and just trying to get global growth as the growth rate in your portfolio, or whether you are taking a more tactical approach and trying to outperform and generate some alpha. You are requiring them to have faith in a model and in an approach that they are just not used to.

Meg Green believes the key to explaining asset allocation is to "lay things out the way someone needs to see it." In particular, Meg finds that clients relate to the metaphor of different asset classes within a portfolio having different "jobs," as the following real-life example shows:

> Consider the situation we just had today. This is someone who had sold a very, very large piece of property and who had never really handled money before. Suddenly, there's a lot of money from a piece of property. I told them that they were very lucky that the piece of property was in a wonderful place, in New York City, and that they had owned it for the last 60 years. But, going forward, we have to take this money and basically give each portion of it a job, and the job of some of it is to be very, very steady, still, and reliable. The job of some of it needs to be very income oriented to send you a check, and then we also need some of it to have the job of gently growing for the future, for the family. And all the categories that you assign jobs to cannot work in the same asset class. You are not going to find steady and easy income in the market, and you are not going to find growth in a Treasury bill. And that's where we basically start: Instead of explaining asset allocation per se, I like to give the different asset classes jobs for these people, based on what they are looking for.

Joe Jacques appeals to what clients already know, that is, their experience of the last few years in the context of what they already know about diversification. "The biggest thing I say is that everybody is from the school of hard knocks. They understand what happened with Enron. They have gone through the 9/11 event. A lot of them had their own company stock decrease tremendously in value. Those clients want their retirement protected. They want their education fund protected. And they realize the markets go up and down, so the best protection is through proper asset diversification."

Shelley Bergman (Bear Stearns, New York, New York) works with everyone from high-net-worth and ultrahigh-net-worth individuals and families to corporations, foundations, and endowments. Shelley likes to use a "shock absorber" metaphor. "We are proponents of asset allocation, so when clients say that they want to be 100 percent in equities, I tell them that they should consider other asset classes as well, like bonds, preferred stocks, closed-end bond funds, or other income-producing securities such as REITs and utilities. Depending upon a qualified client's specific needs, we may also consider using alternative investments such as hedge funds. I explain that these investments are like shock absorbers on their car. 'When you're driving down a nice smooth road you may not be concerned about your shock absorbers. But when you hit one of those streets awash in potholes, you're glad to have them.' Unfortunately, people don't realize the risks of nondiversification until you get into a period of time like 2001 to 2003, and then it's too late."

MAKING IT COME ALIVE

To whatever degree an advisor chooses to convey the basics of asset allocation to a client, it should be done in a way that captures his attention and, if possible, his imagination. Meg Green, who taught fifth grade coming out of college, says she "had to figure out a way to teach the Constitution of the United States of America to ten-year-olds so that they would not only understand it, but remember it." When asked if was easier to teach clients about asset allocation or ten-year olds about the Constitution, Meg says "That's the job of the teacher. I think either one is easy, as long as you make it come alive."

Most of *The Winner's Circle* advisors agreed that the place to start is with charts and diagrams—in short, pictures. Kathy Tully shares some of her process: "I think the 'why' it works is very easy, because I use a chart of the S&P going back 15 years and show my clients how everything they made in the 90's bubble, they lost. And then I go back to the long-term Ibbotson chart that shows all the asset categories. *So, I'm a firm believer that pictures are worth a thousand words. My clients might not comprehend everything I say without the charts."*

Mark Curtis (Smith Barney) feels that it's critical for clients to grasp what is being presented to them. He tries to keep things simple, yet informative: "When the client leaves our office, if he or she can't explain what it is we are recommending and why, we have only done part of our job. So, one of our goals is to make our presentation as simple as we can. We need to make it tangible to the client. We've got to make things real to them. We have to present concepts both in writing and, if possible, with illustrations. Our clients deserve our best and most sophisticated advice, but we also need to do whatever we can to make it as easy for them to understand."

Michael Johnston (Smith Barney) knows how to maximize client understanding by using a single chart that is simple, straightforward, and to the point: "There is a two-page piece within a managed futures presentation," he says, "that takes two asset classes and shows what their expected return is going to be going forward. The expected returns are very close to each other. It also shows what their expected risk is going to be, going forward, and those two expected risks are very close to each other. But then, when you combine them in a portfolio that's 50/50, all of a sudden the return stays the average of the two, but the risk decreases dramatically, and the reason for that is due to the negative correlation between the two asset classes."

Joe Jacques likes to use a simple, easy-to-demonstrate example: "I usually use a pencil when I am talking with clients. I say, here's one pencil; it's very easy to break. But if I put 100 pencils together, you can't break them. And that's the main principle of asset allocation. Through diversification, you have some investments that do well and some that do poorly. But the vast majority together will do better than the marketplace, and via a proper asset allocation formulation we are trying to consistently beat the market and add value to the portfolio."

Jim McCabe found that a real-life example—those clients who had done better by having a diversified portfolio—gave him a new type of evidence that he could share with other clients. "In 1998 interest rates rose and portfolios that were 100 percent fixed income had a negative total return, but if you had a 25 percent equity allocation you had a positive return. This was the first time I could give empirical evidence that a counterintuitive theoretical strategy actually worked."

Perhaps best suited to somewhat more sophisticated investors, another kind of real-life example—the live optimization—is favored by Tim Kneen (Citigroup Institutional Consulting): "Every single one of our clients has an actual live optimization that's saved in a virtual file. They know that an optimization/asset allocation is only as good as the inputs, and they understand our cash premium model. They understand correlation and how it works, and how the optimizer selects and specifically allocates assets. They understand our internal personal biases toward mean regression in asset allocation. This all leads to clients who make more informed decisions. Through the optimization process they don't just get a model; instead, they get a data set that they can use to make the right investment decisions. For example, they can figure out the net effect on expected return, best case return, and of course, worst case return, of adding more equities to a portfolio."

Must clients have substantial technical knowledge to understand the live optimization? Tim says that they generally don't have the technical knowledge, and, in any case, it's his job to educate his clients with the help of the live optimization: "Most of the foundations and endowments we serve have very strong accounting people. Sometimes they have very strong legal people, but many of the committee members are regular professionals, such as doctors. But by the time we are done. I think they all really do understand. Could they write a paper on it like we can? No. But I think they understand the basic concepts of correlation. They understand the basic concepts behind why we allocate to one asset class and when. And if they don't, then we've failed in our job as an educator and as a consultant."

Similar to the use of a live optimization is the way that Jon Goldstein uses software to illustrate basic asset allocation concepts. "We utilize software that illustrates portfolio theory and the building in of the efficient frontier. We show clients different portfolio plots on the efficient frontier. We tell them that if we are not at least on the frontier, we are giving away risk and not getting return for it. We stress very heavily various scenarios where there are no wrong answers—it depends on client circumstances or objectives—what is appropriate for each investor. They can be very conservative or very aggressive; it doesn't mean that one approach is better than the other. That's important for them to understand, and I think the efficient frontier exhibit allows them to see that."

THE WELL EDUCATED CLIENT

Jim McCabe is quite clear about the value of an educated client: "The best client is an educated and knowledgeable client." Jim Hansberger echoes a very similar sentiment: "If there is one thing that comes through, it's the importance of education, of making a client really understand." Louis Chiavacci makes a slightly different point as to the value of client education: "I think a majority of clients 'get it.' By the time we are through with the education process, I think that there is a very comfortable level of understanding."

Raj Sharma (Merrill Lynch, Boston, Massachusetts), who specializes in asset management, estate, wealth, and legacy planning for high-net-worth clients, stresses the value of having an educated and informed client. "We make sure our clients are as educated as much as possible, in the art of investment management and even estate planning and wealth transfer techniques, as well as other services," he says. "When you have a satisfied and educated client, he or she can be your biggest ally, someone who understands your processes, someone who understands the risk inherent in asset classes." With respect to earning referrals, Raj concludes that "If you want them to represent you, they must first understand what you do."

Sanford Katz finds that an educated client is a cooperative client. Since Sanford places great value on working with cooperative clients, he has spent two decades developing an education process that he takes great pride in:

> I'm guessing that a lot of advisors probably agree with what I'm about to say. We really try to stay disciplined about the breadth and type of clients that we work with. We don't really want to work with somebody who wants to use us as a family office, but doesn't want to take any input from us. We don't want to work with somebody who doesn't listen and overexposes himself and puts us in a position of being accountable yet not able to make decisions. That's about the worst thing an advisor can have: a client who forgets everything we've taught him, has his fingerprints all over a portfolio outcome, and then holds us 100 percent accountable for what happens. You end up taking all the blame and you get none of the credit when things go well. So in every situation we want to have least a 50/50 collaborative effort. We don't have to have an argument, even a constructive argument, or to have to convince a client or educate him on all the tactical reasons why his input might be illogical or might undo what we've already done.

So, part of what we do that's different is we spend a lot of time educating clients. I take a lot of pride in educating people because I enjoy it and I feel like I've developed two decades of knowledge to share with people. I try to use a sensible approach that a client can understand, whether it's their first time entering the securities markets or whether they've been doing it for years and need to get to a different level. One thing clients have been very complimentary about is the level of education we continue to provide. They will often acknowledge this when they say to us, "I'm really glad you showed us this. I don't know that we want to integrate it into our portfolio, but we realize that it's unfamiliar to us and it would have been a lot easier for you to not bring it up." We don't just keep things chocolate and vanilla. We try to stretch our imagination a little bit.

To ensure that his clients are well informed, Jim Hansberger and his team follow a three-pronged educational approach that involves face-to-face education, recommended readings, and sponsored conferences. "I don't think there's anything better than just a teacher and a pupil," Jim says, "so it's really a face-to-face education. But, very importantly, we ask our clients to read a lot. One of the books sent to every client was David F. Swensen's *Pioneering Portfolio Management* (Simon & Schuster, 2000). David is the chief investment officer of Yale and its endowment, which along with Harvard and a couple of others has been recognized as carrying asset allocation to its fullest extent—to an art form. We've given that book to everybody and certainly in the last few years a great deal more that's been published. We are constantly trying to keep our clients informed and aware of how things are changing. We have an annual conference that the Hansberger Group sponsors. Two years ago in that conference we focused 100 percent on alternative investments and had various hedge fund managers, real estate people, and private equity managers as speakers. So our clients really learn not just from us, but from reading and from coming face-to-face with other purveyors."

Tim Kneen (Citigroup Institutional Consulting), who we previously learned is a fan of the live optimization and who takes his job as an educator and consultant very seriously, makes sure that his clients receive a very thorough education before any specific choices as to money managers or specific funds are made. "It's rare that we will talk about a money manager with a new client," he says. "I know this sounds strange, but it's not unusual for us to move through the consultation process—from setting a required rate of return and producing preliminary asset allocations to creating live optimizations and Monte Carlo simulations—to the point where we are ready to actually implement, without having even discussed any of the money management organizations. Clients know by how we process their risk and reward constraints that we have designed a thorough asset allocation."

EXPLAINING RISK, RETURN, AND CORRELATION

John Rafal (Essex Financial) uses both conversation and charts to get the basics of asset allocation, including risk and return, across to his clients: "We do it through a verbal discussion and also use charts. We have a discussion about the allocation between stocks and bonds and the interplay between return and standard deviation. So we can show a client directly that the more they have in equities, the higher the return but the more volatility they will have. We have that discussion. It's a long conversation, including discussions of the efficient frontier. We also use a fairly standard chart from Ibbotson that shows, on the left-hand side, 10 percent increments allocated between stocks and bonds. It has historical returns from the beginning of time, for 40 years, 20 years, and 10 years. It shows the number of down years, average return, and standard deviation."

Michael Johnston uses charts to deliver a variety of core information to his clients. "I have them consider a chart containing our firm's expected returns and expected standard deviation for up to 30 different potential asset classes. Then I show them a matrix sheet showing how a given asset class's historical correlation has compared to another asset class. I explain what correlation is. Next, I show them their current asset allocation and where it shows up on the efficient frontier, and then I show them what our proposed asset allocation is and where it shows on the efficient frontier. And then I compare their current and proposed asset allocations on an expected return and expected risk basis."

Ron Carson (Linsco/Private Ledger) also uses charts to explain correlation and diversification. "I do use charts to show clients the risk metrics. 'Here's where each one of these individual asset classes fits on the efficient frontier. And then here's where your portfolio actually resides. As you can see, by mixing these together we have offsetting movements in the asset classes so that the overall volatility of your portfolio is less, but look, you are not giving up that much return on it relative to these other classes." Ron adds that the key question is whether a portfolio component "adds risk or takes away risk. Everything here is about managing the downside. Sometimes clients come to us with 100 percent in bonds and they just don't understand that by adding two or four more volatile asset classes, they have the potential to reduce risk and still have the potential for higher returns." Ultimately, Ron says, "I want to tell a simple story about asset allocation, covering the average mean returns of asset class correlations and coefficients and how they offset one another, and then demonstrating all that in pictorial form."

Mark Sear prefers to describe correlation and returns by using actual returns from a variety of money managers and funds:

> We have a page that shows how A correlates with B, but I never use it because it's too complicated. The best way I've found to explain correlation is to use a page that we have in our presentation that takes a look at different managers going back as far as we want to go. Let's say we went back seven years. Then you will have all the managers on the left and their portfolio performance for each year at the bottom. For example, the portfolio is up 8 percent; some of the managers are up and some are down. So perhaps the bond guys are down and the stock guys are up. It's much better to hand that page to a client and say, "Look, let's walk though what happened in 2000. We know it was a tough year for the market. The S&P was down ten, and down at the bottom it says the bond market was up 2 percent. Let's go through and look at what happened here. Hey look, these guys had a lousy year. These guys had a good year. Look how they play off each other. Now, let's go to another year, 2003, which was a great year for stocks. Look at then how the value guy did 40 percent, the growth guy only did 10 percent, but the bond guy was down 7 percent. See how they correlate off each other?"
>
> We have found it more successful to go with actual results as opposed to the pages that say Investment A at a 100 percent correlates 68 percent with Investment B. We have it, and it's certainly a good page to be used in the right situation. But in most instances, I think people see, "Oh my gosh, that's interesting that the value portfolio, this large-cap value fund, did really well that year. Look at the small-cap aggressive growth fund, it was actually flat that year. That's interesting. I see how bonds did. Look at the very next year. And yet, look at the portfolio at the bottom. Up 8, up 12, up 7, up 9." Overall, we have very smooth results, with a very low standard deviation. And yet, in every year, you can go down the columns and see how people are doing, and it's frequently two or three years of good and then a year of bad.

EXPLAINING THE PERFORMANCE OF INDIVIDUAL PORTFOLIO COMPONENTS

One thing many clients have a very hard time understanding is that in a diversified portfolio containing less than perfectly correlated assets, when some or most components are performing well, other components will by necessity be performing poorly. Joe Jacques agrees that this is a difficult concept to communicate and he tries to let clients know about it early on:

> No. They don't understand it at all. You really have to educate your clients about that principle because they feel that every aspect of their assets should be performing at the same level. That's just basic human nature. We are all greedy. We always want all our assets to go up. But at the very first meeting, I sit down with them and give them an analogy: "Some of the investments we are going to put you in are going to do really badly. And you are going to be so mad you are going to want to throw a brick through my window. I encourage you to do that, but when you throw the brick through my window, make sure you attach a check to it because that's the best time to invest."
>
> Essentially, I emphasize that through asset allocation we diversify, and that is because I don't have a crystal ball. I am not smart enough to know what classes are going to be up and what classes are going to be down. What is going to be in and what is going to be out. So by putting yourself in a little bit of gold, and bonds, and value, and growth, and international ... all are different asset classes and will perform differently. But at the same time, if one asset class does not perform as well as the others, we will analyze it. We may not diversify you out of it because we still need that hedge in case another London bombing occurs or another hurricane hits the coast. You have to have the resiliency to be able to bounce back. Now that people are seeing those things happening, they are more able to relate to the strategy than they were before 9/11.

Louis Chiavacci takes a somewhat different approach. He has clients focus from the very beginning on the performance of their entire portfolio: "We try from day one to encourage them to focus on the bottom line, and realize that there will be very volatile components and relatively benign components to the portfolio. By definition, some parts of the portfolio will be performing better than the entire portfolio. And some parts will be performing less well. We have found that telling stories of how we've done in the past—what we've done right and what we've done wrong—helps them to understand exactly what we are trying to accomplish for them."

To help him explain this concept to clients, John Rafal has borrowed a phrase from a friend: "An author and good friend of mine spoke to our clients last April at our Market Forecast Seminar. He had a phrase that I've stolen, which is 'Being fully diversified means you will always be upset with one portion of your portfolio.' I think that's really the educational message that we have to start with, right from the beginning. You have to expect that you will be unhappy with something at some point. It's so obvious to say that, but it has needed to be said for many years of my practice. Not everything is going to work all the time. What we are trying to show people from the beginning is they shouldn't be piling into oil stocks at the peak or home building stocks at the peak. They should be fully diversified and stick to their allocations and sector weightings no matter what happens."

Mark Curtis prefers to use an easy-to-understand analogy. "Suppose you came to me and said, 'I own an air conditioning business, and every summer I can't hire enough people. My business booms and we are very profitable. The phone rings off the hook. Yet every winter, I lay off half my people. We sit around with nothing to do. What do you think I should do?' I would say, 'Let's go into the heating business. In the summer, when your heating business isn't doing very well, your air conditioning business will do very well. And guess what? You are going to be employed 12 months out of the year. Something is going to be doing well all of the time.' That's what we are trying to accomplish by diversifying a portfolio."

For Meg Green, the idea that some portfolio components will be up while others are down is just "part of the package. And that's part of the hard sale too," she says, "because if everything is working all at once, that means that it could all *not* be working all at once. If people looked at the downside as well as the upside, asset allocation would have to be part of their agenda." Meg continues, "If there is always going to be something working, that means that there will always be something that isn't quite working. But if we do our job well enough, we can trim the losses and ride the gains and know that there are going to be many times when we are going to buy low and sell high, as opposed to what people normally do, which is buy high and sell low, chasing last year's winners."

Paul Tramontano feels that most clients do not understand the concept of varied performance within a portfolio at first, but with education they often come around: "I don't think most people understand in the beginning, but when we start to teach them about portfolios and what diversification is, and how it operates, they begin to get an understanding of what we are trying to accomplish. We work very hard at building portfolios with assets that are non-correlated. We want assets that go up in different types of markets, and we want some things that go up when other things go down, and so on. Then we show them charts and pictures of how different asset classes have acted through the years during different market cycles. We will show them pictures from the '70s, and we'll show them pictures from the '80s. We'll show them pictures from the 1930's. It's easier for people to visualize and understand concepts when they look at pictures."

Ron Carson (Linsco/Private Ledger) tackles this issue in a very direct and almost directive way with his clients: "I always cover this with a prospective client. 'I don't want you to judge the individual parts of your portfolio.' I never want to hear about it, and I'm pretty blunt with them about this. 'Don't come in and say, oh, XYZ Fund or stock is down. I want you to judge your satisfaction by how the overall portfolio has performed.' And when they get their reports, of course, we've got the detail of every account and every security and every fund. But to me, the front page is all that matters. 'Here is the period covered. Here's what you gained or lost. Here's the percentage of change. And that's the only thing I want you to focus on. Because there are going to be times when some of your individual asset classes do go down by a significant percentage.' "

Tim Kneen also communicates quite directly with his clients about varied performance. "We educate them very strongly about how the various investments in their portfolio should work together. We measure that relationship on an ongoing basis through a line chart that shows how each investment works independently against the others. Then we tell them that by definition, if all the components of their portfolio are going up, we have massively failed somewhere. This might sound wrong, but it is what diversification is all about."

Shelley Bergman has certainly succeeded in educating his clients to look at their entire portfolio. "I encourage my clients to not look at individual stocks anymore, but to look at the bottom line. They don't even look at the short-term bottom line—like over a quarter or a six-month period of time—but do they look at it over a two- or three-year horizon." Shelley attributes his success partly to the fact that his clients have a realistic understanding of what to expect. "We try to underpromise and overachieve. We don't promise anything that we don't feel we can deliver. We like to say that our forte is not that we are right all the time, but that we strive to be right over time. This philosophy has permitted us to retain existing clients while growing our business through referrals. Our investors are very patient. We don't get a lot of calls from clients when a specific stock or sector is down."

USING INSTITUTIONS AS A MODEL

Chapter 2 discussed some of the differences between institutions and individual investors with respect to the overall suitability of following an asset allocation approach. But do advisors actually refer to how institutions invest or otherwise explain some of the basics of asset allocation in terms of what institutions do? Some advisors simply don't use institutions as an example. Ron Carson straightforwardly states, "I really don't get into what the institutions are doing."

Other advisors, however, do use institutions as a model. For example, Sanford Katz says that "There are many instances where I've sent clients annual reports for the Yale endowment or the Harvard endowment or another large successful institutional investor. I like to use them to educate clients if they are completely green and cynical about the investment process, or if they are completely averse to a particular asset class. The best example would be alternative investments. They don't like the illiquidity of a private equity fund. They don't quite understand the black box nature of hedge funds. And when you show them that, particularly in the Yale case—and I think Harvard is similar—alternative investments are actually a relatively high proportion of their portfolio approach. It helps clients see that this is something they might want to learn a little bit more about. As far as results, it's fairly common for many of these institutions to generate above-average annual returns. My client can't go out and buy 5,000 acres of timberland. Harvard might. But at least it gives them an idea to think outside the box."

Jon Rafal acknowledges that institutions have many advantages over private investors, but he still feels there are valuable lessons to be learned. "I've attended several lectures as to how the Princeton, Harvard, and Yale endowments are invested. And I've read the book by Jensen, Yale's brilliant money manager. The one thing I take away from all of this—and they all say it, and Jensen says it in his book—is that they rigidly allocate assets. Clearly, if you look at the Yale and Harvard and Princeton endowments, only about 35 to 40 percent are allocated to stocks and bonds. They have venture capital. They have private equity. They have all kinds of private businesses that they have started. They do commodities. They do hedge funds. They do all these things. Most average investors will not have access to, or the stomach for, these types of investments because they involve illiquidity and large purchase prices. So I think there is a lot to be said for following what institutions do, but not everybody can do this."

There is, however, something that John does "borrow" from institutional-level clients. "We try to run every client's portfolio like a pension plan or an endowment," he says. "We create an investment policy statement containing broad allocation outlines—the relationship between stocks and bonds and cash. Once we agree to that, we try to stick with it. But in down years we do spend a lot of time reminding them of our original agreement when they want to make adjustments."

How, then, do advisors actually get to that original agreement with their clients? Having given an overview of asset allocation in Part I and an overview of understanding and communicating with clients in Part II, it is now time to turn to the actual mechanics of asset allocation in Part III, set forth in three steps:

1. determining your client's needs, goals, and risk tolerance;

2. constructing, that is, actually putting together your client's portfolio; and

3. rebalancing, in all its many flavors and time frames.

Chapter 6: The First Step: Determining Needs, Goals, and Risk Tolerance

The first step in asset allocation is simple enough to state: *An advisor needs to determine a client's needs, goals, and risk tolerance before putting together an appropriately diversified portfolio reflecting and addressing these factors.* You can't put the cart before the horse, and you can't put together a portfolio with a reasonable, responsive, and sensible asset allocation until you know what you are attempting to accomplish with that portfolio. Once again, we are brought back to Chapter 3's wealth management approach: The key is to comprehensively, consciously, and holistically address the life needs, dreams, and goals of the particular client at hand—the unique individual who has entrusted the management of his or her wealth to an advisor—in the overall objective context of the client's financial, legal, and other relevant circumstances. (Mark Sear, Merrill Lynch, delights in pointing out that "given historical data, there is mathematically an optimal asset allocation for every person.") Therefore, thorough two-way communication, including an in-depth examination of the client's internal mind-set and external financial and legal affairs, is the critical and inescapable first step in asset allocation.

For Paul Tramontano (Smith Barney), the process begins with an intensive front-end interview:

> We start asset allocation from the ground up. We will spend a lot of time on the front end of the relationship, understanding people's financial goals and thoughts. In our initial interview I tend to spend as much time as I can, sometimes 45 minutes, sometimes an hour, asking every possible question I can about the family, their investment history, where all their assets are, how they are titled, their investment experience, their estate plan, if they have wills, if they have generational planning in place, and who their advisors have been. We really get to understand, first and foremost, where somebody's assets are and how they are allocated currently. We find that many times the way people are allocated and the way they think they are allocated are two very different things. Then we'll get into the allocation, after we spend some time understanding and deciphering the

numbers, and after we understand a little bit more about what the clients want out of their investments.

Paul has faith in his clients and believes that if they are asked the right questions, the necessary information will be revealed: "Our business, as you know, is about the folks that can ask good questions. The people who ask good questions are generally the people doing a more thorough job. We try to communicate as much as we can—even in our initial meetings and then during follow-ups—about the client's thought process. I always have said to clients, 'Most of our clients know the answers. You don't really know the questions, but you know the answers. You might not know the name of the investment you want to be in, but if I ask you enough questions and understand enough about your family, you will be able to give me a pretty good idea of how your portfolio should be set up. And then we can set it up accordingly." Paul adds, "If there is anything I would like to improve on, it is our communication so that we can attain a deeper understanding of what people's needs are."

Especially at the early stages, it is very important to keep the fact finding personal. Ron Carson (Linsco/Private Ledger) encourages this by having his clients focus on their previous investing experiences: "In the first meeting with a client, we spend a lot of time talking about risk and return, but I always like them to share past successes or past failures, things that they feel were failures, either with past advisors or with themselves. I want them to relate a personal experience so we can see why something may not be a good fit for them. Talking about something that's specifically happened to them brings it down to a more personal level."

John Rafal (Essex Financial) begins his personalization process by gathering details about who the individual members of the client's family are. In this way, he can develop a strong relationship with the client by seeing the big picture of the client's family and its overall goals: "The first thing we do is take down very extensive data—names, dates of birth, things like that—but also who are the kids and where do they go to school? Where did the client go to school? In other words, we want to get to know these people very intimately. We want to develop a long-term relationship that isn't going to be disturbed over time by competitors. We don't want it to be based on performance. A relationship is based on understanding clients' goals and helping them succeed."

WORKING BACKWARD FROM NEEDS, GOALS, AND OBJECTIVES

Hank McClarty (Gratus Capital Management) starts with the end in mind, then spends a great deal of time up front talking to his clients: "We try to determine what it is we are trying to accomplish with their money. Then we spend a great deal of time just talking about their past experiences, their goals, and what kind of income they are going to be looking for from the portfolio. For example, a lot of our clients are trying to give their money away before they die, so what are their philanthropic desires with the portfolio? Then we start trying to get a feel for their comfort level. 'If you invested $10 million in the market, and it went down by 20 percent in a year, you would be left with $8 million. Is that something you would be comfortable with?' I start throwing out different scenarios to them and try to get a feel for where they would be comfortable. And then I combine that with what they actually need from the portfolio, income- and growth-wise, and come up with an asset allocation based on that."

Jim McCabe (Wells Fargo Investments) also starts with the end in mind as he tailors his asset allocations to a client's specific needs: "Our asset allocations are dependent upon the client's objectives. Everything is tailored to the client's needs. Because my largest client's risk is in his business, which he knows very well and controls, the portfolio we manage is 100 percent fixed income, 90 percent of which is prefunded municipal bonds. His objectives are obviously very different from the average client's. Most clients have a balanced portfolio. Those who are younger generally have higher-equity allocations because time allows them to weather downdrafts of the equity markets. Asset allocation is tailored to each individual client's needs and objectives."

For Martin Halbfinger (UBS) the focus is on the big picture vis-à-vis the client's unique investment objectives: "What's most important to us is understanding the client's full financial picture. I don't think you can come up with an asset allocation model in the abstract, and every model probably ought to be different for every family, based on their risk tolerance and their goals and objectives for their money. Once you have that data and you really do understand how the family is currently invested, you then have an opportunity to create a beginning asset allocation model. I don't believe everything is formulaic, where it should be 5 percent or 10 percent of this particular asset class or that, because I think we're pursuing a moving target all of our financial lives. Things change all the time."

Brian Pfeifler (Morgan Stanley & Co. Incorporated, New York, New York), who works with ultrahigh-net-worth clients and foundations, focuses on the individual needs and concerns of his clients. "There isn't one asset allocation that's meant for everyone. We spend a lot of time with each client, really figuring out what they are trying to achieve. Some have very specific goals. It goes without saying that you have to tailor solutions specific to each client. Every one of my clients is different and I work with them individually to provide solutions that reflect those differences." Brian adds, "It's not overly complex, it's just that you have to be very thoughtful about each client's individual situation and needs."

Like many *Winner's Circle* advisors, Michael Johnston (Smith Barney) starts out with a questionnaire that is oriented toward uncovering the gamut of the client's wealth management needs, including risk tolerance (discussed in detail later in this chapter). "We use a questionnaire that is not limited to asset allocation, but is more slanted toward understanding the client's overall wealth management needs. It looks at their liabilities, their risk management issues such as insurance, their estate plan, and their charitable intentions. It's understanding what the client's views are in many areas, from risk management to estate planning to charitable contributions to income needs, asset allocation being just one area. All of that helps answer the questions: 'What type of investor is this individual? How much risk can she take? What objectives does she have?' This makes the asset allocation decision-making process easier because you've got a full picture of the individual, as opposed to asking her how much risk she is willing to take without understanding anything else about her."

The best advisors are crystal clear that the client's goals and objectives come first and that the actual asset allocation and specific products come second, almost as an afterthought. John D. Olson (Merrill Lynch, New York, New York), who works mainly with high-net-worth clients and corporations, couldn't be clearer about the focus that he and his team put on clients' goals:

> We talk to clients about asset allocation as part of our overall process, but it's not the first thing. It will come up early in the conversation, but it's not the first part of the process. We are very, very goal oriented with our clients. A lot of individuals will come to us really just wanting to make money. They haven't focused on their goals enough. So we are extremely focused, and we

push them to focus on what their goals are, such as retirement lifestyle—how much and when.

Whatever their goals may be, we explain they are going to help drive the asset allocation and that we really won't know how much risk or what the allocation should be until we have focused on the goals and used the software to flow everything out to see how much risk they have to take. What we don't do is have a conversation and have five asset allocation models, one for capital preservation, one for income growth and income, etc. We will do the goal analysis first, then see generally where people fit, and then fine-tune it and customize it.

Joe Jacques (Jacques Financial) is adamant about focusing on client education first, with choosing proper products a distant second. "It's basically just an education from the very beginning. You sit down and go through all your client's assets and liabilities. You try to identify all their goals and objectives. Once you identify where they are going, you educate them on the proper way of investing; the primary area that I educate people in is asset allocation. *And then the least important step in the entire process is the products that you are dealing with. You basically establish what the clients want, their goals and dreams. Putting them in the proper product is then kind of an afterthought. It's not really what drives the investment; the product is the last thing you do.*"

GATHERING OBJECTIVE FACTS, FIGURES, AND DOCUMENTS

Louis Chiavacci (Merrill Lynch) and his team begin with collecting and organizing all of a client's financial documentation and with the follow-up to make sure that nothing is missing: "Part of organizing an investment strategy is getting their financial lives in order. Our process therefore involves getting a copy of every document that governs their financial lives. That means every bank account and every brokerage statement, as well as wills, trusts, family partnerships, and all of that kind of material. We will build out and model their entire consolidated balance sheet, including every entity such as grants, trusts, etc. The first meeting is about establishing the personal relationship. In meeting two, they give us all this material. We then spend maybe 100 to 150 team hours understanding their entire financial situation. Then we come back to them with a series of follow-up items sorted in terms of urgency."

As Chapter 3's discussion of the wealth management approach mentioned, it is important for an advisor to know what all of a client's assets are. To make sure that he has complete information, Martin Halbfinger gathers relevant information by taking a "financial X-ray." He says that with respect to clients, he and his team "really want to understand the mix of all of their assets, not just those assets that they are considering working with us on. Unless we take all of those assets and put them in a format that shows where their total allocation is, we're working without a complete picture. Most of our clients don't get there on their own. They come to us with five spreadsheets, all different and never combined, and never with a percentage in each asset class."

Paul Tramontano gathers necessary information from clients by asking them in great detail about their financial history.

> I ask them for their entire financial history. I start with what real estate they own. How is it titled? When did they buy it? What was the cost basis? What do they intend to do with it? What do they want to do when they retire? Where do they want to live? Do they want to stay in New York? Do they want to move to Florida? Do they want to have two smaller houses instead of one big house? I ask them about their bank accounts. I ask them how they do their banking and if they write checks or pay online. I'll ask them where all their savings and investment accounts are. I'll look at all their mutual fund accounts. I'll look at their limited partnerships. I'll ask them about personal assets, jewelry, artwork—if it's titled, if it's insured, how its been passed through generations, if that's appropriate. I'll ask them about retirement accounts. I'll ask them about investments in gold, silver, or precious metals. I'll ask them about custodial accounts, trust accounts, outside business ownership. I'll ask them about their will, when it was updated, who did it, and whether they have an estate plan in place.
>
> This takes some time, delving into all of these questions and really digging down into understanding how every asset is titled. Sometimes you meet somebody and they say they have 100 shares of XYZ that their grandmother gave them. They want to keep it forever. We have to allocate around that. And so there could be a lot of subquestions in these major areas.

John D. Olson does not require that a client have all his financial assets with him, but he does make sure he and his team take them into account. "It's not a requirement, but if we don't have it, we want to know about it. It's part of the overall analysis. We include it because the process is meaningless unless we take everything into account. We can now add external assets to the Merrill review package we use."

GOING BEYOND QUESTIONNAIRES

While many advisors use a questionnaire or some other written document to determine both subjective information (e.g., risk tolerance) and objective financial and legal facts and figures, others feel that questionnaires are too limited, especially for the subjective information. John Rafal uses a basic questionnaire, but then he relies mainly on talking with his clients. "There are a lot of questionnaires I've seen over the years, but they are usually made to be fed into a commuter to produce a plan, and we think many of these plans are too canned."

Jon Goldstein (Smith Barney) tells us that his clients generally do not work well with written questions, but instead prefer to have conversations: "I don't give a form to a client and then have them fill it out. Our clients tend to be very wealthy and they are not going to have the patience for that. I'm just not going to get thoughtful, complete answers. But I'll use those sorts of questionnaires as a guide for a discussion, and my clients are happy to talk about things like 'This is what money means to me. This is what we worry about. And these are our concerns, and these are our hopes and goals.' After doing it for this long, it's pretty straightforward for me to translate those answers into a plan that gives us a high probability of meeting their goals."

In explaining why he asks scenario-based questions rather than using a formal questionnaire, Sanford Katz (UBS) compares the interview to an accountant's attempt at gathering tax return information. "I would say we never really use a questionnaire because it's just not personal enough. It's sort of like when my accountant sends me the year-end questionnaire so he can prepare my taxes; it goes in the garbage every year, and I later send him a shoebox full of semi-organized stuff. I suppose for people who have very straightforward W-2 wages and reoccurring deductions, it works. But I think we spend more time just talking with clients about their balance sheet, preferences, and needs."

Mark Sear asks written questions, but tries to make sure that he doesn't waste clients' time by sending them questions that he already has the answers to: "I hate the word 'questionnaire' because it's too impersonal; we like to ask questions. We don't have a formal set of questions; we just ask questions. We met with a guy in Denver who had already done a lot of trust and estate work, and so he didn't want a form that came in the mail with questions on trust and estate planning. We really don't want to ask about what we already know. I guess I am not a big fan of just mailing or e-mailing a list of questions. I want to get some information first so that I don't waste your time."

With respect to whether he uses questionnaires, Hank McClarty says, "I did for years. Now we go with the information that we have learned over the years. The questionnaire gives us much of the same feedback, but there is no personal experience to it. Instead, we sit down and explain to clients in real-life scenarios exactly what would happen and how it would impact them to determine how they would feel about it."

Jim McCabe says "I've never used a questionnaire. It isn't that simple. It's as much of an art as it is a science. At day's end, it is a combination of things." Jim and his team focus on "bringing our collective experience, asking the right questions of the clients, and combining market conditions with the client's long-term needs." As an example of how varied clients needs may be, he cites a family that recently inherited considerable wealth:

> The mother and father were our clients. They died within a year of each other and passed $100 million to the next generation (undiminished by estate taxes because of superb estate and life insurance planning). The beneficiaries were four daughters and a foundation. Today, the allocations are as follows: The foundation is two-thirds stock and one-third fixed income. One of the daughters is 100 percent fixed income. The other three daughters all differ with one primarily allocated to equity and two that are more equity but differently balanced. Even within this family, the allocation varies greatly across the board. The demographics are the same. They are all women in their 50s to early 60s, yet each of their portfolios is different. They should be very similar, but they all have different objectives, obligations, risk tolerances, fears, goals and market experiences.

Jim Hansberger and his team rely on what he calls "face-to-face profiling" to really understand a client:

> We have an extraordinarily detailed profiling session, face to face. It's not a pat questionnaire by any means; there are lots

more questions than standard Wall Street questionnaires. Face-to-face profiling simply tells us who we are dealing with, because you certainly have to know your client. You certainly have to know their level of risk tolerance. You certainly have to know their experience. You certainly have to know their goals. If they themselves don't know their goals, you have to identify them. Is this, in fact, a person who cares a great deal about leaving assets to charity and/or to their heirs or not? Is this someone who is a big spender or not? Is this someone who is a true consumer, who is going to run through their money? Does he want to make a lot more money? And it's not just about asset gathering; it really truly runs the gamut. It is a real discussion of how you feel about your children, philanthropy, who are you going to be responsible for in the future? If something were to happen to you, how would you want assets disbursed? Where do you see yourself ten years from now? And there's a great deal of attention paid to the whole issue of goals and risk tolerance.

Brian Pfeifler gives us an in-depth explanation not only of how he and his team get to know clients over time, but how this long-term knowledge can reveal surprising investment objectives and tendencies among clients:

> If a new person comes in, we want to spend time with them, get to know them, and understand particular data points regarding their situation, such as their family obligations and short- and long-term investment, donation, and spending goals. Important questions to ask include where is the money going both during the client's lifetime and upon his or her death? What current charitable obligations are there? What are the anticipated spending needs of the client and other family members? What prior investments has the client been in? What has the client's career been like?
>
> We try to gather this information and an understanding of the client's risk tolerance, and then discuss the asset allocation and its implementation. In evaluating investment opportunities, we generally discuss potential money managers available to implement the client's desired asset allocation. Our review generally goes through in considerable detail historical performance, the potential impact of different market conditions on the strategy, and ultimately what sorts of investment strategies the manager can help the client achieve. There is some quantitative analysis

that we typically do with clients relating to asset allocation and investments in funds and third-party money managers.·

At the end of the day, I learn a lot about the lives of my clients. I do not rely on a standard list of questions. Instead, I spend time with my clients and get to know them as people. During the "get to know you phase," I typically have two to four meetings, easily lasting one to five hours each. If you spend ten hours with someone, you really get to know them. For example, suppose a client has sold a big position and has a lot of cash. In that sort of situation, I will typically recommend that they slowly move into the markets and evaluate a number of available alternatives. We carefully look at specific money managers, put money with those managers, and see how they do. It's a gradual process. Along the way, we sometimes find out more about the client and what his true risk tolerance is.

I think there's an element of psychology in what we do to try to understand our clients. It's a process by which we dig deep into their personal lives and, through a number of meetings, come to a point where we better understand what they are looking for, what their obligations are, and what their financial and investment history has been. Together, we come to a decision about what is going to be done with their investments, and then, over time, we can make appropriate recommendations regarding adjusting their portfolio when their circumstances or situations change over time.

For Jim Hansberger, the key to uncovering what clients truly need and want is not only in the art of listening, but in paying special attention whenever clients state how they feel about something: "Asset allocation is definitely an art, not a science. There are certain scientific approaches to it, but it is definitely an art. A word that not enough people in the advisory business use is 'feel.' One of the things we always try to say is, 'How do you feel about X?' And I can tell you that if there's any one thing that I've tried to teach our entire group for a long time, it's that if they ever hear that terminology—'It's the way I feel about something'—just stop talking and listen. If you hear 'I really like this, but I just don't feel comfortable,' or 'I just feel like I should do X,' then let your ears perk, because that's when the client is really starting to tell you something that matters."

The bottom line for Jim McCabe, who doesn't use a formal questionnaire, is also that asset allocation "over the long run, is as much an art as it is a science. To purists this may be heresy, but I think being too quantitative sometimes loses the humanity (and the client), and, therefore, it doesn't always serve well. At day's end, part of what we hope to deliver is peace of mind and a good night's sleep."

ASSESSING RISK TOLERANCE

Both mathematically and practically, risk tolerance and associated topics are at the heart of asset allocation and modern portfolio theory. The whole point of diversifying a portfolio (by including less than perfectly correlated assets) is to reduce risk, measured as volatility, without greatly diminishing return. Put differently, the whole point is for an investor to take on no more than an acceptable amount of risk while still maximizing return. Two questions arise: What is an acceptable amount of risk for an investor, and how can an advisor work with clients to help them understand and identify their true risk tolerance?

It's important to remember that while the efficient frontier (see Chapter 1 and Appendix B) describes a line containing diversified portfolios that maximize the risk/return trade-off for any given time period, this line can only be drawn retrospectively. That is, modern computing power combined with widely available data on the actual performance of stocks, bonds, and other investable assets makes it relatively easy to retrospectively calculate a set of hypothetical portfolios that show where individuals of different risk tolerances would ideally have been invested. But going forward, despite the most earnest attempts at prediction, there are no guarantees that any given asset class or investment will continue on its past or current trajectory. In other words, going forward over time there really can (and will) be substantial volatility and investment losses, and that's why it is so very important for clients not to be invested beyond their risk tolerance. (As pointed out many times in this book, investors tend to make the absolute worst timing decisions when they are pushed beyond their cash flow limitations or psychological comfort zone during downturns, thereby further compounding their losses and in some cases making it difficult for their portfolios to recover.)

As a first principle, many advisors make sure that their clients do not assume unnecessary risk in order meet their needs. John Rafal says that he and his team "try to develop an investment allocation based on the return the client needs to earn in order to achieve his objectives. We don't want clients taking on any more risk than they have to. I am working with clients right now who probably need to earn $3 million on their portfolios to achieve their retirement objectives. They have $5 million. To avoid problems, we are not going to take the same level of risk that we would take if they had $2.5 million. A lot of advisors take on more risk than they have to. We try very hard not to do that."

John D. Olson also espouses a policy of having his clients take on as little risk as possible. "We really want to advise clients to take the least amount of risk necessary to get to their goals. So we really have to know their goals, and that drives the asset allocation. How could we possibly know how much should be in the different asset classes unless we really understand their goals and risk tolerance? So, once we know their appetite for risk versus their goals, we will look at it within the framework of their current asset allocation. We can then fine-tune it as to how much should be in equities, bonds, cash."

Quite often, an advisor will have to remind a client forcefully to minimize risk, as Mark Curtis (Smith Barney) recently had to do with one of his clients:

> I have a very wealthy client who is a widow. Her husband was a financial professional and while he was alive, she had little to do with managing their financial affairs. Once her husband passed away she assumed responsibility for her finances. Some years later we were looking at her portfolio and her allocation was something close to 20 percent traditional equities and 45 to 50 percent fixed income, another 20 percent in asset classes like natural resources, REITs, emerging markets, and hedge funds, and the balance in cash equivalents. She sent me an article about what a model portfolio looks like for different people at different ages. Then she said, "Based on this, I should be 50 percent equities and 50 percent fixed income."
>
> My response was, *"We've discussed your lifestyle and we've gone over your needs, and what we've discussed is that in order to look after your best interests, we only want to take the amount of risk that you have to and not more. And that's all we are doing. We are taking the amount of risk that is necessary for you to achieve your goals and no more. The goal is not to take more risk to make money; the goal is to find that fine line where you are taking just enough risk to achieve your goals, and hopefully no more than that."*

In many cases, however, "taking on as little risk as possible" begs the question of how, exactly, to balance the trade-offs between clients' goals, objectives, and dreams, and the amount of risk they are willing to take. In other words, in some cases, especially with particularly wealthy clients, an advisor can simply say, "Given your needs and goals as you have described them, here is a portfolio that will very likely achieve those needs and goals and that has as little risk as possible." In many other cases, however, especially with less than extremely wealthy clients, a conscious trade-off will have to be made between the amount of risk taken and the desire to achieve higher returns in support of various goals and objectives. Over the long run, more risk means more reward, but more risk also means more real chance for loss and, as mentioned above, not all clients are financially or psychologically equally suited for bearing much loss.

How, then, can an advisor determine a client's true risk tolerance? This is inherently a difficult task because, as Sanford Katz says, "It's just human nature that people's own estimate of their willingness to accept risk is not that well calibrated to their actual tolerance for risk. We need to find their actual tolerance for risk, because we don't like to take any chances." Interestingly, Sanford finds that some of his older and wealthier clients find out over time that they are actually less risk averse than they originally thought they were. "I would say that at least half the time, with an older client with a substantial wealth level, inevitably they are willing to take more risk than they think they are. Sometimes it's the concept of 'Why don't you bifurcate your approach to this and take $10 out of $50 million, or $20 out of $50 million, and be at least moderate with it? Not necessarily aggressive. And let's pretend the other $30 or $40 million is pure principal protection, meaning the money almost doesn't exist — it's just there to generate income.' Over time, I find those people will often move toward the middle of the risk spectrum."

After Martin Halbfinger and his team take their "financial X-ray" to gather hard facts and figures, they then move to an "interview of the client, assessing what kind of risk they are willing to take. We define risk as not about making or losing money, but about what they can stomach in terms of volatility. We think measuring volatility is a very, very important process in order to understand the risk to the portfolio. We need to understand the risk tolerance, the ability to withstand volatility, how long a period of time these assets need to serve this family, and what kind of major expenditures they think they are going to incur."

Meg Green (Royal Alliance) starts with a risk tolerance questionnaire but her real aim is to understand her clients on an emotional basis. "We have a risk tolerance questionnaire that we like to use with most clients. I won't say all clients, because some will just sit there and stare at you. 'What do you mean? I don't want to lose any money! But yes, I want to make the most money I can.' Then we'll sit and talk about it. When the markets were being so absolutely awful, and a lot of people were scared to death, I would say to them. 'Okay. Let's deal with this position. Would you feel worse if we sold it and it kept going up, or we didn't sell it and it went down?' Now, I am making it emotional. That's how they are going to make their decision. Not intellectually, but emotionally. That's what risk tolerance really is. Some people just don't care, and then other people care too much."

Sanford Katz, tackles the risk tolerance area with clients right from the start, to set expectations, avoid client disappointment, and to get a feel for what the client's true risk tolerance is:

> The first thing I do is test and back-test their tolerance for risk. Especially early in the relationship, I will call them in either good performance times or bad performance times when the markets aren't cooperating. Particularly when they first put money to work, people hate to see their portfolio go from a dollar to 90 cents. And so I will constantly reach out and take their temperature, in terms of their understanding and comfort level. Doing this is very important because it avoids surprises. It avoids client disappointment. In the process you really get a sense for how people feel about it. We'll ask a client early on, for example, 'How would you feel if we had a diversified portfolio that conformed to an asset allocation that we agree on, and within a period of 6 or 12 months, you never achieved a new high water mark? Say the markets don't cooperate and we have a slow or a rapid 10 percent loss of capital? How do you feel if it's 20 percent? How do you feel if it's 30 percent?' What we find is that people often answer these questions one way and then behave very differently when it happens.

Ron Carson (Linsco/Private Ledger) embeds his risk tolerance questions in the "personal and confidential financial profile" that he has each client fill out:

> We sometimes spend a lot of time on this to see if they are consistent in the way they answer their questions. If a client says, "I'm a conservative investor, but you know what, I would invest in a speculative startup," or "I'm an aggressive investor, but you know what, I can't stand to have my portfolio go down by more

than 15 percent," then I've really got to spend some time with this person. I'll ask, "Do you really understand that seeking higher returns increases the likelihood of downside exposure?" If I can't get through to them, and they really believe they can get a high return without taking on risk, then I won't take the conversation any further, because we are not going to work well together.

Although Kathy Tully (Morgan Stanley) has doubts about some questionnaires, she uses them in concert with her knowledge of her clients to help expand their horizons and determine their true risk tolerance. "A lot of forms really don't ask the questions the way a client would understand them," says Kathy. "Normally, clients are with me when we fill them out. Sometimes, though, I will send out the questionnaire ahead of our meeting, saying, 'Go ahead and fill it out on your own.' When we get together, I'll walk them through it. In knowing the client, I know how they might answer something based on the black and white question. Then I will explain a lot more to them. Sometimes we have to look at what this particular answer would result in, and we find out that's really not what they meant. So it's a constant educational process about what kind of risk there is and what it can do later on. I have to expand their horizons. As for risk tolerance, my favorite question is, 'Do you want to maximize your return in the good times? Do you want to maximize your return in the good times ... or minimize your loss in the bad times?' That proves to be a very thought provoking question."

LOSS AVERSION AND AVOIDING TIMING MISTAKES

"Loss aversion" is an important aspect of risk tolerance. Tim Kneen (Citigroup Institutional Consulting) says that he and his team "spend time talking about what drives individual people to answer questions in certain ways." He then has clients focus on their worst-case scenario: "We ask clients to define for us what their worst-case acceptable scenario would be. One client might say 'not achieving our required rate of return,' another might say 'a loss of 10 percent,' and another might say 'any loss at all.' We then have to put that into numbers for them by showing them worst-case scenarios in different environments for different mixes of financial assets."

Ron Carson is very up-front with clients about this issue: "The first question we ask a prospect when they come in—and I did this, this morning—is 'How much can you afford to lose?' And the prospect looked at me as if to say, 'Well, I don't want to lose any money.' So I continued, 'At some point your portfolio is going to go down in value. I don't know if it's going to go down the first quarter you invest with me, or if it's going to happen three years from now. But I promise it's going to go down. And if we can have a percentage of decline that you are comfortable with, and you don't do the wrong thing at the wrong time, such as sell out at the bottom, the upside will take care of itself.' And he looked at me and said, 'You know what? You are right. Because in the past when I was not successful, I've had a good stock or a good fund and I got scared out of it, only to sell it and check on it three years later to just kick myself for not sticking with it.' "

Louis Chiavacci finds that when he asks clients to respond to a variety of scenarios in which their portfolios decline by different amounts, they will usually respond honestly and direct him to the right amount of risk for them:

> We discuss risk tolerance, not in technical terms, but in layman's terms, and we are very clear about it. The discussion might go something like this: "Suppose we invest and construct a portfolio that appears to be appropriate for you. We put our best thoughts into it, our best managers, all of our best reads on asset class valuations, etc., and you entrust us with $20 million. And then it's a year from now, and we come to you and we say, 'Congratulations. We've had a terrific year. Your portfolio is worth $19 million. And at the same time, the Dow, which was at 10,600, is at 8,000. How do you feel?' "
>
> Well, that's where we see if they squirm in their seats a bit. Usually people are pretty honest. "Well, I'm not going to feel good, but because the market was down so much, I guess I'm okay." And the conversation will continue, "Well, what if we were down $2 million, or 10 percent, and the market is down 30 percent? Are you okay with that?" "Well," they might respond, "the market is down 30 percent, I'm still okay with that." "But what if we come to you at the end of year two and now after being down 10 percent, we are down to $17 million but the Dow is at 6,000." "You are fired," they say. So then we know that's too much risk.
>
> We have them fill out surveys and really get to know them. But really, the discussion is about losing money and their willingness to stay with a thoughtful, sound long-term investment strategy in the face of temporary losses ... because you never know when the

losses occur that they are truly temporary. You really don't know. We try to get them to come to grips with this concept of losing money. And when we do have this discussion we really find that people will very honestly answer your questions and will help steer you toward the right portfolio for them.

Louis continues with an explanation of why, especially during downturns, it's critical for a client (and the client's advisor) to have made an accurate risk tolerance assessment:

> If we go back to what Ben Graham and Warren Buffett have taught us, good investing is 20 percent intellect and 80 percent temperament or psychology. And so, trying to get the right portfolio in place to avoid a big mistake is really one of our primary objectives. The biggest, most expensive mistakes that we have watched investors make were usually decisions that were made under financial stress, for example, four trading days after 9/11, after the market had already dropped 25 percent. Rarely do we get a client that comes to us after a 2000 up move in the Dow and say, "You know what, I really think it's time to reduce my exposure to equities." It just doesn't happen. Yes, people do panic after the markets have already gone down meaningfully. A good, thoughtful, well-constructed portfolio is a great friend of time. For somebody who is taking more risk than they really can stomach, it's only a matter of time before they panic and sell out at an inopportune time.

Michael Johnston echoes a similar theme, noting that clients tend to underestimate their risk tolerance, that this often leads to substantial timing errors in selling stocks, and that special consideration must be paid to those clients who have previously been successful entrepreneurs:

> They can give us some idea of what their risk tolerance is, but it isn't until we get to where we are looking at different asset allocations, expected returns, and standard deviations, and seeing what their worst-case versus best-case scenario is in a given year, that we begin to realize what it really is. They may say they are an aggressive investor up front, but when we put out an aggressive asset allocation analysis, they will look at it and say, "Oh my no, I don't want that much."

Mark Sear has a well elaborated theory of loss aversion framed around three types of wealthy individuals and how important it is for each type to know whether they are satisfied with what they have or whether they want to reach for even higher levels of wealth:

There are three kinds of wealthy people. First, there are those who are wealthy and can pretty much buy whatever they want. But the minute the money stops, they are poor. I call that "A" kind of wealth. Then there is "B" kind of wealth, which is a guy who has enough money in his investment portfolio to replicate the life that you have in "A." For example, consider a guy who is spending half a million dollars a year because he's earning a million and having a great life, and then he amasses enough wealth to have a portfolio that throws off half a million dollars a year after taxes. It's a different kind of wealth. He can now stop working and live the same kind of lifestyle as in "A." "C" is the wealth of a person who has so much money he can influence government. He can influence sports. He can influence society. He can influence markets. He can buy an island. He can buy an airplane. That type of wealth is completely different from the guy who has enough assets to retire and replicate his professional employment. Those are three very different kinds of wealth.

We try to say to people that if they are lucky enough to ever get to "B," they should never take enough risk in their portfolio to ever send them back to "A" unless they are driven to be the big guy, that is, to rise to "C" level. If you have $15 million after taxes, you can invest that in absolutely conservative high-quality assets and have a very low probability of losing money over a long-term period of time. You'll never have to go back to work and you can live a great life if you invest wisely. But if you want to have an island and a baseball team and influence politics, you better take all $15 million and put it in one idea. Then you pray you were right, and maybe it goes to $300 million.

If you want to be that kind of guy, hey, go for it, take your $15 million and roll the dice. But if you don't care about that, and what's really important to you is preserving all the work you've done to get there, then make it bulletproof and don't risk going backward. I've seen way too many people in the tech bubble get to $40 million and go back to $5 million. And you know what? $5 million is great. But try to retire on $5 million of 3 percent tax-free bonds. Just so you know, that's $150,000 after-tax per year, and these guy are used to spending $150,000 a month. That's a problem.

The marginal utility of money is very important in what we do. The marginal dollar you make when you are rich already is less valuable than the dollar you make when you don't have any money. The exact opposite happens when you are rich. When you are rich, you don't need that extra buck. This is the thing we talk to clients about. Once you get to a level you are comfortable with, tell me if you want to buy the baseball team, because we can advise you or send you somewhere else. But if you are happy with what you've got, we can protect it.

It's very, very important to have the right mind-set. To get to $15 million, you are the gunslinger. Right? You've taken the $100,000 that you got from your grandfather's passing and put it all into one company. Then you bought another company, and then you merged with something else. Then finally, after 30 years of work, you sold this company for $20 million, pretax. After tax, it's $14 million or $13 million. And you can invest that all and have half a million bucks in cash flow and go fishing whenever you want or have a house in Cabo San Lucas. You've done it. Well, don't take it and put it in risky stocks. It could take you back to $6 million so you have to go and buy another company and go back to work. That's what we talk about.

Historical events can change an investor's appetite for risk. Joe Jacques has seen a change in the risk/return equation since 9/11 (an event whose repercussions will be discussed in greater detail in Chapter 12). "The whole strategy has changed since 9/11," says Joe. "Before then everybody was willing to take a lot of risk because they didn't think there were any downside consequences. Now people are much more sensitive. Then, somebody would come in and say they wanted me to guarantee them 15 percent. Now those same people are saying, 'If you can get me a 5 percent return, I am happy. I am willing to give up my upside if you can protect my downside.'"

Hindsight can also show that even if an advisor correctly pegs a client's risk tolerance, it's still entirely possible to make the wrong decision. Paul Tramontano relates the following story: "It was New Year's Eve in 1999, and I had a client who had taken a bunch of money out of the market because he was worried about Y2K, and now he wanted to put his money back in the market because it looked like Y2K was not going to be a problem. I said, "Perhaps this isn't the right time to get reinvested. You took money out and the market is running away from you. Would you feel worse if you put money in and it went down and you had to wait a long, long time to break even, or if you waited and didn't put any money in and the market went up without you?" He said, "I'd feel worse if the market went up without me. I need to reinvest." So that's how we made his decision to be invested. It turned out to be the wrong one. But, I really spent time trying to understand his psyche and getting him to where he wanted to be. Fortunately, I didn't let him invest as much as he wanted to, so we saved him some money."

For Paul, as for many of the advisors, the ultimate key is to create an opportunity for clients to disclose their true risk tolerance. Paul says, "I ask questions like, 'Would you feel better if the market went up 20 percent and you weren't part of it, or would you feel worse if the market went down 20 percent and you were invested in it? Tell me your feelings and how you would react to those things.' I try to get some subjective points into our discussions so I can really understand how somebody is thinking about their portfolio."

In the end, what clients say about their risk tolerance, and what they truly believe, may be two very different things. As Jim McCabe says, "The acid test is when the market drops 20 or 30 percent. That's when their true colors will come out and they will let you know of their discomfort or whether they are fine with that. Nobody minds upward volatility, but it's surprising how little most people can tolerate downward volatility."

LIQUIDITY AND CASH FLOW NEEDS

Reaching an illiquid financial position can be so devastating that many advisors start with a client's liquidity and cash flow needs, make sure that these needs are handled first, and then "back out" the rest of the asset allocation. Sanford Katz attempts to anticipate a lack of tolerance for illiquidity, which is something that can otherwise greatly surprise both clients and advisors: "When things are great, people have tremendous tolerance for illiquidity because they usually have excess cash coming from other sources. There are returns from liquid sources. Principal and income become fungible, and you can always create needed cash flow by simply harvesting gains. When we get into down markets, we find that equation to be very different. We try to prepare people for both scenarios ahead of time."

Jon Goldstein points out one reason why it's important to avoid a cash flow shortage: "What we say to clients is that you want to decide when to sell investments, you do not want circumstances to tell you when to sell them. Because when that happens it's often a bad time to sell." Jon's discussion of the difference between individuals and institutions with respect to liquidity issues sheds some further light: "In developing an appropriate asset allocation for an individual client, the approach is different than for an institution. Individuals are mostly guided by liquidity needs—money when they need it. So, there's an awful lot of lifestyle planning that you have to extract from clients before you can come up with an investment plan. That's very different from what I would do for a large endowment, for instance." Finally, Jon explains that what he and his team do differs from traditional asset allocation, because of their central focus on liquidity needs:

> We have a theory that since all of our clients are individuals our practice is a bit different from traditional asset allocation, which really grew up out of the defined benefit pension plan market where there is a pool of capital and obligations that need to be met for many, many years hence. The idea there was to smooth out volatility by combining different asset classes. We think that's definitely appropriate for individuals, but people are more emotional and while they may say they've got a long time horizon, they certainly behave differently in periods of extremes, especially on the down side versus the upside. We tend to focus very heavily on downside volatility. I've yet to have a client complain about upside volatility, which everyone enjoys.
>
> So, cash flow and the ability to fund lifestyle—which we call liquidity planning—tends to be as important as asset allocation, and is where we always start. If we can insulate a client from the peaks and valleys of the market by providing plenty of liquidity to fund their day-to-day needs, they can be coolerheaded and allow the principles of asset allocation to work. We therefore spend a lot of time with clients determining how much money it takes to meet their goals. If we provide it with a fixed income portfolio, we will let a lot of this process drive the percentage allocated to fixed income, rather than trying to optimize a certain rate of return or risk. In some cases, clients' needs are well beyond what a fixed income portfolio can generate, and then we get into the heart of what asset allocation tries to do, which is combining asset classes that are less correlated to one another to smooth out volatility.
>
> So, we do an awful lot of work in figuring out how these asset classes perform when the markets are under stress and the last five years have given us pretty good data for that kind of stressful market.

Michael Johnston reveals how he and his team, instead of focusing on risk tolerance directly, instead start out with their eye on the client's liquidity needs and work backward from there:

> We find it more difficult to determine clients' risk tolerances up front. We sort of work backward to reach what we think the asset allocation should be. First of all, we try to determine how much income they need to live off of, taking into account their tax rates and itemized deductions. From there, we determine how large of a bond portfolio, or how large of an income-generating portfolio, they need to meet their lifestyles. Then we determine if that represents too large a part of their portfolio, such that the rest of the portfolio is not able to grow above the inflation rate and keep the overall portfolio from growing.
>
> In other words, if they are spending 5 percent per year on half of their portfolio for living expenses, then the other half of the portfolio not only needs to generate enough return to stay above the rate of inflation for that half, but it also has to generate enough return to stay above the rate of inflation for the bond portion, which may be distributing all of its money in the form of income. So, you don't want to have it too lopsided, where you've got 80 percent in bonds to meet their income needs and only have 20 percent in equities or alternatives, and there's just not enough growth-oriented assets to make up for the declining value due to inflation over time. So, once we've looked at what their income needs are on an after-taxes basis, and backed into what we think would be an appropriate amount in fixed income, then we take it into the asset allocation model.

Drew Zager (Morgan Stanley & Co. Incorporated, Los Angeles, California), who works with ultrahigh-net-worth clients, finds that there are some interesting twists in working with very wealthy clients around cash flow issues: "Our clients generally have more money than they need for their ordinary course of spending and lifestyle needs. From a portfolio management perspective, it comes down to a question of what portion they need to set aside to meet their lifestyle spending needs. For the ultrawealthy, I have noticed that many will pull out an arbitrary amount to set aside for their cash flow needs and keep, let's say, $10 million liquid. I don't necessarily want to drag down their portfolio's overall performance by keeping too much liquid—so we often work with the client to establish a separate discretionary account that is designed to manage liquid assets in a way that is customized for the customer's own goals and risk tolerance."

RETIREMENT NEEDS AND ESTATE PLANNING

Simultaneously taking retirement and estate planning needs into account is one way advisors help to manage all of their clients' wealth. Ensuring a comfortable and desired lifestyle and then leaving a positive legacy to future generations and philanthropic causes are both important goals which can best be met with the help of an advisor who maintains a pragmatic, holistic, and long-term perspective.

With respect to retirement, Mark Curtis focuses on the client's future liabilities: "If you spend $100,000 a year today, but once in retirement you are going to need today's values of $80,000 and you no longer have earned income, then your portfolio has to provide 100 percent of the needed income. Now keeping in mind that that liability grows somewhat with inflation every year, what do you need to save? And at what rate does it need to grow? You've got to have a plan that is indexed toward your future liability. It's similar to a defined benefit kind of assumption. The analysis is a combination of how much do we need to save per year, and how should it be invested to fund that future liability?"

Paul Tramontano endeavors to take retirement needs into account by keeping his clients' asset allocation strategy as simple as possible: "Our strategy is very simple; in fact, we try to keep it as simple and as short as we possibly can. In its simplest form, if we are providing for a retiree, we will not use a lot of fancy programs for asset allocation. We will build an income stream for that retiree which meets his needs and we might use fixed income or dividend oriented companies or perhaps an alternative investment to create an income stream." Once again, we find that for the best advisors, it's the client's needs that drive the asset allocation. Paul continues: "Once we've created the income stream that they need in retirement, we will generally invest the rest around a growth-oriented strategy or an inflation protection strategy, depending on their level of risk tolerance. And so, we really back into our asset allocation strategy in the simplest form, based on what the needs of that client are."

In the context of understanding a client's retirement needs, it's always important for an advisor to set reasonable expectations on the client's part with respect to total portfolio return. Hank McClarty says, "We explain to clients what a real return is, and what they should expect from the portfolio. A lot of people are assuming 10 or 12 percent net return. We've got to tone that down, because the compounding effect can skew the end cash flow result if returns are assumed too high, especially when you account for taxes."

In addition to taking advantage of scenario planning and managing for total return, long-term retirement planning may require ongoing changes to the client's strategic asset allocation. According to John Rafal:

> We tell people that long-term projections in retirement have to be redone every year, because all these functions change every year. Everybody does one of those spreadsheets where you inflate your income by 4 percent a year for the rest of your life. Well, your income needs and your earnings do not work in a linear fashion. You will never return 8 percent in any one year, but you may average 8 percent a year. So, we do a projection as to how much you need to retire on. We do some Monte Carlo planning. For example, how much do you need so your portfolio can sustain three down years in a row? Then we try to develop an investment allocation based on the return they need to earn in order to achieve their objectives. We don't want them to take any more risk than they have to. I am working with clients right now who probably need $3 million to achieve their retirement objectives from returns on their portfolio. They have $5 million. They have no problems, so we are not going to take the same level of risk that we would take if they had $2.5 million.

Echoing Hank McClarty's concerns about total return, John explains how he and his team explain these matters to clients:

> We talk yield versus total return. With yield so low, in order to achieve your income objectives, you have to manage most portfolios for total return. Your payouts will come from a combination of income and growth, not just from income alone. That's a constant theme when rates are 4 percent. In other words, you could take all of your money, put it all in Treasury bonds, and still not be able to meet your income objectives. So we take the asset allocation and then equate it to a historical return. What we try to do is take out half and reinvest half. That's something that I do with all clients. So, suppose we are going to generate a 10 percent return based on a 60/40 allocation, and we are going to do a draw of 4 to 5 percent against the portfolio. We are not sure where it's going to come from. It could come from dividends, and it could come from growth, but obviously it will have to be a combination. And we will reinvest the rest. So what we want is income that increases annually from a rising capital base, because otherwise, how can you keep pace with inflation?

John then offers the success story of a client who followed his advice along the lines just described:

> We have a client who retired in 1985 with $685,000, and we were drawing $2,500 a month from his portfolio. He claims he now lives exactly the same, but we are sending him $9,500 a month, 20 years later. I know he lives better. He's got a plane, he's got two houses. He's done very well. His capital is $1.4 million. And that's because it grew over time, allowing us to pay out more income. We talk a lot about rising income expectations over time to keep pace with inflation. We've had a lot of guys retired now, 20, even 25 years. So it's important to be able to show that income can rise over time. You can't do that by putting all the money in bonds.

For Joe Jacques, "You make sure you learn what the client wants. You educate the client and set their expectations; I think that's the key thing. You educate them not to expect a 15 percent return. I educate my clients by saying, 'I'm trying to get a 6 to 8 percent return. And when you are ready to start taking an income stream, we are not going to take out more than 5 percent. Because, once you retire nowadays, life expectancies are 20 to 30 years. And we have to constantly increase our assets to adjust for inflation going forward.' That requires educating your clients so they realize how important this whole concept is."

A thorough advisor should also always take estate planning into consideration. As Martin Halbfinger puts it, "Part of our asset allocation model brings in estate planning, and it should. How you are planning for the future includes planning for future generations, and some of your asset allocation decisions should be based on this." Michael Johnston and his team start with a thorough questionnaire to determine a client's needs and objectives, with a special focus on integrating estate planning needs into the overall asset allocation:

> A 15-page questionnaire that our team built takes into account all of the information that we need to understand clients' financial situations. We go through it with every client, not just to look at asset management, but to understand their liability needs, their risk needs, and their estate planning needs. *When it comes to asset allocation, we need to take into account their estate plan.*
>
> For example, a lot of our clients have grantor-retained annuity trusts as a part of their estate plan that allow the future appreciation of the assets in those trusts to be passed along to their

children, above a certain government rate of return that's required to be given back in the form of an annuity to the grantor or the parents. In creating the asset allocation, those specific asset classes that have the highest growth rate potentials over a given time are more suited investment in the grantor-retained annuity trusts because we want as much of that appreciation as possible to go to their children, without estate taxes or gift taxes.

With respect to the overall asset allocation, Michael is careful to make sure that it matches up with the client's estate planning needs: "A number of our clients have charitable remainder trusts, some of which are net income makeup trusts, some of which are just straight out charitable unitrusts. If those are going to be used as a source of income for them, then first we've got to determine how to invest inside the CRT to generate that income for them, and we have to take into account that income stream as it relates to the asset allocation for their personal portfolio. So, in this first stage, we are looking at how we invest in each component of their estate to maximize each piece and make sure that they are working together."

AN ADEQUATE TIME FRAME

Whether considering retirement and estate planning needs or simply trying to preserve capital or maximize returns with minimum risk, what time frame should an asset allocation strategy embrace? For Martin Halbfinger, at least a three- to five-year time frame is desirable: "I think a mistake a lot of people make is they try to model something and then they decide they only have a year or two because they are going to use the money for something else. You can't have an asset allocation model really work that way. The way we've modeled our practice is that when we sit down with anyone, what eventually evolves has to be a three- to five-year game plan. That's the only way you can give your asset classes enough time to behave in relationship to what they have historically done in the markets. If you only have a two-year time frame, I don't think you can create a model that works." Martin explains his reasoning in more depth:

> I think a three- to five-year time horizon is what you need for any model to work. Not necessarily for any asset class. What an asset allocation model really says to you is that the reason you want to be diversified is because certain things are going to be working while others aren't. So that can never be in a one- to two-

year time frame. I really think that five years is ideal. And three years is on the short side. Ten years would be nirvana, but it's difficult to get there because clients can't really focus on a ten-year game plan. We show them a ten-year historical chart that is a very quick slide in our presentation. When we get to the five-year chart, it's a lot more meaningful because it's really right in their mind-set. When you talk today, it's very clear about what happened in '01 or '02. And that's really what you need. You need the balance. So, I think five years is right, but three to five years is the minimum for us in terms of the way we ask our clients to look at something and give it an opportunity to really kick in.

The other part of it is this: Nobody buys an asset allocation theory in two minutes. This is an evolutionary process. That's another reason why you can't just come in with a game plan and say, "This is right for you." There are also trust and integrity factors that have to come across and that takes time.

Mark Sear starts out from another perspective—a 40-year plan—but also realistically focuses on discussing three- to five-year periods with clients:

The customized model we build is based on 40 years of time. We only look at the first 15, and we try to talk to clients in three- to five-year year chunks, in terms of "It's going to take at least three years to know that the process is working." What we try to encourage clients to do is to take a longer-term approach to this, both to sticking with managers and giving themes time to play out. As to the asset allocation, we build it, but certainly changes happen. For example, if we build an asset allocation with a Fed funds rate of 1 percent and nine months later the rate is 3 percent, we may need to take a serious look at how we're utilizing our cash, so we always give time to let our original thesis play out. Some changes are made because of changes in market conditions. Absent that, we try to take longer time frames and build an asset allocation and give it time to play out.

John D. Olson puts his thoughts about time frames into the context of retirement planning: "The time horizon is their goal. So, it's kind of a lifetime time horizon really because, let's say, the retirement goal is in 12 years. One of the things we'll say is 'That's not the finish line.' That helps with the asset allocation because with some people, their mentality is 'Okay, I'm retired now. I should be entirely in bonds.' Life expectancies, as you know, are being extended, and so there may be an additional 30 or 35 years in retirement. It's important to talk about an asset allocation that includes having equities in retirement. So, I think the goal is maintaining their retirement lifestyle for the rest of their lives. This is why we meet every quarter to make sure we are on track, and why we monitor their portfolio's performance versus the kind of goals that they have."

GIVING ALL CLIENTS THEIR DUE

In Chapter 3's discussion of wealth management, the question arose whether advisors could afford the amount of time necessary to really get to know less affluent clients. Jon Rafal, who was previously described as "welcoming all comers," says that "ideally, you want to treat everybody equally. There is a cliché that you can spend just as much time on a $10 million account as you can on a $100,000 account, and this is probably not untrue. Our business is all about service, so what I try to do in the case of smaller clients is to share the relationship with other advisors. I become one of two advisors on the account, and the other advisor takes control so they have more time for the client."

Paul Tramontano makes the point that the greatest time commitment generally happens on the front end of the relationship, regardless of who the client is: "It's a case-by-case situation. There are some wealthy people who have been with us for a long time. They don't require a lot of work, because we've done a lot of work on the front end. My feeling is that there are 24 hours in a day. And we will work all 24 if it's necessary and if clients need us for something. We engage in a kind of 24/7 thought process. If people need us, they will get us at any time: day, night, weekday, or weekend. We are in the advice business, and our time commitment is not always related to the amount of money a client has."

Meg Green says that she discourages clients who don't meet her minimum account size: "We can certainly do a plan for you, but it's going to cost you more money than you should be paying for a plan." If the potential client persists, Meg says that "If they are going to come in as a client, then they get the full weight of a client. We are going to get to know them, whether or not they are an appropriate client for us. Not only is it the right thing to do, but each client goes out and spreads our reputation. So are we really who we say we are or not? We are. We are the real deal. So everybody gets his proper time of day."

Joe Jacques has a large, often middle-class client base. (Willing to help anyone, he tells us—tongue in cheek—that he has no minimums: "My minimum is that the client is breathing, and then I'm flexible even on that.") Despite his large client base, Joe still takes the time to really get to know each client's situation so he can come up with an appropriately individualized asset allocation:

> When I sit down with a client, I take a questionnaire and go over all of their assets, liabilities, their company's pension plan, and anything else that is pertinent. Then we discuss their true goals and objectives. Retirement and college education are important, but other people want to buy a larger house or a beach house. Others are supporting other people in the family. So you have to kind of look at their individual situation. Are they looking for retirement savings? Are they looking for liquid savings? Each have different products that fit different circumstances. Even though I deal with a large client base, I individually tailor my investment strategy on a client-by-client basis. Because I am with more of a middle-class clientele, the assets that a typical client has are a little less complicated than those of a business owner or very wealthy family. Basically you are not dealing with as many elements as in more complicated financial planning situations, and you are still within about a two-hour time frame. You can pretty much understand these clients' situation and then tailor a plan specifically for their needs.

INSTITUTIONAL DIFFERENCES

Do advisors who work with institutions, from pension funds to nonprofits to corporations, have special procedures for these organizations? On the one hand, it is incumbent upon the advisor to determine the needs, goals, and risk tolerance of institutions, which, while they might be confined to a smaller range than individual clients, are still unique to the institution at hand. On the other hand, working with institutions typically involves communicating with at least two layers of infrastructure, staff members, and trustees or board members.

Tim Kneen says, "We treat staff and trustees differently. At the staff level, we spend a lot of time talking. At the trustee level, we use questionnaires or 'polls,' as we call them, to get a solid feel for where the board is coming from on a lot of different issues. But even at the board level, we will spend time talking as well, because a piece of paper can never get a trustee to truly understand the net effect of some decision that he or she is making. Once trustees understand that there are consequences to any decision that they make, they make better decisions." Tim also makes the point that each institution has different "problems," and that it is his job to identify and help solve those problems:

> Institutions are all different. Everybody is managing a different liability. When I say liability, sometimes that's a future cash flow, such as a pension that is underfunded, or it's a current cash flow issue, like a foundation that has payout requirements. Regardless of which one it is, each institution has a unique situation that we need to solve for. *People think that we are in the investment business. We are not. We are in the problem-solving business.* My job is to find and help solve the client's problem. My job is to use asset allocation and manager selection. The rest of my toolbox has been built through almost two decades of experience in helping solve these problems.

In the experience of Mark Curtis, when a foundation is first being set up, there are similarities to the kind of thought process that an advisor goes through when working with an individual client. Not surprisingly, a good deal of communication with the individuals providing the funding is necessary to make sure that the foundation can accomplish its long-term goals.

> I have a well-known entity that has just created a foundation with $25 million in cash, and the foundation has a requirement to pay out 5 percent every year. The three principals who set up this foundation—all wealthy and successful individuals—are technology people and not really financial people. So, they sat down with their family office CFOs and came up with an investment policy that they pulled offline. The investment policy said that since we have to pay out 5 percent per year, we want to earn 5 percent with as little risk as possible. And accordingly, we want no more than 35 percent of the portfolio in aggregate ever to be in equities, with a targeted asset allocation of 35 percent equities and 65 percent fixed income.
>
> I went back to that client and said, "Let me add some perspective here. For example, your probability of success and that asset allocation with that payout rate is about 30 percent. Your probability of failure, which means depleting the foundation's funds over time, is about 70 percent." We then put together a

series of questions that was sent to each of them individually, and asked each of them to individually respond. First of all, what's the gifting policy going to be? Second of all, how would you feel if and when the fund started to become depleted? What would you be inclined to do? Would you be inclined to put more money in? Would you be inclined to cut back on expenses and gifting? What would be the strategy?

They then asked me a series of questions. I came back to them and said, "What this should mean is that you would only make variable grants, and that you may not want to make a specific commitment to any significant dollar amount because your goal is not to deplete the fund. Why not say, instead, that you will make various entities grant in percentages per year of the portfolio's value and in aggregate, not to exceed 5 percent per year? Now given your goal of not depleting the fund over time, here is what your allocation should be … ." It's interesting, because in some ways this is a very similar discussion to what we might have with an individual: What are my income needs in retirement as a percentage of my portfolio, and what therefore are the implications on my asset allocation?

CHAPTER 7: THE SECOND STEP: CONSTRUCTING THE CLIENT'S PORTFOLIO

After determining a client's needs, goals, and risk tolerance, the next step in asset allocation is constructing the actual portfolio itself. But how does this happen? How does the advisor actually "make it come together"? What is required to effectively turn an understanding between client and advisor into a well allocated portfolio? A famous one-panel cartoon shows a bearded scientist writing an extremely complex formula on a blackboard; near the bottom of the blackboard, instead of more numbers and equations, are the words "and then a miracle happens." Constructing a portfolio is not miraculous, but moving from an understanding between advisor and client to the purchase of the right variety of actual investments does take some careful consideration and effort. This chapter will explore how top advisors actually "make it so."

Importantly, many—if not most, or even all—of the best advisors rely heavily on their team members during the process of portfolio construction. The critical roles that team members play can be seen in the multistage process that Meg Green (Royal Alliance) and her team undertake on behalf of each client:

> We have two basic divisions that are closely related: the financial planning division and the investment division. We process the information from the client and create a financial plan; we know who they are, what they've got, and what they are looking for. Once we take a look at the whole financial plan, we are then looking at all of their investments.
>
> By this point, we've done a risk tolerance assessment, and we focus on what they are looking for. Is it growth? Is it tax sensitivity? Is it income? Members of my team sit down—usually four, maybe five people—and we have an investment committee meeting on this particular client. One of our investment specialists will put together a layout. Here's their current portfolio, and this is where they are. We look at the taxes, as well—gains and losses, and potential gains and losses. What's embedded, and what isn't? So we know what, if anything, we can move. And then as a group we will put things together and ask, "What do

you think about this? I think they could use that." Then some-body creates a spreadsheet so we can all see the organized data, then show it to the client: "This is your current portfolio. This is your proposed portfolio."

Jim McCabe (Wells Fargo Investments), in reviewing his process of actually making portfolio choices, says, "I work with a couple of partners as investment consultants. We don't have a formula, but we function well together as part of a very high-level team."

SOME INITIAL ALLOCATIONS AND STARTING POINTS

Assume that an advisor has done his or her best to understand a client's needs, goals, dreams, and objectives (including family needs, retirement and estate planning needs, and liquidity needs), as well as the client's risk tolerance and loss aversion, along with anything else that is of particular importance to the client's unique situation. What, then, is the next step? Where does an advisor begin in putting together an appropriate portfolio?

For Jim Hansberger (Smith Barney) the process has already begun during the needs assessment stage based on what he is "hear-ing from the client. It's very clear to me," says Jim, "which people are not comfortable with a lot of illiquidity versus those who are gener-ating huge amounts of income and cash and have no reason to be concerned about liquidity. So, it starts with liquidity, as well as con-victions about taxes, family, philanthropy, and so on. You never ever want to put people in a box, but you can start to get a real feel for the four main asset classes—stocks, bonds, commodities, and curren-cies—and levels of risk early on."

Jon Goldstein (Smith Barney) sees portfolio construction as tak-ing place in two major phases, what he calls "two cuts": "Well, there are two cuts: One would be strategic, and one would be tactical. Strategic is the liquidity planning that we go through. Every client situation is unique, and you don't necessarily have to force owner-ship in each major class of cash, bonds, and stocks. Some clients don't hold any bonds, because they simply don't need to. And some have significant portions of their portfolio in fixed income because that suits their goals best. What it then leads to on the bond side is pretty easy. We buy safety and we buy the type of bond that opti-mizes after-tax returns, so that might be tax-free municipal bonds. It might be government agencies. It's very rarely corporate bonds. We just don't want to take credit risk. So that's the first cut. The next cut is on the more exciting side of investments, which is growth investing. This can entail things as straightforward as stocks, but also hedge funds, futures, private equity, and all kinds of other investments. The majority of the time is spent, on how to optimize returns in these kinds of portfolios. In this second cut, on the growth side, there is some uniformity across our client base, and it stems from what our view of the capital markets is over the next two or three years, and sometimes even beyond. If two $10 million portfolios come to me and they are both growth portfolios, they are going to be very similar in approach."

As mentioned in the last chapter, the guiding light for Paul Tramontano's (Smith Barney) portfolio construction is simplicity: "What we are really trying to do is to keep our asset allocation very simple. And so we will talk to people about their income needs out of their portfolio, and most asset allocation discussions on income needs center around retiring. When people are retiring, they need to start annuitizing what they've put together as a nest egg, so we will first build an annuitized portfolio as the fixed income part of the portfolio, and then invest around it. That's how we back into our asset allocation."

Michael Johnston (Smith Barney) also works backward into his asset allocations, starting with income needs and also relying on optimization software and a close look at what asset classes are available and how good they look:

> I would say that my rule of thumb is to work backward. If a client tells me that he or she has after-tax income needs of $250,000 a year, then what percent of their overall portfolio would need to be in municipal bonds? The first calculation I do is for that individual to be 100 percent in AAA-rated municipal bonds on the part of the yield curve that's appropriate given the current interest rate environment. Then, from there, is the size of the remaining part of the portfolio large enough relative to the municipal bonds for it to grow at a rate above inflation on an after-tax basis in order to feed into the municipal bond portfolio so that the purchasing power of the bond portfolio grows over time as opposed to decreasing? If the client can meet those objectives based upon their income needs, then one asset class (the municipal bond portfolio) of the overall portfolio is determined as far as its percentage of the overall portfolio, and that is whatever amount needs to be in bonds to generate $250,000.

Then for the rest of the portfolio, we have models that look at the expected return, expected risk, and expected correlation between other asset classes in order to provide the appropriate mixture between those asset classes. But then, at times, certain asset classes and the strategies that we have might either be available or unavailable when we are looking to invest. Or the percentage that's allocated to a given asset class may be below the threshold or minimum size to actually get into an investment in that particular asset class. So you have to make some decisions of either rounding off or excluding a given asset class or two for either not meeting minimums or lack of availability at that particular time and then set the cash on the sideline until a later date.

Now, if the client's income needs are greater than what an AAA municipal bond portfolio can generate without taking too much interest rate risk, then we look at finding other ways to generate income in other parts of their portfolio. In that case, we might provide more exposure to structured credit strategies that generate income without having as much interest rate risk or in some cases, a strategy that is negatively correlated to bonds in an increasing interest rate risk environment to help offset the interest rate risk of the bond portfolio. Within the equity markets, we might overweight large-cap value stocks that pay high dividends to supplement that or, within the international equity markets, we might select a manager who is more value oriented and who tends to have a higher dividend payout than other international equity strategies.

Ultimately, it comes down to some basic math. First, based upon their income needs, we try to figure out how much income the portfolio needs to generate. Next, we use some asset allocation programs to preview some possible optimal portfolios. And then, looking at each of the asset classes that are being suggested, we see what's available and what the required minimums are.

Michael further summarizes his whole process, from start to finish (and even goes into rebalancing, the subject of the next chapter): "So, in the first stage, we are looking at how we invest in each component of their estate to maximize each piece and make sure that they are all working together. The next step is developing the asset allocation model. The last stage is just more of the maintenance stage of monitoring the managers, monitoring the client's needs, monitoring the tax implications, and determining when to exit an asset class or when to reduce exposure to an asset class or increase it, given changes in market conditions."

Ron Carson (Linsco/Private Ledger) starts out with a set of five basic models into which clients generally fall, although there are exceptions that need special attention: "We have set up five basic models, and all of our clients fit into one of these models. There's aggressive growth, growth, growth and income, growth and income plus, and conservative income. Then there are exceptions: Suppose someone transfers in stock with a low basis, and it's in the large-cap growth sector, and it's too much of their portfolio. We'll utilize a sell stop or some sort of hedging strategy to protect them. But then we won't buy any more of that particular asset class and as we sell the stock over a period of time, we'll eventually try to get them into the model that best fits what they are trying to accomplish. Probably 90 percent of our assets here reside in the growth and income model. It seems to fit almost everyone. It really boils down to what kind of percentage decline can you stand without panicking, without giving up on the process, and most people are in that 25 to 30 percent range."

As for how he actually chooses asset classes and individual securities, Ron makes use of optimization software, exchange-traded funds (ETFs), and a broad base of asset classes: "I use optimization software to identify the asset class. And then I have some exchange-traded funds that I monitor on a weekly basis. Not that we are making changes weekly, but I look at them every week. How have they performed relative to the indexes? For example, right now, with the growth and income model, I have 10 percent of the portfolio in convertible bonds, 6 percent in high-yield bonds, 14 percent in international equities, 8 percent in REITs, 10 percent in large-cap growth, 5 percent in large cap value, 7 percent in mid-cap growth, 4 percent in mid-cap value, 7 percent in small-cap growth, 7 percent in energy (this is a pure play on energy), 8 percent in emerging markets, 8 percent in small-cap value, and 6 percent in international bonds."

Sanford Katz (UBS) looks at many sources of information and pays attention to them all, but keeps a special eye out for information relating to "mean reversion" of asset class returns:

> There are so many sources, so many smart people and some not so smart people, who model these things and give suggested allocations. We listen to strategists all over Wall Street. The opinions never seem to match up because they are all predicated on a variety of differing assumptions. We look at everything that we hear with an open mind. I am particularly interested anytime I see an asset allocation shift change that's recommended by a reputable source. Usually those changes are small—"shift 3 percent

to cash" or something to that effect—so it's hard to make sense out of them.

Asset allocation reports are frequently published, whether they're based on tactical opinions or just on a mathematical relative valuation model. I do tend to like a mathematical valuation approach; I don't necessarily do a lot of the math, and I don't always even try to interpret it, but I like an approach geared toward relative asset class valuation. I grew up in this business with a relative value understanding of the bond markets—everything was based on spread relationships between securities. So, in my mind, the same principle applies across asset classes because future returns are somewhat finite in nature and hide in many places.

What do I mean by that? Well, the work that we do within UBS is very good, especially our global asset management group, which is really a world-class institutional money manager. I like to look at their quarterly reports and what their models are saying about small-cap versus large-cap, about international versus domestic, and about currency valuations. I haven't seen how the Federal Reserve operates firsthand. But to me, much of what the Fed looks at and much of their language relates to this same type of approach. They are looking at where capital flows are moving asset valuations, whether it's housing, commodities, precious metals, equities, or fixed income. I think the idea is that without some secular change—and we do have secular changes over time—there is some reversion to a mean return. Because the world is not perfect, asset classes will contribute to that return disproportionately over time. If you start with that framework, you can come to some pretty reasonable conclusions and potential strategies.

It's important to note, however, that just like virtually every other top advisor, Sanford considers the individual client's needs first and foremost during the entire process: "It's obviously unique to every client, particularly with the high-net-worth segment we deal with. When a client first starts with us—whether it's with cash or slow diversification out of a concentrated holding of stock—we have the ability to approach each situation in a relatively new way. We start by taking a snapshot of the current environment and opportunities. It's not just deploying a simple equity and bond balance or percentage split, but obviously involves utilizing alternative investments and so forth. With every new money mandate we have, we try to take a look at what's really working, and what's likely to work for the next 3 to 24 months."

Joe Jacques (Jacques Financial), who has a broad client base with a variety of retirement needs, starts by letting his clients know that he uses his personal investing experience as a touchstone for making recommendations to them: "One thing I always tell my clients is that I don't put them into anything that I'm not personally invested in myself. Because, if I don't believe in it enough to invest in it for myself, how can I recommend it to them? Basically, I am that same upper-middle-class type of person, so I'm trying to accomplish the same things that my clients are—retirement, education, and other important factors. So, these are the same products I'm dealing with myself, and as I monitor and manage my own portfolio, I do the same thing for my clients." Joe then constructs his client's portfolios by combining his knowledge of their objectives with his reliance on a group of familiar, well performing mutual funds and managers:

> As an investor with over 25 years of experience, I have done my homework and learned what family of mutual funds I am most comfortable with from a performance standpoint, because basically I look at performance. I talk to the fund managers within the selective mutual fund families that I deal with, and I also deal with the companies. As an investment advisor, I know what products my clients need and the goals and objectives they are trying to accomplish. A lot of times, if my clients are into a retirement type of product, I have certain products I know will fit their situation. If they want liquid investments, I know a couple of products that will fit with that situation. There are 9,000 different mutual funds and probably just as many annuities, and you can't analyze and evaluate everything. I pick out just a few of them. So I pretty much have my own portfolio of products that I deal with, and when I know that a client wants to accomplish a particular goal or objective, I've dealt with that situation many times in the past and it's very easy for me to know which product to utilize.

For Brian Pfeifler (Morgan Stanley & Co.) and his ultrahigh-net-worth clients, making decisions on portfolio choices comes down to a combination of many factors: "A number of different things come into play when the actual decision is made—client objectives and needs, risk tolerance, product balance, leveraging expertise from within the firm such as research views, putting my own views in there, and then combining them all."

Brian provides an illustration of how he brings this all together: "As an example, our firm recommended that it may be appropriate for some clients to have an overweighted position internationally. However, I also wanted to provide some of my clients with the opportunity to have some exposure to emerging Europe as well. So, for the appropriate clients, we went through and looked at the various investment choices, and settled on a money manager who has maybe a 15 to 20 percent exposure to emerging markets in Eastern Europe. In the end, the client made his investment decisions based on analysis by both myself and by the firm's asset allocation specialists. That analysis was customized to address the client's situation, objectives, needs, and risk tolerance, and incorporated an evaluation of the temperament and suitability of the investment to the client."

Brian's approach is in some ways a bit different from that of most advisors. He has an internal sense of where he believes his clients should be invested, and then he tailors his recommendations to each client's individual needs and capacities:

> As a result of keeping a close eye on the pulse of the markets and having consulted with specialists, I have sense of where I believe my clients should be invested. Then I have a healthy discussion with them individually about the pros and cons of incorporating my ideas within their specific portfolio and seeing what they want to do—if it's appropriate for them, if they have the ability to do it, and if it's right for them on an individual basis.

"LIKE BUILDING A BUSINESS PLAN": ONE ADVISOR'S DETAILED PROCESS

Mark Sear (Merrill Lynch), who works almost exclusively with ultra-high-net-worth clients, shares his overall asset allocation process, which he compares to building a business plan or a business model:

> We start with this idea of building a business plan or a business model. Many of our clients have just sold their companies. They founded a company and sold it to a public company, or they sold it to a private company for cash. So, if that's our new account, we will talk to them in the language that they speak, the language of running a business. So we need to build a business plan, and the variables in this business plan are not meaningfully different than what you would build into a corporate business plan. In a company, you talk about sales growth; here, the

growth problem is how quickly we can grow the portfolio. Expenses in a company are not unlike expenses at home. What are you going to spend? Are you going to retire? Are you going to continue to work and if so, for how long? So we show them a spreadsheet model that incorporates their every year going forward. How much are their taxes? How much is their mortgage? How much is their tax deduction against their mortgage interest? We try to build a pretty close model to what their life is going to look like. And that allows us to have an educated discussion about asset allocation.

So when we talk to clients about the process, we tell them we are going to build a model just like they would in running a business. It's going to be for their personal family, their family business. And we are going to know how much they are spending; if they are spending more than they are earning, that gap needs to be made up in the investment portfolio. Any future liabilities—college, funding their parents' new house, funding a new home for themselves, renovating an existing home, starting a new company—all those future liabilities need to be built into the model. We need to have a sense of when they are going to buy the new house for their mother- and father-in-law. Whatever they are going to do, we build it into the model.

Once Mark and his team have created the model, they begin their asset allocation analysis:

So now we have this road map that allows us to say, "Okay, now I know what we need to do. We need to generate a return of X to meet your cash flow needs because you are going to earn this amount of money, and spend this other amount of money, and then in year three, you are going to have this big negative because you put a million dollars in your house. Year five, you are going to start a new company, so that's going to be a million dollars; we need to make sure we have a reserve set up for that. And, just as you do for a company, you have an expense budget and an earnings budget." Then we overlay our asset allocation themes on this and we look at different asset allocation possibilities. So, we say, "Here are our themes. Here's what we believe in. Here's what we are trying to mimic in our asset allocation." That is how we explain our process to the client. We are not going to talk to them about what we like or don't like until we have a sense of what our options are.

After the model is built, Mark communicates it to the client, and engages him or her in finishing and perfecting it:

> Once we've built the model in a spreadsheet and email it to them, they can say, "Wait, this isn't right. My property taxes are more than that." Or, "I'm not going to spend that much. That's insanity." So they can change the model, and then we can work with it and say, "Okay, this is our negative or positive cash flow." Obviously if it's positive, it gives us a lot of flexibility. In many cases, 90 or 95 percent, they are either going to earn less, be completely retired, or spend more than their historical expense. In those instances, it's a negative cash flow, and the difference needs to be made up from the investment portfolio.
>
> Often you meet people whose starting assets aren't actually cash assets. They might be nondividend-paying stock, because they sold their company for stock. So we have to work through the diversification strategy and find out what makes the most sense because, obviously, how you liquefy a concentrated position will affect how much tax are you going to pay. You might use some charitable techniques, or you might use some derivative securities to get out of a position. There's a big overlay on the front end as to how you get to a liquid position. I haven't gone through this process with many people without their becoming very engaged. They comment by email, saying, "You've got to change this and don't forget that." Then I check it one more time before sending it back to them. Once we've gone through the whole process, it's so involved and it's so customized, I think they feel good. We can now sit down and say, "Okay, here's our business plan." And now we know exactly what we need to do once we get to the asset allocation.

The next and final step in this process is to make specific asset allocation decisions in accordance with the "business plan," starting with an assessment of where the various markets are today:

> Today, for example, bond yields are very low, and we don't like high-yield bonds because currently their spread to high-quality bonds is too narrow. So it's very difficult for us to get a yield out of fixed income. However, we do like nondollar bonds, which currently have a higher yield. And we do like high-dividend-paying stocks. So, an asset allocation that we might show you today might have a little bit more weighting toward high-quality, high-dividend-paying stocks, and a little bit more

weighting toward nondollar-denominated bonds, but no weighting to high yield. We may forgo a little yield, but keep the duration short because we think interest rates are going to rise. And we have no weighting toward real estate investment trusts, because we currently think they are expensive.

We take the needs that the client has articulated for us and we come up with a couple of different strategies. For example, in some instances, we talk to the client about other assets they may have, about how to generate more income in the early years because yields are very low today. Is there anyway we can cut down the cash flow in the early years to grow the portfolio a little bit more?

It's an iterative process. We go back and forth, with us doing the work and showing them alternatives. They'll sort of favor one, so we tweak that one a little bit. We'll come back to them three or four times until we finally have something that we all agree is going to give them the cash flow they need, be the least likely way to incur losses in the portfolio, and be the most certain way of creating returns that are acceptable to them. Most importantly, it has our viewpoint imprinted on it. It allows us to have the flexibility to say, "We do like this, we don't like this. And here's why."

The most important three things are: We've met the cash flow needs; we've taken as much risk out of the portfolio as we can given the client's risk tolerance; and we've allowed our thought process to be worked on. One advantage to having a 15- to 40-year model is that, like a company, we can sit down on a quarterly and annual review basis and say, "Okay, here's our business plan. In order to live your life, with what inflation is now, you need to have this kind of income. I can give you a couple of models if you want, if it helps. If a year went by and we didn't hit our target, we need to make some adjustments in the model." That's our typical asset allocation process. That's typically what happens.

NUMBERS AND TYPES OF ASSET CLASSES IN SOME TYPICAL PORTFOLIOS

At a certain point, the discussion turns from the overall asset allocation plan—the business plan or model that Mark Sear speaks of—and moves into the realm of specific asset classes and actual funds, managers, alternatives, and investments. How many classes of investments do advisors typically recommend and use in their diversified portfolios? The answer differs considerably. Some advisors use investments in a half dozen or so classes, and others go up to two dozen or more. This depends partly on the type of client. Even though asset allocation is appropriate for many middle-class and retail clients (see Chapter 2 on the benefits and suitability of asset allocation), their needs will generally be far simpler than those of wealthier clients and institutions, and can typically be met with the use of fewer asset classes. Wealthy and institutional clients, on the other hand, depending on their precise needs, may wish to take advantage of as much diversification as they can, thereby dividing their portfolios into investments from a great many asset classes, including certain alternative investments that may be difficult for noninstitutional clients to get into.

Terminological differences are important to notice. For some advisors, there are ultimately only four asset classes: equities (stocks), fixed income vehicles (bonds), cash (currencies and cash equivalents), and alternative investments (which include everything else). As Mark Sear puts it, "The main themes are cash, bonds, stocks, and something alternative, and that could be hedge funds, commodities, or even managed futures (although we don't use them). It could be a variety of things. On the macro level, those are still the main areas."

Mark Curtis (Smith Barney) takes a more expansive approach, saying that it is important "to really broaden your sense of asset classes. For example, natural resources, real estate, emerging markets, these are classes that a lot of individuals have overlooked. I think one of the first things we need to do as financial professionals is to determine what asset classes are appropriate to put into an individual's asset allocation." In short, there are many advisors who find that both for purposes of discussion and purposes of portfolio construction, it is useful to think and act in terms of more than four major asset classes. Ultimately, as indicated in Chapter 1, there is no "right" answer here, and the meaning and level of granularity that "asset class" typically takes on becomes perfectly clear in context.

Sanford Katz's thought process is instructive here:

> We'll usually talk in terms of what I would call major asset classes. So there are equities, bonds, and cash, but taking it a little further there is domestic versus international, small- versus large-cap, and so forth. And then there is the value versus growth continuum, a distinction we may favor after the initial

allocation in steps. We don't want people to bite off more than they can chew, so making allocation decisions one "dimension" at a time is a more sensible approach I believe.

As for the number of asset classes that he and his team typically use, Sanford says it's usually not less than eight to nine and not more than 14 to 15: "I would say we try to keep things simple. When we format our preliminary presentation or a potential asset class summary for a new client, or recommend changes for an existing client, if we drill down into the subclasses we are usually deploying at least ten to twelve. Rarely does that number go below eight or nine. And at some point, when we get beyond 14 or 15, it can be overkill. But, of course, Wall Street can define asset classes and subasset classes in increasingly microscopic ways. So at some point, it becomes more semantics than statistical benefit or reality. So we try to keep it simple, but at a level where there is proven benefit to separating sub-asset classes."

Different advisors will typically make use of different numbers of asset classes in their clients' portfolios. For Meg Green, "If you are going to consider all the different stock classes, you are going to be talking about maybe 12"" in one of her typical portfolios. For Joe Jacques, to achieve "proper asset diversification" a portfolio should include at least "growth and value, small-cap, international, real estate, and bonds." Joe adds: "For my retirement portfolios, I have as many as 15 different asset classes, and for my nonretirement portfolios, probably in the neighborhood of eight to ten different asset classes."

Michael Johnston pegs the number of asset classes that he uses as being between seven and 15: "In a given portfolio, there could be anywhere from seven to 15 asset classes represented for a given individual. Within the bond market, at least if they are in the top income tax bracket, they are going to have some exposure to municipal bonds in their taxable account. In the tax-deferred accounts (401ks, IRAs), they are probably going to have some high-yield bond exposure. Within the equity markets, we break the world up into large-caps, mid-caps, small-caps, growth-oriented investment styles, and value-oriented. Within the international markets, we break it up into four categories, large-cap developed growth, large-cap developed value, small-cap international, and emerging markets. And then in the alternative space, managed futures, various levels of volatility within the hedge fund world, and various types of credit structures. So you can see we can easily get to anywhere from seven to 15 asset classes."

Louis Chiavacci (Merrill Lynch) says that his clients typically end up with four to ten different asset classes, depending on how you count them: "A typical client will have municipal bonds and high-yielding municipal bonds. Both of those are fixed income, but that would be two. We do categorize large growth versus large value, and small growth versus small value, and international versus emerging markets. We do categorize REITs as a separate asset class. We categorize hedge funds as an asset class, even though in their true sense, they are not an asset class. We are usually looking for something that is market neutral, with respect to hedge funds, as opposed to market directional. And we do often have exposure to private equity. So, depending on how finely you want to count that, it's four to ten different asset classes."

Martin Halbfinger (UBS) finds that he typically puts his clients into what he sees as six asset classes: "They all have a piece of the model at some portion. Cash and then fixed income are two. It used to be that it was only fixed income, but cash and cash instruments have become a much bigger part of the model today. Then equities. International—in our view—is a separate asset class because it's clearly underutilized in most investors' portfolios. Alternative assets, which include a combination of hedge funds and private equity, are an increasing percentage of an allocation model. There are obviously subsets within equities (such as large-cap growth and mid-cap value) depending on how you want to use them, and we combine our alternatives as part of our equity allocation."

STYLE BOXES

In the mid-1980s, the mutual fund reporting and analysis company Morningstar introduced the idea of the "style box." Consisting of a 3 × 3 grid, with size on the vertical axis (from top to bottom, Large, Medium or Mid, and Small), and "Investment Valuation" on the horizontal axis (from left to right, Value, Core or Blend, and Growth), the style box categorizes stock funds into a total of nine basic types, as follows:

Large Value	Large Blend	Large Growth
Mid Value	Mid Blend	Mid Growth
Small Value	Small Blend	Small Growth

These styles can apply to both mutual funds and privately managed funds, although in both cases there may be variability or "style drift," that is, certain managers are harder to classify and do not necessarily stay mainly within one or even two styles. (A related discussion of manager selection and performance follows later in this chapter.) In theory, the upper left box has the most conservative stock funds, and the lower right denotes stock funds that are the most aggressive and riskiest. Other style boxes have since been developed—for example, style boxes that apply to international funds or bond funds—but references to "styles" usually mean the preceding Morningstar equity funds style box.

When making asset allocation recommendations within the overall class of equities, some advisors pay close attention to this grid, and others do not. Meg Green, for example, uses styles to make sure clients are properly diversified: "I want to be very style specific. I have people who will look deeply. We will do footprints. What a lot of people don't realize is that they might be in four different funds and the top ten holdings are all the same. Well, that's not asset allocation."

John Rafal (Essex Financial) has had a similar positive experience with the style box, and incorporates it into his discussions with clients: "We've been in a period for the last five years when style diversity has actually worked. Mid-cap, small-cap, and international—without those, your returns were much, much lower. In the '90s, there was only one style that worked, and that was large-cap growth or large-cap value. But in the last five years, clearly without small-cap, mid-cap, and international, your returns were significantly lower. So yes, we talk about it."

Sanford Katz, on the other hand, has a definitional issue that pertains to the entire grid: "I don't know that there is a huge difference over time between value and growth. I think that's more of a Wall Street marketing phenomenon. Or at least an investor classification phenomenon." Jim Hansberger uses even stronger language: "You should be focused on the price you pay, whether it's for a piece of real estate or a common stock or whatever it might be. That's why I don't buy into so-called 'value' and 'growth.' We diversify portfolios by asset class rather than by style."

Although Ron Carson feels that the styles represent meaningful differences, he finds that going deeply into them is unnecessary: "We don't go that deep. I want to tell a simple story about asset allocation, covering the average mean returns of the asset class correlations and coefficients, how they offset one another, and then demonstrating that in pictorial form. So I don't get as deep as style difference. Obviously, there's been a huge dichotomy with value outpacing growth, and now it looks like growth is poised to take off. But we already include that in our process, so I don't get that specific when explaining it to clients."

For other advisors, finding the best possible managers is more important than making sure to "hit" all the style boxes. Mark Sear says, "As for going through the style boxes ... we don't do that. We go within the equity box, and we try to find the best managers we can." Mark adds that given his goal of not losing money for individuals, he is not interested in the "style box game":

> There is a distinction between style boxes and what we try to do. If you go and pitch to a university foundation, for example, they probably want something in every box. They've probably got large-cap value, large-cap growth, mid-cap value, mid-cap growth, small-cap value, small-cap growth, international, alternative investments, and so on. So, they want a manager in all those classes, and then they tweak the amounts. But I don't deal with institutions. I deal with human beings. And I want investment managers who have a low likelihood of losing money, and who tend to do well when times are tough. And yes, if the market is up 20 and we are up 18, I can live with that. But when the market is down 20, I want to be down 2. Those are the kind of managers that I want to affiliate with because we have the same mind-set. And that's not a style box game.

Jon Goldstein echoes a similar sentiment. With a focus on the typically backward-looking analysis at the heart of asset allocation, Jon finds that over time he and his team have moved away from strict adherence to the style boxes:

> We've gained a certain perspective on the so-called Morningstar Box over time. The markets change over time, and asset allocation in general is a backward-looking science. We are looking at data that's already occurred in order to draw intelligence today. If the future is like the past, then these conclusions are okay; the problem is that the future is usually not like the past. So, we've grown a lot less strict about staying in style boxes. To the contrary, we find ourselves attracted to managers who don't necessarily fit neatly into the style box, which is how the bulk of serious money gets invested. And we don't get discouraged by style drift as long as it's within the manger's mandate. It's something we are used to seeing, and we look

forward to it. If they are closer to the investment markets and the trends that they may anticipate or even observe, we want them to be able to change the portfolios in accordance with that. Some of our most successful ideas have come from managers who simply don't fit neatly.

So, to give you a hard example, for a long time all-cap managers just didn't fit in the style boxes. Today, I would rather have an all-cap manager versus a targeted cap, whether it's large, small, or medium, almost anytime. Again, I want those particular stock-picking managers to have the freedom to weight that portfolio where they see the best opportunity for either preserving wealth or growing it. And I'll take a portfolio of those kinds of managers any day.

We certainly don't try to populate all of the style boxes. It's exceedingly tough to pick the sectors of the market that are going to perform. And it's no different in asset allocation, trying to pick the asset classes that are going to perform. You are going to miss the optimal mix. So I don't try to own all of them. I try to concentrate on where I think the bulk of returns is going to be generated. We spend a lot of time around here debating what the major trends are going on in the capital markets, trying to be a bit more forward thinking.

As an example of "forward thinking" processes, Richard Zinman (Smith Barney, New York, New York), whose specialty is wealth management for high-net-worth clients, has developed a novel approach to the opportunities inherent in style box distinctions. Richard describes what has led up to his development of the "core satellite" approach:

I've found that the vast majority of our competitors approach opportunities by selling the style box approach, or the proverbial tic-tac-toe board. The problem with this approach is that it ends up comprising nine active managers, which starts to resemble an expensive index fund with a great deal of overlapping and tax inefficiencies. Once you analyze the performance, you may have three managers who will outperform their respective indexes, three who will perform in line, and three who will underperform. Then the advisor will fire those that underperform with no guarantee that they are going to hire managers who will outperform. This is all very costly, because the client will pay deferred capital gains tax and incur transaction costs—selling on the bid and repurchasing at the offering price. Ironically, the managers who tend to do well are often punished because they attract greater assets but are unable to manage their asset growth properly. Consequently, we've developed a new paradigm, the core satellite, which is elegant in its simplicity and makes more sense for our clients.

Richard indexes the core equity component globally by using a tax-enhanced index manager who has very little tracking error with indexes such as the Russell 3000 and the EFIA. "The manager we seek," says Richard, "will be able to harvest tax losses on an ongoing basis, which ultimately can act as an asset to offset tax-inefficient aspects of the portfolio. Additionally, we seek alpha, or manager-added, performance, in those asset classes that are perceived to be inefficient, such as small- to mid-cap equities as well as certain emerging market equities and alternative investments. ["Alpha" refers to the excess return an investment manager will seek to add above a given index.] This approach makes the whole portfolio simpler, far more cost efficient from an expense standpoint, considerably less expensive from an administrative standpoint, significantly easier to rebalance, and meaningfully more tax efficient."

Rebalancing the portfolios is based on "our view of the world," Richard continues. (See Chapter 8 for an in-depth discussion of rebalancing.) "We may make small tactical shifts but the strategic allocation, what triggers the rebalancing, is the portfolio values." He offers cash as a simple example. "We tend to hold no less than 5 percent cash, and no more than 15 percent. If the portfolio, particularly the equities portion, is doing extraordinarily well, we mechanically sell equities because cash as a percentage of the portfolio drops below 5 percent. We do the same thing when cash exceeds 15 percent. Acting in this counterintuitive way has tended to be rewarding over time."

EXCLUDING ANY ASSET CLASSES?

Are all asset classes worth considering? Should any asset classes be excluded from a client's portfolio? Michael Johnston brings the focus back to the client as he explains why he feels that all asset classes are worth considering: "Every client's situation is different. Given certain market conditions at the time, there are asset classes that we would exclude. But just because we are not using an asset class today doesn't mean that we wouldn't use it one year from now. I wouldn't say that any asset class is off limits, even though certain asset classes are going to be inappropriate for certain investors for tax-related or other reasons. But for other investors it might be appropriate. So, we keep all avenues open."

In some cases, it is the clients themselves who either approve of or nix specific asset classes. Tim Kneen (Citigroup Institutional Consulting) says that a great deal is up to the client here. "We will discuss what asset classes can be included in the portfolio. Different clients will feel differently. Some clients would never allow a hedge fund into their portfolio, while others openly welcome that possibility. Some clients would never allow commodities or derivatives, while others would. So one of the topics we spend time on at the beginning is the advantages and disadvantages of each asset class. We look at the expected return and the expected standard deviation—that is, the risk or volatility—of each asset class. We've now got a list of asset classes that we can consider."

Jim Hansberger was quoted in Chapter 1 as saying that "there are basically only four asset classes." With respect to including and excluding different asset classes, Jim concludes that the "devil is in the details; the devil is in the execution" and that things may not be as simple as they seem. His overall analysis is well worth considering in depth:

> When we sit down with a prospective client, we often state that we believe it is the allocation of assets that creates and maintains wealth. Certainly, in the equity management portion, we think sector selection is more important than whether you own Coke versus Pepsi or Home Depot versus WalMart. At the asset class level, however, it is the allocation of assets that creates and maintains wealth. I buy into that one hundred percent, but that does not automatically mean that very broad diversification of assets makes sense and is the best way to create consistency of performance.
>
> Many people interpret asset allocation to mean simply that you've got this broad risk spectrum and it includes untold numbers of different asset classes and subasset classes, and you just broadly spray across that. They claim that is the new paradigm, and with it you are automatically going to accomplish your goals. I do not think that's true.
>
> It's not nearly that simple. Let me take it a step further. Something that we throw out there for everybody is that there are basically only four asset classes. Equities. Fixed Income. Commodities. Currencies. That's it. Everything else falls as a

subsector. All cash is a currency. Every form of debt and bond and credit structure is fixed income. Every form of equity, whether it's venture or private equity or common stock, is an equity. A real estate trust could be an equity or fall into a commodity, but real estate is a commodity. There are only four.

Consider the risk spectrum, the traditional risk/return chart starting on the bottom left with cash and going up to the upper right to venture capital. There's no telling how many subclasses there are along the way, but there are really only the four main asset classes. And, in identifying traditional risk/reward ratios for those four asset classes, one of the things I've noticed in this move toward asset allocation is that an awful lot of people are not paying enough attention to liquidity versus not. It's a big deal. And what kind of taxes versus not? Ordinary income versus capital gains tax? Suppose you tell me about a private equity or real estate investment that has capital calls for five years in a row and is completely not salable. If you are expecting a 10 percent return in comparison to a 10 percent return in a common stock that pays a dividend, that's salable every day, and that has only 15 percent capital gains, are the two equal? I don't think so. I put a huge premium on liquidity.

Again, it's just not that simple. Projected total returns broken down by asset class or by risk level are not enough. It's got to be taxes. It's got to be liquidity. It's got to recognize whether we are talking about a foundation, a trust, a taxable account, or a tax-free account. Are we talking about investing for heirs? Many of our clients today are investing not for themselves, but for their heirs. They are investing for foundations. They are investing for family partnerships at a later date.

SEEKING BETTER RETURNS

For advisors, the "artistic" part of portfolio construction involves balancing both the desire for safety and the desire for high returns. For Sanford Katz, the first crucial part of the equation is making sure that a proposed asset allocation is "calibrated properly to the client's objectives. That's the first step," says Sanford, and "then it's a question of the second part of the equation, which involves taking our personal views and gathering quantitative information, and then overlaying some tactical preference. So we will sit down and start with what's been our team's historic asset allocation baseline for a moderate type investor of a certain profile and age with a certain level of liquidity. We'll have that in our head—it's already implemented with our existing clients—and we are constantly refining it over time as we live and learn from experience. But clients don't hire us just to be closet indexers. That said, they don't want us to deviate too far in a risky direction. We have to work at the incremental opportunities, the fine line between being too far out there, or conversely, just indexing. We need to find some tactical overlays that will hopefully generate alpha. And do it on a relatively consistent basis. If we are not consistent, clients will eventually ask themselves if they are better off indexing."

Louis Chiavacci utilizes a proprietary relative value analysis that incorporates Merrill Lynch's quantitative research and triggers the team to rebalance portfolios at opportune times. Louis describes the asset class orientation: "Simply put, is growth expensive relative to value?" In 2002 the team determined that the high-yield bond sector represented compelling value as compared to investment-grade bonds. "We incorporated this value-based discipline into each client's overall investment strategy, with the exception of those clients for which we felt these bonds were not suitable." Louis continues to discuss the importance of his asset class strategies: "Asset allocation is by far the greatest contributor to a portfolio's total return. This is one of the drivers of the investment strategy that we produce."

The late 1990s was a time when investors were chasing high-growth stocks, not more familiar investments like real estate investment trusts (REITs). In Louis's mind, that was the best time to enter that market. "Historically, REITs have traded in a range of 68 percent of net asset value, or NAV, at its trough to a peak of 130 percent. The mean is around 102 percent right now. In 1999 we were buying the REITs at approximately 70 percent of NAV" Louis compares the spreads, or price differences between the different sectors, adds economic variables, and determines where value exists. Over the next several years REITs became one of the best performing asset classes. "In retrospect, investing in REITs instead of technology stocks in 1999 and 2000 was a product of our capital allocation process," he says. "This disciplined approach helps to preserve our clients' wealth."

"We have very frank discussions with clients about how painful it is to lose money," Louis explains. "Of course by the time the late '90s arrived, investors seemed to forget the meaning of losses." During the discussions, Louis builds models to show clients the impact of losses on their portfolios. Additionally, the team's detailed quarterly reports act as a reminder of the disciplined approach, the need to rebalance, and the importance of sticking to the long-term game plan.

For Rick Blosser (Morgan Stanley), whose goal is to achieve positive returns regardless of market conditions, it's necessary to understand how asset classes are correlated: "What we try to focus on is not only outperforming the market, but absolute returns. For example, we generally do not manage in a way that simply benchmarks to the market. For many of our clients, they are not aiming to be down, for example by eight, if the market is down ten. Of course we can never guarantee performance or positive returns, but we design our strategy in a way to aim for absolute, positive performance in any given market environment. To be able to achieve that, we believe that the investment strategy not only needs to have good underlying performance across different asset classes, but the client needs to start with a model that looks at correlations among asset classes and how those correlations may change over differing market environments."

Rick further explains the process that he and his team use in analyzing different asset classes, both individually and in comparison to each other:

> As I said before, I believe that developing an appropriate asset allocation model is 75 percent of the battle in terms of really creating a comprehensive wealth management strategy. To achieve that end, there are several different things an investment representative needs to do for his or her clients. The investment representative needs to be realistic and have a good understanding of the underlying return and risk characteristics of different asset classes. My team helps me to get there by utilizing the firm's resources as well as external resources to help understand what the different categories of securities and other assets are potentially going to do going forward. Firm research helps us to analyze volatility for different types of securities, and how that volatility has changed over time.
>
> For most publicly traded equities, we can go back over the last 50 years and work through their return and risk profiles and correlations to the equity markets. We try to condense down that historical information as well as make predictions about future behavior. For example, for particular securities we try to project what the return and risk profiles are likely to be for the next ten years. This gives our clients and us a more informed basis to

work from when developing an asset allocation strategy. Then we look at the relationships between different asset classes. For example, we might ask how equities perform versus bonds or alternative assets, like hedge funds, private equity, commodities, and real estate securities, over different market environments.

Mark Sear works at achieving better returns through what he calls a "theme" approach," and points out that having investments in every style box is not important: "A big part of what we do now is a whole thematic approach. For example, the utilities theme—we currently like utilities. We found the best manager to drive home that theme. When we had high-yield bonds as a theme back in 2002, we had a closed-end fund and an open-end fund. We liked the closed-end funds because new money was going to work right then. It wasn't some of the older bonds that had been floating around for a while. We wanted fresh money, and you know you get it through a closed-end fund. We like that. But we also had an open-fund option, because not everybody likes the closed-end fund. That's the way we played the high-yield fund game. Those are both themes, and that's a big part of what we do, as well as having the best managers. Never do we say 'We have to have something in every box, because we are the asset allocation specialist.' "

Brian Pfeifler emphasizes a realistic perspective on success and seeking better returns potential. "In my view, it is essential to have a portfolio properly allocated across different asset classes and to invest with a long-term view. How do you make that extra percentage of return with managers and manager selection strategy? In my view, the answer is by correctly scaling the risk/reward trade-offs and making sure the recommendations are appropriate for each client's specific needs." Following Brian's lead, we now turn to money manager selection and performance.

MANAGER SELECTION AND PERFORMANCE

With respect to overall portfolio performance, while asset class choice is of preeminent importance, the choice of investment managers—especially private fund managers who specialize in specific asset classes and typically manage mainly on behalf of institutions and the very wealthy—is also of considerable importance. Most advisors regularly monitor the performance of these managers (compared both to other managers and to index funds), because their performance affects both the recommendations of managers to clients and also comes into play during rebalancing (see Chapter 8).

Michael Johnston gives us an in-depth explanation of how he chooses managers, what he is looking for in terms of performance, and how he tries to avoid what he terms "closet indexers":

We have recommended managers within each asset class based upon the historical performance of the people who are managing those portfolios. And within a given asset class, we might have several different managers, depending upon the client's objectives. If a client were looking for income from stock dividends, there is a manager that we would recommend within large-cap value who is different from the manager we would recommend if a client didn't need dividends but was looking for more long-term capital gains growth. What we recommend really depends upon the client's objective. And at the same time, if the manager's strategies are no longer doing well, then we might remove that manager from the portfolio.

More managers than I would like tend to stick to a given set of percentages for the economic sectors within an asset class. You have a lot of closet indexers out there who are just trying to replicate or to perform slightly better than their given asset class. We try to find managers who are going to add alpha to whatever asset class we have them categorized in. We want them to stay within the parameters of that asset class or stay pretty close to it and at the same time add incremental value on a risk-adjusted basis. And it's very hard for a closet indexer to meet those parameters. So you've got to have a manager that is willing to look at an asset class and say, "Well just because the index says that I should be 20 percent exposed to financial stocks, I, as a manager, can still believe that this asset class is undervalued relative to other industry sectors. I have no problem putting 35 percent or 40 percent of my portfolio into financial stocks."

How strongly I believe an active manager can outperform a given index depends on the asset class. As you move down in market capitalization, my belief grows stronger. In other words, I believe that a small-cap value manager can do a much better job than its given index in performing on a risk-adjusted basis. I believe it is more difficult for large-cap growth managers to outperform the S&P 500 or the Russell 1000 growth just because there are fewer market inefficiencies within large-cap stocks than within small-cap stocks. I believe it's easier to outperform in the international markets with a good manager versus an index. So, you have to really break it down by asset class to fully answer that question.

As for showing clients actual managers in each of those asset classes, we pick managers in each of those categories that have shown a prior history of doing well relative to their peer group, doing well relative to their benchmark, on a risk/return basis, with the objective of the actual portfolio generating greater return and less risk than what the model asset allocation is doing. The asset allocation model is using projected returns and projected volatility, and we are trying to find managers who can do better than that. And even though Citigroup is the world's largest financial institution, we don't believe we have the best investment products internally in every asset class. So we rely upon a consulting group inside Smith Barney that goes out and identifies very good managers in each of these asset classes. On occasion, there are asset classes where Citigroup has something unique to provide that is either better than outside providers or we can't get access to outside providers. We invest our clients' money wherever it's the best fit for them, whether it's with Citigroup or an outside manager.

One of the first questions that arises in the minds of many clients is whether some managers are consistently better than others. Sanford Katz (UBS) relates his thoughts and experiences with this issue: "I believe that better managers can outperform the market, but I also believe that 70 or 80 percent of managers probably don't outperform the market. When we meet with them, a lot of clients will ask about that, and we'll say, 'Why should we care about them? Shouldn't we only care about the 20 percent that consistently do best?' So the next logical question is, 'Can we find those 20 percent?' I think that eight out of ten times, they are identifiable." In some cases, in order to increase the likelihood of finding those best managers, Sanford will use more than one manager per asset class. "We may have three managers in each, although we generally try to avoid that. But in riskier asset classes, I do like to do that. In emerging markets, for example, I like to have a few bets on different managers, because I think the dispersion of returns is much higher in these less scientific, or smaller market cap sectors."

In many cases, it's a question of familiarity, reliability, and long-term results. Brian Pfeifler says, "Once the client, in consultation with me and my team, determines that he or she wants to have exposure, let's say, to international, we'll generally recommend using money managers whom we're familiar with and who, based on our diligence, have a good track record."

John Rafal begins by keeping close tabs on the performance of managers: "When we are recommending money managers, part of our presentation to clients is to show the performance of the manager by year, individually and then blended. There are charts that go along with that, and it really pops out very quickly." John says that with respect to their performance, "We try to give managers three years to fail, and we try to adhere to that rule—a full market cycle, if you will—although market cycles are arguably a lot longer than three years. But if you fall below the 50th percentile for three years or longer, we pretty much have to address your performance and get you out of the portfolio. That goes for mutual fund managers, too."

For Mark Sear, the key is hiring the best managers rather than feeling obligated to have investments in each style box:

> Within the equity box, we try to find the best managers we can. We go out and find best in class managers. So, yes, we don't want to have all our money in guys who only do large-cap. But it's not because there's a style box. If we want international, we want the best international manger. There are managers we use who are spectacular investment managers with phenomenal track records. There's one manager who's not classified in any section, but I just know he's very, very good, and extremely conservative, and does very well in down markets.
>
> When we go through the process of looking at managers, we measure how they do in down markets. We would rather have a manager who captures most of the upside and has very little downside exposure when the market is weak. First, we like to invest with managers who have a lot of their own skin in the game. We typically will not invest with a manager unless he or she has his or her own capital in the fund. Second, we want to know that the manager has the ability to have as much cash as he or she wants to have. If the manager can short stocks, that's great. We want people who have been able to show a long-term track record of having very good performance in very difficult environments. And I'll give up upside for that.
>
> So, there are no style boxes, it's more like we find managers we believe in and who are spectacularly talented, those we believe fit our profile of having relatively low turnover, and who are relatively good performers in difficult environments. And they have their own money in the fund. They do what they've always done. They don't shift around, depending on what the market likes. They aren't so big that they really look like the

market in terms of scale. Those are variables that we like. When we find managers like that, whom we like, we continue to use them until they are either too big or they close. We've had three investment managers close in the last six months because they got too big. That's a critical thing for us. But we are always going to hire somebody who's a great manager. If we can't find somebody we want to invest with, we don't have to fill that style box.

Jon Goldstein works to maximize return for clients by evaluating managers in terms of their performance vis-à-vis the efficient frontier: "If we can find individual managers who execute better than their indices, then we can perhaps add a little more value and find a portfolio that performs above the efficient frontier. If we are getting excess return for no increase in volatility, that excites us a lot. It's harder to get clients excited about it because it's more of an academic concept. But we spend a lot of time looking at that and plotting real manager returns and showing those portfolios. Again, this is all historical and the future is not like the past. In our case, we are trying to find managers who we think will continue to add value."

For Dana Jackson (Smith Barney, Menlo Park) the key is simple: choose managers who are less likely to lose money, especially in down markets. "Trying to predict the stock market, or trying to pay attention to what environment we think we are going into, affects the types of manager we like. Given our clientele, we always have a bias toward managers who are good at protecting capital during down markets. That tends to be the first thing, or one of the major things, we look for. At the end of the day—I'm sure you've heard this before—you make more money by not losing money."

Hank McClarty (Gratus Capital Management) takes a different approach, at least with respect to the equity component of his clients' combined portfolio since 2000 he has run this portfolio himself, and he and his clients have been very pleased with its performance:

> At some point in, about six months into 2000, I switched my entire equity portfolio to one portfolio that somewhat mirrored the S&P 500. We decide on those stocks as we narrow it down within the sector. We have small- and mid-cap growth and value in there, up to 30 percent, and the rest is a large-cap core portfolio. Our clients have been absolutely in love with it since then, all of them.
>
> Now our clients are ahead of what they are seeing on the news. They have really built up some sizeable capital gains, and there is very low turnover. They have gotten to know these

stocks, and they like that much better than owning 26 shares in a 100-stock portfolio, which was one of our five equity portfolios. They didn't know any of the stocks, and they were just bought and sold at whim. They had no relationship with the equities.

I think you can make rocket science out of anything. The bottom line is that every single quarter since we started running this equity portfolio, it has handily beaten the S&P 500 on a risk-adjusted basis. There wasn't one quarter when I was using four or five managers that I could ever say that. We had them for purposes of "diversification," but there was always at least one manager dragging it down.

TAX CONSIDERATIONS

Winner's Circle advisors keep tax considerations in the forefront of their minds. Advisors must consider the tax consequences of buying and selling different types of investments and how different parts of a client's profile may require different types of tax-related treatment (e.g., money in tax-exempt or tax-deferred retirement funds). Louis Chiavacci puts it simply: "Our clients are by and large taxable. So the after-tax implications of everything we do helps to drive the decision-making process." Similarly, Ron Carson says that he and his team work on taxes "through the whole process. We employ an in-house CPA. Anytime we are looking at making a change, we consider what kind of impact it's going to have in general for the firm—do we have a loss or do we have a gain?—and then individually for our clients as well."

Joe Jacques is himself a CPA, so he is able to provide his clients integrated tax planning and investment planning advice. "With a majority of my clients, I am also preparing their tax returns. It's a great asset, because whenever you do an investment, there are tax implications. Or vice versa. By having both a CPA and a CFP®, I can go through both a tax planning strategy and an investment strategy when I am working with a client."

Jim McCabe sees taxes as a factor worth considering, but he doesn't let them become an overriding concern: "Taxes are always one of the factors. We always look for the highest after-fee, after-tax returns, consistent with the client's risk tolerance. When there's a liquidity event, taxes are a significant factor. There are federal taxes, state taxes, alternative minimum taxes, and estate taxes. However, we never let the tax tail wag the investment dog." Jim adds that while tax planning typically plays "a very important part" in the strategy he recommends for each client, taxes are actually less of a factor than they were a few years ago: "As time has gone on, rates—especially the capital gains rate—have come down and taxes have had less of an impact. People used to do far more tax planning. In the past, tax deferral or tax avoidance would have been a much bigger factor than it is now. Income and capital gains tax rates are down and the estate tax exemption is increasing."

For John Rafal tax considerations accompany but are distinct from the general discussion about asset allocation: "We talk about tax consequences, in terms of the investment vehicles that we are going to be considering. We talk about tax management, if you will, including harvesting losses. We want to get a good return, but we want it to be tax neutral or actually not create an ordinary income or capital gain. This has to do with activity, with whom you select to manage your money, and with whether we are going to use funds or separate account managers. If we use funds, are we going to use tax-oriented funds? And are we going to use funds that strive for a lot of activity or a little bit of activity? So we have that discussion, but it's sort of separate and apart from the asset allocation discussion."

Mark Sear points out that a vigorous "tactical" approach to asset allocation and to rebalancing (see Chapter 8), can be tax inefficient: "With a tactical approach, the more you try to micromanage and the more you try to split the allocation, the less tax efficient it becomes. With more turnover, with more activity happening, with more stuff going on, it is more difficult to be tax efficient. Perhaps the only drawback to being very tactical is that it can be tax inefficient, and yet you don't ever want taxes to drive investment decisions." Dana Jackson makes a similar point: "We don't rebalance portfolios as often as institutions do. We don't go in quarterly and semiannually and rebalance. Simply, I think the tax effect of doing that tends to negate the advantage you get from rebalancing."

Michael Johnston (Smith Barney) points out that special tax considerations often come into play with respect to estate planning: "A lot of our clients," he says, "have grantor-retained annuity trusts that allow the future appreciation of the assets to be passed along to their children, above a certain government rate of return that's required to be given back in the form of an annuity to the grantor or the parents. So, in creating the asset allocation, those specific asset classes that have the highest growth rate potentials over a given time are more suited for being invested in the grantor-retained annuity trusts because we want as much of that appreciation as possible to go to their children, without estate taxes or gift taxes. So, we have to take the estate plan into account." Michael also addresses tax concerns *structurally*, with respect to the types of accounts he sets up for his clients in the first place:

> Specific to the way in which we invest in each of the asset classes, within the equity markets we try to always use separate account money management to give us tax lot control for each client. This relates to their cost basis and their purchase dates, so that at the end of each year, we can do an analysis of the year-to-date realized gains and losses for the portfolio, and estimates for their K-1 or limited partnerships. For those clients who have assets or other gain-generating investments outside of Smith Barney, we talk with the client's CPA or accountant to determine what their net taxable event looks like outside of us, as well as taking into account any tax loss carryforward from prior years. We then analyze each of our separate account managers to identify tax lots with unrealized losses. We sell the unrealized loss tax lots to help offset realized gains in other parts of their portfolio. We use a separate account structure to give us more tax control, since most of our clients are either in the top income tax bracket or subject to alternative minimum tax. Proactively managing the realized gains of our clients' portfolios can play a big part in their net returns.
>
> Within the alternative world, most of those structures are in limited partnerships and we don't have the ability to go in on a tax lot basis and realize losses at the end of the year. So, from a tax perspective, that world is more like mutual funds in that you don't necessarily have control. You don't know what's going to show up on that K-1 at the end of the year, from a taxable event perspective. But we can make estimates and accommodate that by controlling what we do within the equity portfolio and bond portfolio.

Hank McClarty also has an eye on the structural tax advantages that have come to clients since they started managing the equities (as previously described):

> Let's say a client comes to us with $5 million worth of Coke stock with a basis of $5 and they want to slowly diversify it. Many managers will liquidate 100 percent of it on the first day and invest the proceeds. Now, suppose our portfolio calls for Pepsi. As long as we've got a decent rating on Coke and we don't think the stock is in trouble, although my client's portfolio may not have the exact same return as the rest of my portfolios, on a

tax planning basis it certainly makes a lot more sense to hold it and slowly sell the stock off over a period of time. That's one more benefit of portfolio customization and trading around a concentrated position.

Lastly, Louis Chiavacci advocates regular "tax harvesting" for his clients: "Several times a year we will go through client portfolios and instruct the managers to harvest losses. Not just wait until December, but if we bought Coke and we bought Pepsi at the beginning of the year, and it's now April and Coke is down and Pepsi is up, we might tell the manger to sell the Coke and rebuy it in 31 days. We will do that numerous times a year so that by the end of the year we've accumulated tax losses. This dramatically improves the after-tax returns of clients' portfolios."

DOUBLE-CHECKING WITH CLIENTS TO GET IT RIGHT

Before an advisor moves forward with actually constructing a new client's portfolio (or reconstructing an existing client's portfolio), it is incumbent upon him to make sure—to double-check—that he and the client are in fundamental agreement. Many clients trust their advisors both implicitly and explicitly, and the advisor will only need to get agreement as to the rough parameters of the asset allocation. Other clients will want a good deal of detail, sometimes down to the exact names and numbers of specific asset classes, managers, funds, and individual stocks, bonds, and other investments that may make up their portfolio. Ultimately, it's the client's prerogative to approve the recommended asset allocation, and it may take several iterations or more until final approval is reached. (Of course, even then things can, and will, change over time, leading us to rebalancing, the subject of Chapter 8.)

Brian Pfeifler is in full agreement. "By working together with a variety of different themes, we come to an initial asset allocation proposal and then we present it to the client. The client will give feedback, and they can still tell me, 'No. Thank you for that, but I am going to do this.' And that's okay so long as he or she knows where I stand and what my recommendation is. We are very clear on that. We get an asset allocation started, and then the client and I go back and forth on it. It's a pretty regular role of ours to adjust to the client's feedback. Not every client is comfortable with the initial allocation I propose. We will simply scale back the exposure of a particular asset class until the client is comfortable with it."

Dana Jackson, who works with ultrahigh-net-worth clients, stresses that in the end, the client must be comfortable with the asset allocation: "We go through the process of educating our clients to make sure they understand the risk/reward trade-offs. We focus on getting them to say, 'Yes, this looks right for me.' We are constantly revisiting and making sure it's still right. It's not worth losing any sleep. Being very comfortable and having the correct expectations is what asset allocation for individuals is really about."

Jim Hansberger, after first determining detailed client information from the "face-to-face profiling" method described in the last chapter, then checks in with his clients to make sure you are on track: "We submit the profile itself to them at this point. In other words, this is what we've found, and we want to make sure you are in agreement. Is there anything we've gotten wrong? Is there anything you would like us to elaborate on? Keep in mind, they never saw the questions; they just heard them. So when it comes back to them subject by subject by subject, it feels a heck of a lot more detailed than signing a signature card to open a checking account. It's at that point, when we have finalized it, with or without any changes, that we promise them a proposal in a short period of time. At that time we provide a breakdown by asset class and projected targeted returns per asset class, and then specific recommendations per asset class."

After asking relevant questions, Mark Sear comes up with a model that he shows to his clients to make sure it's right: "First we ask the relevant questions. How much income do you earn? How much do you spend? How much do you have in mortgages? We ask the questions that are relevant, and then we will build a model in and we will email it to them. 'Look, this is all the data you gave us. Does this feel like and look like your income statement? Does this look like your balance sheet?' And if it does, then we know that we've got good data, and we go forward and then model different scenarios to try to help them understand—given their liabilities, assets, expense rate, and income rate—what kind of portfolio makes the most sense."

As described in Chapter 5, Tim Kneen uses a computer-based "live optimization" process that lets him work with his clients in real time to come to an agreed-upon understanding of how to go forward: "We go through the optimization process, but we never get to a point where we say, 'Okay, we've listened to you and here's our proposal. You should put 20 percent with this particular manager and so on.' Our proposal process is really done live with the client, and it's all done through asset allocation. The client is agreeing to certain risk and reward parameters of a portfolio. He is not agreeing to 20 percent in large-cap growth, 13 percent in small-cap value. He is agreeing that the target return is X, and in the worst-case scenario he is willing to accept Y once the risk/reward trade-offs are known."

For John D. Olson (Merrill Lynch), it's important to "drill down" and show clients exactly how the different asset classes will be used in their portfolio: "Once we have the asset allocation, then we are going to implement the investment strategy and fill the buckets. We'll fine-tune the asset allocation. We spend a lot of time on size and style. The large-, mid-, and small-cap; growth, value, and alternatives. I think international is especially important now. Most people are probably underinvested internationally, even though there is now more awareness of it. Then we will show the client or the prospect the allocation, and we will drill further into it and show how we will allocate among the asset classes. And finally we will choose how we are going to position the bonds, equities, alternatives, and the overall diversification."

PRESENTING RECOMMENDATIONS AND GETTING THE GO-AHEAD

Ultimately, of course, as has already been hammered home many times in this book, specific investment choices must begin with the needs of the particular client. Martin Halbfinger is up-front about this as he tells his clients what the key determinative is with respect to choosing assets for their portfolio: "We basically tell them that the asset allocation model should be based mostly on their goals, objectives, and risk tolerance, first, and the environment second."

When he is ready to make his recommendations to a client, John Rafal simply has a frank talk with them: "We say, for example, 'Okay, here's what you say your long-term objectives are, and these are the assets you have. We think you either need more assets, or we need to reallocate what you have in order to better achieve your goals.' It's also not that uncommon to find a really great portfolio in front of you, where things are basically fine, in which case we talk about fees and expenses and what they are paying. So it's kind of a moving target."

Sanford Katz will sit down with clients and show them a several page presentation, with each "layer of the onion" revealing more and more detail:

> We typically put together something that's simple and easy to understand. Often we'll start with a pie chart, so people can see

how their assets will be divided overall. We'll do this without even indicating dollars, because that can warp the client's opinion. Instead of saying, 'We want to put $4 million into this,' we tell them the relative percentage, so they see it doesn't look like such a big deal. in the context of the bigger picture. Then we'll have things by sector and by dollars, again showing percentages. Next will be a spreadsheet that will usually fit on one page— sometimes it will go to two—with probably 10 to 20 line items that show asset classes and subclasses, but without getting into actual managers or products. Then we will have the third, and usually the final, layer of the onion allocation where we will show them a page that is actually product or manager specific. And that seems to work very well because you are drilling down to one level, and then another, and then you proceed into an actual implementation plan.

For Meg Green, it's important not to put clients (or potential clients) under too much pressure. For that reason, Meg typically charges an up-front financial planning fee, and then gives clients a choice as to whether they want to go ahead with the proposal she and her team have arrived at:

We charge a financial planning fee so that people aren't sitting there holding their sides, saying, "Oh my gosh, they are selling me something. Oh my, I have to buy something. I have to make a decision." They can suddenly become overwrought. "What do I do? How do I answer? I don't think I want to do this. This is scary." They could be thinking all of that as opposed to "Look, I've paid a fee. I can sit back and relax. Okay. Talk to me."

Paying attention to what they are being "sold" or not takes too much energy. So when we present the plan, we've already had a first meeting, we've done all the digging we can, we've done all our research, and we've put together a proposed portfolio. When we give the person our suggestions, we have told them right up front, "We do not expect anything of you. You do not have to make one move. If you choose to do anything, you can certainly do it anywhere you like. You don't have to do it here at Meg Green & Associates. And we want you to know that. So sit and relax. Because we have no expectations of you, and what we want to do is lay it all out for you so that you get the answers you came for."

Does Meg "lose" some potential clients at this stage by not asking for an up-front commitment (other than the financial planning fee)? She says that her likelihood of winning a prospect is "probably at 90 percent," and, that in any case, she is much happier working with prospects and clients in this way.

CHAPTER 8: THE THIRD (AND ONGOING) STEP: REBALANCING THE CLIENT'S PORTFOLIO

A s a very quick review, the practice of asset allocation consists of three steps. (These, of course, follow the preliminary step of understanding why asset allocation works and why it is the dominant modern investment methodology.) First, determine the client's needs (Chapter 6); second, based on those needs, construct an appropriately diversified, well–asset-allocated portfolio (actually purchase the necessary investments) (Chapter 7); third, over time, periodically rebalance the client's portfolio. But what, exactly, is rebalancing, and how often, for what reasons, and in what manner, should a portfolio be rebalanced?

Rebalancing, also known as "asset reallocation" or "portfolio rebalancing," consists of the sale or liquidation of certain assets in a portfolio to enable the purchase or holding of other assets. In *The Art of Asset Allocation* (McGraw-Hill, 2003), David Darst, Chief Investment Strategist of Morgan Stanley's Global Wealth Management Group, defines rebalancing as "the process of selling a portion of assets and, with the proceeds, buying other assets, usually to align the overall portfolio mix with a specified asset-allocation policy or targeted asset-allocation weightings." Similarly, Richard Ferri, in *All About Asset Allocation* (McGraw-Hill, 2006), simply defines rebalancing as "the means by which you get the portfolio back to its original asset allocation target, thereby remaining adequately diversified." Rebalancing does not take place as part of a simple "buy and hold" strategy.

While the actual function of rebalancing is easy to describe, some confusion arises because advisors will rebalance portfolios for a number of different reasons, as follows:

- *Regular, or "return-to-target allocation," rebalancing:* As David Darst indicates, the usual and most essential reason for rebalancing is to return a client's portfolio to the originally agreed-upon asset mix. What drives this regular, ongoing rebalancing is the simple fact that some assets will perform better than others and thus will become more heavily weighted in a portfolio over time. If stocks outperform bonds over a ten-year period, the client's portfolio will become overweighted in stocks, compared to bonds. This type of regular rebalancing takes place on a variety of different time schedules, depending on the advisor, but most often seems to take place yearly. It can also be triggered if a particular portfolio component becomes overweighted by a certain percentage, say, if equities rise to more than 5 percent of their target allocation.

- *Strategic needs rebalancing:* If there is a substantial shift in the needs, goals, circumstances, or risk tolerance of a client, then the original strategic or long-term asset allocation plan will need to be adjusted. This type of rebalancing may take place on an immediate or ad hoc basis, or the need for it might be evaluated on a regular schedule (such as half-yearly or yearly), depending on the advisor. Significant personal or financial changes in a client's life—for good or ill—can precipitate this kind of rebalancing.

- *Strategic outlook rebalancing:* Based on the advisor's analysis of and feel for long-term trends in various asset classes, capital markets, and other economic and secular factors, a portfolio may be rebalanced to preserve capital, increase return, or otherwise serve a client's needs. This type of rebalancing usually takes place on an infrequent basis (such as yearly). To the degree that an advisor will be moving a portfolio outside the original strategic asset allocation parameters, it usually requires the client's assent. In certain cases, major disasters or other world events may necessitate an immediate or nearly immediate rebalancing along these lines, although it can be hard to distinguish such strategic rebalancing from tactical rebalancing.

- *Tactical rebalancing:* Tactical rebalancing is similar to strategic outlook rebalancing, but takes place in a shorter time frame. An advisor may use his or her experience, intuition, in-firm and out-of-firm quantitative analyses, reports on manager and fund performance, and a variety of other means to rebalance a portfolio to improve returns or reduce volatility. Sometimes this is done as often as weekly (or simply on an ad hoc basis). Some advisors see tactical rebalancing as counterproductive—a movement away from the essence of asset allocation—because both timing the market and asset class picking (like stock picking) are thought to be extremely difficult if not impossible. Other advisors find tactical rebalancing to be near the heart of how they regularly add value to their clients' portfolios.

In addition to returning portfolios to their agreed-upon mix or target allocation, *regular rebalancing has at least three distinct advantages.* First, it enforces a type of "sell high, buy low" discipline, because assets which have performed well will be overweighted and thereby will need to be sold to purchase assets that have not performed well and that are therefore both underweighted and relatively inexpensive. Hank McClarty (Gratus Capital Management) says it this way:

> I think the single most important thing in asset allocation is rebalancing. If you don't rebalance annually, and you let one part of the portfolio get overweighted over time, an awful lot of your return could be lost, and you could have a lot of risk. Rebalancing forces you to buy low and sell high because you are always reducing the part of the portfolio that has outperformed and adding to the part that has underperformed. And since all these various asset classes move in cycles, you are going to win over time.

The second advantage of regular rebalancing is that it puts the attention of advisors on their clients and portfolios, thereby giving advisors and clients a regular prompt to get together and discuss the portfolio and the client's overall circumstances, This regular communication is also essential because changes in the clients' circumstances could affect risk tolerance levels. Jon Goldstein (Smith Barney) is very clear about the importance of checking in regularly with his clients:

> We are religious about meeting with our clients quarterly. We spend a great deal of time and effort producing a quarterly report that evaluates performance and asset allocation and the client's entire balance sheet. And for newer clients, those whom we have worked with for only two or three years, we kind of force this quarterly meeting. It's an opportunity to get to know them better, to educate them as to what's going on in the markets, and to let them feel more comfortable with the process. And it's a great opportunity to learn how to refine where the portfolio should be. It's a great opportunity for us to check in and make sure that what we are doing still is in the client's best interest.

The third advantage (although this blends into tactical rebalancing) is that rebalancing gives advisors and their clients a chance to regularly assess the performance of funds and fund managers, and then shift assets within asset classes, from underperformers to outperformers, when necessary or desirable. The monitoring of specific managers and funds will be discussed later in this chapter.

There are also disadvantages associated with rebalancing. First, it can be expensive for the client, both in terms of transaction costs and tax consequences. In general, the more frequently rebalancing occurs, the more transactions costs and tax consequences can be incurred, but this varies widely depending on the types of investments being sold and bought, the types of accounts the client's assets are held in, and the client's overall tax situation. (For example, there will be no or few tax consequences for a nonprofit institution regardless of how often investments are bought and sold.) As Dana Jackson (Smith Barney) says, "We don't rebalance portfolios as often as institutions do. We don't go in quarterly and semiannually and rebalance it. The tax effect of doing that negates the advantage you might gain."

Another disadvantage is that, especially where tactical rebalancing is taking place, an advisor may be moving a portfolio beyond its original asset allocation targets. This can amount to a moving away from the general principles of asset allocation by not allowing enough time for the long-term positive returns of the asset class in question to kick in. Arguably, an overly enthusiastic use of tactical asset allocation may move the management of a portfolio entirely out of the realm of asset allocation and into the realm of asset class picking and market timing. If asset allocation has become the dominant modern investment methodology, as discussed in Chapter 1, then detractors may make the claim that too frequent rebalancing of any kind is simply a way of bringing in stock picking (or asset class picking) and stock timing (or asset class timing) through the back door.

A caveat about rebalancing is pointed out by Hank McClarty: "Regardless of how often you do it, it takes time and effort, especially in separate account portfolios. Many financial advisors aren't willing to do it because it's generally not something that generates fees for them." Hank adds, however, that it's unfortunate that some advisors think that way, and that he believes rebalancing "actually generates better relationships in the long run," which, after all, is the key to success for any financial advisor.

In the rest of this chapter, distinctions will not necessarily be made as to which type of rebalancing an advisor is practicing. In fact, the different types blend into each other, and there is generally no functional difference (no difference in what actually happens in the real world, with real investments in real accounts) between rebalancing for target allocation return purposes or rebalancing for strategic or tactical purposes. What's most crucial here is that the overall importance of proactively rebalancing, by any name or time schedule, should not and cannot be underestimated. The full promise of the asset allocation approach to investing can come to fruition only if rebalancing is thoughtfully, consciously, and regularly undertaken.

TACTICAL REBALANCING

Given the criticisms leveled at tactical rebalancing, how do the advisors themselves feel about this activity? Tim Kneen (Citigroup Institutional Consulting) says that he and his team practice both strategic and tactical rebalancing: "We do both. Strategic is kind of the model, if you will. And we are always trying to stay around the model. We like to call tactical 'tilting,' so that we don't confuse it with market timing. Market timing is the decision that we will be predominantly out of large cap or all the way out of stock. Tilting is saying, 'We are going to put a bit more into growth stocks versus value stocks or a little bit more into large stocks versus small stocks.' But we will always be invested in those asset classes. We practice tilting, not timing."

Jon Goldstein explains that return to target allocation rebalancing and strategic needs rebalancing "are far more common. Tactical rebalancing," he continues, "is more the role that our investment managers follow. We run a consulting practice, so we tend to be the manager of managers, and we allow these managers to rebalance inside their own portfolios. We've been well served by finding multicap managers who have the freedom to make these choices for us. So, in a growth portfolio, we'll spend some time rebalancing among styles, based on where we see the capital markets going. For example, we'll look at how small caps perform versus large caps, value versus growth, and so on. Depending on what's going on, we'll either defend against it or take advantage of an opportunity. *But by far the biggest issue is if a client's situation has changed, or their goals have changed, or their need for access to liquidity has changed.* And that absolutely influences how we are positioned." Jon adds that with respect to those who tactically rebalance as frequently as weekly, "No. I think they've gone down the road too far. They are tying to optimize something that at a certain point takes you past the point of diminishing marginal returns, creating tax liability but dubious portfolio benefit."

When asked whether he thinks tactical rebalancing might be at cross-purposes with asset allocation, Michael Johnston (Smith Barney) makes some useful distinctions:

I think it depends upon the degree in which that over weighting is taking place within a given asset class. If you are saying, "Okay, out of my 100 percent of assets invested in strategic asset allocation, I am going to take 20 or 25 percent of that portfolio and tactically overweight and underweight relative to the long-term strategic asset allocation," that will hopefully add incremental benefit to the client, who will still be diversified because of the fact that 75 percent or more of the portfolio has not changed. But if somebody is sitting there and tactically changing 95 percent of the portfolio, investing it in two different asset classes because the investment advisor believes that those two asset classes are undervalued relative to the rest of the world, then yes, I think that destroys the asset allocation. I think there's a fine line where tactical asset allocation crosses over into being less beneficial to a client, first, because of losing diversification, and second, because of tax consequences. If you are constantly rotating from one asset class to another, you've got to generate 20-plus percent better returns to make up for the difference between long-term capital gains and short-term capital gains and other associated fees and transactions costs.

Michael adds, "I wouldn't say that all advisors implement tactical strategies. There are a number of advisors who look at their firm's long-term strategic asset allocation and then keep their clients pretty close to that model. They don't tactically overweight or underweight specific asset classes. But I believe that most of the advisors who focus on high-net-worth and ultrahigh-net-worth clients go through the tactical rebalancing process."

John Rafal (Essex Financial) makes a related point, saying that for those advisors who frequently and actively rebalance, "it's more sector analysis than asset allocation, because they are reallocating, I think, within the stock-allocated part of the portfolio. I have a friend who has a business similar to mine, and he's got 18 sectors and he rotates weekly among them. To me, that just flies in the face of long-term investing. I am not a big fan of that." Kathy Tully (Morgan Stanley) focuses on the frequency of rebalancing, and feels that rebalancing as frequently as weekly or even monthly "is a lot like trying to do market timing. I don't try to do that. I think quarterly is really sufficient with what's happening in this world. Quarterly is a good time frame, because if you are doing market timing, that defeats the purpose of asset allocation because you want to buy low and sell high. I haven't seen a market timing service yet that's right even 50 percent of the time." Jim McCabe echoes this sentiment, saying that he is "not a big fan" of frequent tactical rebalancing, in part because it amounts to "too much micromanagement."

On the other hand, Mark Sear (Merrill Lynch) explains why he and his team might reallocate a portfolio after one of their regular weekly meetings (described in detail later in this chapter) and gives a solid example of how this might look: "Commodities right now are way, way too hot. And so today, in our weekly office meeting, we are going to talk about 'Hey, we've had some positions that have had huge movements. Let's get in front of those clients and make sure we are doing the right thing.' We want to make sure that we are taking advantage of what we think is a short-term phenomenon here to extract some value. So, if we started with 10 percent commodities and now if it is at 16, 18, or 20 percent, let's take 5 percent off the table and redeploy that into things we still like but that haven't performed as well. So, if commodities have now grown to 15 to 20 percent, now that we've made some money, let's take some of that spread and redeploy it and put another 1 to 2 percent in the bio-tech fund."

Brian Pfeifler (Morgan Stanley & Co.) describes how he and his team have recently made a couple of tactical rebalancing decisions based on real-time events: "A number of years ago, there was an assassination attempt on the head of state in Taiwan and the market went down 12 percent overnight. We went to several of our clients who were interested in investing in Asia and asked, 'Would you consider having some exchange-traded fund [ETF] exposure in Taiwan?' It was a call made based just on the event. Something newsworthy happened, and then the trade happened. Part of our added value is to spot windows of opportunity like that where specific securities or a market generally might be undervalued."

John D. Olson (Merrill Lynch), while he hopes to avoid being a "market timer," fully embraces the idea of tactical rebalancing in response to real-time conditions and opportunities. In fact, he goes so far as to say that these kinds of calls are one of the main reasons clients come to him in the first place:

> Market timing is a real issue that we try to avoid. But, having said that, we will overweight and underweight an allocation when necessary. I guess an example is high-yield bonds, where the risks were rising a while ago and research actually made a very good call on underweighting high-yield bonds. Not every-

body had high-yield bonds, but where they did, we made proactive calls. We didn't necessarily wait for the scheduled client review. If it's something else, it might wait for a review or regular rebalance or we could communicate first to the client. I don't know if "urgency" is the right word, but if we feel something needs immediate attention, we will proactively make calls and make some asset allocation switches.

I think an advisor has to have an opinion that may not be the cookie cutter allocation; that's a lot of the value added by the advisor. For example, underweighting a little bit of small cap and favoring large cap because you've had a big run in small cap and value, then we may want to own very high-quality, large-cap, dividend-paying stocks. When we feel those kinds of influences, we will take a position. I think that as advisors we should do this, and hopefully we have the wisdom that comes from being in the business for 25 years. This is the advice that clients come to us for, and it's the value, too, over something on the Internet that somebody can just punch in on a Web site.

Rick Blosser (Morgan Stanley) and his team use a similar method (tactically overweighting or underweighting based on strategic benchmarks) and also reach the conclusion that this kind of tactical rebalancing can potentially benefit clients:

We start by creating a baseline strategic asset allocation for each client. Next, we create customized benchmark allocations. Each asset class will have a benchmark, for example, U.S. equities, the S&P 500, or for international equities, it might be MSCI EAFA. We'll take the benchmarks for each index, and then we'll work with the client to model projected allocations for the client. Based on the client's decisions regarding strategic allocation, we will work with them to create a tailored, blended benchmark. So, for example, if the client elects to invest 40 percent in equities, 30 percent in bonds, and 30 percent in alternatives, we'll work with the client to create a blended benchmark based on that strategic allocation.

Then, at any given point in time, what we try to do—and where we think we add a lot of value—is to tactically overweight or underweight strategic benchmarks for each client. The value we add, or part of the value we add, is being able to decide whether we should be overweight or underweight in those asset classes for a given period of time. We may be significantly underweight in U.S. equities right now, or overweight in international equities, based on that benchmark and depending upon the particular client's needs, goals, and risk tolerance. What is most important from a value perspective, in my view, is maintaining an underweight or overweight position for a long enough period of time to benefit from the full investment cycle.

We can also add value (as compared to the benchmarks selected by the client) by being more intelligent about how we manage the overall risk of the allocation. We also work to keep clients informed about how their portfolio is performing. We may, for example, use attribution analysis to analyze the effects of tactical rebalancing for a particular client's portfolio.

ONE ADVISOR'S TAKE ON REBALANCING: 75 PERCENT STRATEGIC VERSUS 25 PERCENT TACTICAL

On the question of strategic versus tactical rebalancing and whether tactical rebalancing makes good sense overall, Jim Hansberger (Smith Barney) gives us an analysis that is itself both strategic (big picture thinking) and tactical (reacting to the markets in real-time as events unfold):

> Basically, "strategic versus tactical" in anything means big picture versus small picture. A strategic leader is the person who sets the vision and the overarching tone, a general or a CEO, and the tactical leader is the manager or the person who is carrying out the strategy or the vision of the big picture.
>
> And yes, market timing, quick moves, and so on would seem to fly in the face of really good, long-term asset allocation. But in all fairness, as I look back over the years there have been times when there have been years with more turnover than other years. That's the nature of the times. The stock market, they say, has basically performed at 10 percent a year for 60 or 70 years. But I don't think there have been more than five or six or seven times that the stock market has actually been up 10 percent. It's up a lot more or down a lot less, and typically, that dictates certain things. If the stock market went up 100 percent in a three- or four-year period, that would certainly seem to dictate more asset allocation moves. When things get really heated up, going up or going down, you find yourself rebalancing more often.
>
> Let's take it all the way down to the micromanagement of a single asset class. We know what happened to technology in the

five-year period in the late '90s. It went from some very small percentage of the S&P to 35 or 40 percent. I think that was clearly overdone, and realistically, technology was not going to be 40 or 50 percent of the whole GDP of America. So it was overdone, and we needed to do rebalancing to reduce that.

I'll give you an example of the reverse. At the end of 2004, energy was down to a 5 percent component of the S&P. In the '70s, during the energy crisis, it was 30 or 40 percent. So it was an all-time low; it was way, way underdone. One could have made a case that it was worthwhile to bring it up just because it had gotten way underdone and way underappreciated, without ever seeing any sign of a spike in oil, gas, or anything else.

I do think strategic should outweigh tactical, always. But there are times when you should be very aware of tactical opportunities to make quicker changes within the bigger, overall picture. It makes sense to say the split it is something like 75 percent strategic and 25 percent tactical.

FREQUENCY AND TIMING OF REBALANCING

The frequency of rebalancing can change over time. Ron Carson (Linsco/Private Ledger), states, "We used to rebalance on a quarterly basis. Now we rebalance annually. Not that we won't rebalance if there is some huge change in an asset class. For example, we trimmed our energy position in early 2005 and we trimmed it in 2004 because energy prices had gone up so much; in 2005, that part of the portfolio was up almost 100 percent before the year was over. It had doubled our percentage, so I cut it back. I didn't wait until year-end."

Just as Ron Carson "didn't wait until year-end" to rebalance, Sanford Katz (UBS) explains that, while on the one hand constrained by tax and structural factors from tactically rebalancing too frequently, on the other hand, there are times when he is willing to "drop everything" to rebalance his clients' portfolios:

> Sometimes the temptation exists to be tactical even if you are only slightly off the baseline allocation, yet there are often constraints that make this difficult to do. We find that usually we are looking—not necessarily in a regimented time period or on a calendar basis—to reallocate when there are major market moves. Part of Warren Buffet's theory, as I recall, is you don't need to show up at the table every day to play, but when the market deals you a favorable hand, you should be ready to play. And so

we try to operate under that principle, whereby a massive correction in equity markets, a massive shift in currencies, or a massive change in interest rate or yield curve shape, creates opportunities such that we should be willing to drop everything and reevaluate client allocations account by account.

Sanford further explains that "as much as I would like to do that," it's not possible for him to make rebalancing shifts in all of his clients' portfolios at the same time:

> Everybody has a different embedded tax situation. Everybody's risk profiles is different. There are clearly benign shifts that we can do for all clients consistent with their instructions or preferences. But half the time, quite honestly, a lot of the shifts that we would like to make may only be acceptable to a certain percentage of our clientele.
>
> A good example would be a client that's already over weighted in equities because we bought at the last dip in the market and we are at the outside edge of their equity allocation comfort level. Suppose we get another dip. We are not going to push them over the edge on that allocation. We are not going to take them to a new level unless it's something they really understand and want to do. Another client may not be overweighted in equities and in that case we may proceed with additions.
>
> There are a lot of moving parts to watch, not only within each client account, but across the whole business we manage. The differences across the client base gets challenging when you are watching more than 50 or 100 accounts. A lot of it is just trying to be on the ball, trying to juggle a lot of different variables, and it really does come back to knowing your clients. That can't be emphasized enough.

Louis Chiavacci (Merrill Lynch) says that he and his team do not typically make allocation changes on a weekly basis, "unless there's been some dramatic movement." Louis continues that it would just be too hard to make smart reallocation decisions at such a pace: "It's very difficult to make a lot of smart decisions. I think a big, big part of our job is not making bad decisions. First, do no harm. Also, you are adding some fees and costs. Maybe there are some people out there smart enough to time things to the week, but we are not that smart. So, we are very smart in a couple of small spots and we try to stay close to those spots. We know there are a lot of things we are not good at. If something is too hard, we don't try to do it. And timing markets weekly to us seems too hard." Instead, Louis checks "at least quarterly" to make sure that each client's portfolio has not gotten too far out of alignment with its target allocations, and to make sure that no major shifts have happened in his clients' lives that might necessitate rebalancing. Sometimes, as the following example demonstrates, he finds it necessary to "trim back" or readjust a specific asset class on multiple occasions if is seeing particularly strong growth:

> Back in the late '90s, we were recommending somewhere between 10 and 12½ percent in REITs for a client's portfolio. But in 2001 and 2002, that percentage had grown because equities came down, bonds went up, and REITs went up to where certain client portfolios had 20, 21, 22 percent of real estate. And that clearly was too high if our original target was 12½. And it was still growing, partially because other asset classes were coming down, but mostly because REITs were going up meaningfully in value. So, over time, we trimmed that back. Maybe not back to 12½ percent, but maybe to 15. And then it kept growing. And then we would trim it back again and trim it back again.

For Joe Jacques (Jacques Financial), who defines his client base as middle class, rebalancing, especially tactical rebalancing, occurs fairly infrequently. "It's not really useful for my client base. My client base is much more on a generic type of basis. I deal with general growth funds and highly reputable mutual fund companies. Now, what the individual fund mangers do within those portfolios might be along these more technical lines. But that's not something you do as an investment advisor with my middle-class client portfolio."

Paul Tramontano (Smith Barney) says that even when he and his team have identified opportunities, "we probably would never be tactically asset allocating weekly." Instead, the way Paul goes about tactical asset allocation (which might be closer to what was defined in the first section of this chapter as "strategic outlook rebalancing") can be seen from the following example: "We have thought that there is a wonderful opportunity in Japan and in the Pacific Basin in general. And so we have been, over time, moving assets out of the United States and into those types of assets. We would never do it weekly, because we never want to make the shift for a short period of time. We think this is a multiyear change—something that will take place over the next five, ten, and twenty years—and we want to have exposure there. And so, beginning in July of 2004, we began to move assets into Japan and other places in the Pacific Basin if families didn't already have exposure in that area."

Paul concludes with a fairly negative assessment of frequent, tactical, asset allocation: "I hate to say 'never,' but I have not run into too many people who have traded their way through tactical asset allocation in a way that really builds wealth. Wealth has been built by people who have been longer-term investors, whether it's Buffett, Gates, or many others who have a lot less than they do."

Hank McClarty (Gratus Capital Management) is an advocate of rebalancing not more frequently than annually: "You have to give these asset classes time to work. If you are rebalancing them all the time, you really aren't giving them an opportunity to do what they're going to do. It's important to have a system in place, whether it's every quarter or once a year." Even though he is an advocate of annual rebalancing, Hank nonetheless "reviews their portfolio and its performance with all clients every quarter."

Mark Curtis (Smith Barney) says that semiannually is ideal for overall portfolio reviews, but certain clients do benefit from monthly rebalancing: "Ideally, what you want to do is rebalance at least semiannually subject to market volatility and the client's situation. Of course, whenever a client adds money, you don't make any recommendations until you've looked at their overall situation. For some clients, however, we do rebalance monthly."

Martin Halbfinger (UBS), who is an advocate of "catching yourself" before asset allocations get too far out of alignment, also says portfolios should be checked at least twice a year:

> It's very different for each family, but what I mean by "catching yourself" is that you want an allocation that is within a percentage range. If a particular asset class has a terrific run, thankfully and profitably you've become overweighted in it. As opposed to leaving it overweighted, which many people want to do, you really are obligated to reduce it on the way up, without your having one iota of understanding of whether you are at the top. That's not our job. Our job is not to catch the bottom or the top. Our job is basically to create a model that keeps you balanced for the entire time, which prevents you from getting overweighted or underweighted to too great an extent.
>
> What you have to do is keep checking all the time for when you need to rebalance. It's the rebalancing that will constantly keep you in the right proportions. You can't do it too often, because you are looking to not make too many changes to the portfolio. Our real goal is to create an allocation that's dynamic enough so that the core of it will last for three to five years.

For Mark Sear, the frequency of rebalancing changes and is based on integrating a large number of factors and information sources:

> We certainly review asset allocations on a weekly basis. We meet every Monday and talk about what we are seeing and hearing. There are two parts to that. There's the asset allocation conversation, where we discuss the relative value of different securities, and there is manager review. Then we have a review with clients every quarter. We sit down with each client and talk to him or her. "Here's where you are. Here's where the indices are. Here's where the managers are that we selected for you versus their benchmarks. Here's the asset allocation we put out. Here's the page I gave you for your last quarterly review, which is what we thought was going to happen this quarter. Here's how we did on those investments and here's what we think for the next quarter." Every quarter there's a report card for ourselves and how we've done.
>
> So, never more than weekly would we change something. Very infrequently, we would have changes week to week. But certainly we review what's going on every week, and we have a client review meeting every quarter. Typically, when we do things, we think about them for a while and then tackle them at the quarterly review. Sometime we may not change an asset allocation, but we may change a manager. Or we may change the allocation. That's the most likely time to do it. It may happen two times a year. But we talk about it every week, and we certainly could pull the trigger intraquarter if we thought it was needed.

Finally, Paul Tramontano says that he and his team will rebalance "as often as necessary." Paul says: "We review everybody quarterly. We try to talk to everybody quarterly and look at what they are doing. And if it's appropriate, we will rebalance quarterly. But most of the time, if you set a plan in place, it doesn't need to be rebalanced too often. If values change dramatically, or as alternative investments mature and money comes out of them, or as asset classes get overvalued, we might reallocate. As an example, if it's June 2005 and real estate has appreciated, we might underweight real estate in other parts of the portfolio. We would probably avoid real estate partnerships and private equity opportunities that are invested in real estate and related loans."

Paul adds that one of the advantages to having a large staff is being able to have someone communicate with his clients and get their consent before any asset allocation changes are made. "We have a system within Smith Barney that gives us a quick look at things which enables us to move quickly if necessary. But generally, when we are making significant changes in a portfolio's asset allocation, we are talking to clients often enough where it's part of our quarterly review process to make the adjustments we desire. That's part of the reason we have a big staff. I've got half a dozen people who are talking to clients all day, every day. If we want to make a shift, I can say to somebody, 'go make it happen,' and they make the necessary calls and take care of it."

"AUTOMATIC" REBALANCING TO RETURN TO TARGET ALLOCATIONS

With respect to its core function—described in the first section of this chapter as "return to target allocation"—how often should rebalancing take place? Or perhaps time is not the most critical variable. Perhaps portfolios should be "automatically" rebalanced whenever they grow too far out of alignment with the original strategic plan. Most advisors keep a close eye on the allocation percentages within clients' portfolios, and take special care when regular formal client review meetings are scheduled. As for "automated" or "automatic" rebalancing, this mostly takes place when certain software packages and monitoring programs automatically send "warnings" to an advisor if portfolio percentage allocations stray too far.

John Rafal explains why it is important for clients to regularly rebalance, and how despite their initial agreement to do so, they are often reluctant to keep to that agreement when the markets are moving:

> We try to run every client's portfolio like a pension plan or an endowment. We create an investment policy statement containing the broad outlines of the asset allocation—the relationship between stocks, bonds, and cash. And once we agree to that, we try to stick with it. We meet with our clients quarterly and rebalance if necessary. In the '90s everybody said, "What do you want to rebalance for?" We had stocks going up 30 percent a year and bonds going up zero. So we would say to a client, "In order to meet the long-term objectives in your agreed-upon policy, we have to sell stocks and buy bonds." And invariably, year after year, a client would say, "Let's change the policy." Unfortunately, in many cases during the tech run-up I was not personally forceful enough to make clients stick with their plan.

Louis Chiavacci has faced a similar situation: "At a time when people should become more aggressive in their investment policies and strategies, most people have the natural inclination to pull back. Well, we tell them up front, 'Look if the Dow goes to 6,000 and we started off with a portfolio that's 30 percent equities, and that 30 percent equity has shrunk now because the market's been whacked, we are not only going to be asking you to bring it back to 30 percent, we are probably going to be asking you to bring it up to 50 percent. Are you comfortable with that?' Because we want to know what we are going to do when the market tosses us the fat pitch. And the fat pitch will always come in a different format."

Many advisors feel that it is "important to have a regular system in place." Hank McClarty describes his system as follows: "We have about 40 clients in our practice, and talk to them all the time. But we officially sit down with them, with a bound performance review, every quarter. We use an asset allocation worksheet. It shows, percentage-wise, exactly where they are with their small- and mid-cap and large-cap equities, their bonds, their managed futures, and so forth. During the review we use the worksheet to show how we recommend getting everything back to the target allocation." As to time frame, Hank continues: "Typically, it's once a year. But if something gets really out of whack, if we needed to sell something, if we sold 10 percent of the bond portfolio to generate cash, then we would make the adjustment right then and there, rather than wait until the end of the year. Our rule of thumb is once a year, but we are not bound by that."

Joe Jacques indicates something a bit different: "I am not a big fan of rebalancing just for the sake of rebalancing. I look at it as a flexible discipline." Joe further elaborates as to why he prefers annual rebalancing:

> The principle of rebalancing is to sell high and buy low. That's the principle. It's a forced discipline to always keep your asset classes in line. But rebalancing, with a very narrow focus, on a quarterly or a semiannual basis, is too often. Let's say value is doing better than growth. If every quarter you are selling out on something that's doing better and putting it into something that's doing worse, essentially you are always selling out of something that's doing great and putting it into something that's doing worse. In the short run, that doesn't really make a lot of sense. I look at it on an annual basis and then determine whether reallocating is necessary. If, let's say, we had a 50/50 mix in value

to growth and I feel value over the next couple of years is going to be a little stronger, I might let value go a couple of years and let it build more and more into that asset class until I feel there's a point where change needs to be made and then I rebalance.

For Meg Green, it's a combination of closely watching all of her clients' portfolios and paying special attention to the tax consequences of rebalancing sooner rather than later: "We have certain assets that we mange for our clients that are automatically rebalanced. As for the schedule, it depends. If the portfolio is not tax sensitive, then it's going to be quarterly. If rebalancing is a taxable event, it's going to be less often, depending on when the allocation gets roughly 2 percent away from the model. Primarily, we are all over our clients' portfolios. We've got our systems. We print out every single portfolio and review it twice a year. That way nobody ever falls through the cracks."

Tax consequences also have a major effect on Michael Johnston's rebalancing schedule. Rebalancing is typically done on an annual basis with most of the effort focused at the end of the year:

> Every late October and November, we analyze our clients' portfolios from a tax perspective to determine their year-to-date realized gains and losses. We look at what unrealized loss positions they have in their portfolios in order to neutralize any taxable events as much as possible. At the same time, we also make plans for rebalancing the portfolio. Depending on their tax situation, we might go ahead and do the rebalancing in November to early December. If we expect their tax situation to be better in the following year, we might postpone rebalancing until January.
>
> We have not had any dramatic movements in any given asset class recently that would cause us to do an intrayear rebalancing. The last time I remember doing intrayear rebalancing was in the summer of 2003, when the ten-year Treasury got down to about 3.1 to 3.2 percent. Bond yields had decreased a lot and bond prices had increased a lot. At that point we took some money off the table in the bond market and reallocated it into the stock market or other asset classes. That was really the last time we did an intrayear rebalance.

Importantly, however, Michael also reviews each of his client's portfolios on a quarterly basis, which he says is only possible when an advisor works with a small number of wealthy clients: "We have systems that show what a client's asset allocations are, but nothing automatically tells us, 'Oh, for this particular client, you need to go in and take 5 percent out of one asset class and reallocate to another asset class.' That's one of the reasons why, when you are working with high-net-worth families, you can't have 300 or 400 clients. We work with about 60 households, so we can do this. It's not just looking at what's overweight and underweight in their account relative to some model. You've also got to take their personal situations into consideration and see if making a change is even justified."

Jon Goldstein also stresses the importance of reviewing clients' portfolios on a quarterly basis. "It's a moving target, so we definitely monitor portfolios carefully. Some of the process has to do with our view of the capital markets. Cycles that create outperformances can go a lot longer than you expect, so that rebalancing too quickly might be giving up return. At the same time, we do believe in being prudent and not letting things become too concentrated. So we monitor quarterly. We evaluate allocations and we look at investment portfolios by style, cash, bonds, stocks, and more. There is definitely discipline in our ongoing monitoring."

Tim Kneen makes use of an automated warning system (not an automated decision-making system) that tells him when a portfolio has gone outside of its target asset allocation parameters:

> We have a target allocation that's come through from our investment process. Any time we get more than 5 percent outside of that, it will trigger a review. If the target allocation is 15 percent large-cap growth and we get to 20 percent, it will trigger a review. Nothing may happen, but there will be a review. A warning pops up on my screen and tells me we have a hot spot. A 10 percent discrepancy will trigger an action from the investment committee: rebalance or make an active decision not to rebalance. Of course, we will be pretty proactive about rebalancing. But at times there are reasons not to do it. For example, in 2005 we were overweighted in the mega-cap stocks. Our policy was to be slightly overweighted in the large caps, but we elected not to rebalance because it was playing right into the theory that we were then running with. There wasn't a technical decision to autorebalance at that point; instead, we automonitor and then look at the situation.

Louis Chiavacci also has a software program that helps him to monitor allocations that stray beyond their target range. "It's a little less automatic than it should be," says Louis. "But we do have a supplemental software program that helps us to monitor things." Kathy

Tully takes advantage of an asset allocation system that automatically rebalances portfolios: "Clients receive a quarterly report that shows the original allocation design and where the allocation is now. They can see that it's going to automatically rebalance if the allocation is about 5 percent out of whack. That's what I love about this program."

Raj Sharma (Merrill Lynch) feels that "rebalancing is a concept frequently discussed, but rarely implemented. One reason why rebalancing isn't used or simply fails is because it is very counterintuitive; often you have to sell an asset that is working well for an asset that isn't." To ensure proper rebalancing for his clients, Raj uses a percentage variance system augmented by proprietary software developed by his team that rebalances clients' portfolios on a systematic basis.

> If the variance for an asset class deviates by more than a pre-specified percentage, that's a trigger for us to rebalance. We explain to clients that rebalancing is a counterintuitive tool that helps them buy low and sell high; by following these recommendations over time there's empirical evidence that this can enhance portfolio returns by much as 1 to 3 percentage points. This rebalancing technique, combined with our qualitative strategy, understanding the markets and our overall investment strategy, has been very successful for us in these very difficult times.

For Sanford Katz, when to rebalance depends on the type of asset in question, how large a percentage of a portfolio it constitutes, and simply how comfortable he and his team are with what is going on: "We are openminded about the need to rebalance, within reason. A few percent for emerging markets would be a big deviation and probably would require some rebalancing. A few percent deviation for large cap or international developed countries is less of a concern as long as we are tactically comfortable with it. We will either intentionally overweight areas of a portfolio slightly, or let them drift through appreciation/depreciation to levels that we are comfortable with."

With respect to whether he uses any kind of "automatic trigger" in case allocations get too far out of alignment, Sanford says that "I would say to the extent there is a stop-loss mentality or gain realization level, there's no quantitative trigger. But we do notice when we get into a zone of discomfort. Warning bells will start to ring quietly at 15 to 20% percent on the downside. And I think, the alarms go off when things move down by 25 or 30 percent. At that point, it becomes a very difficult decision, because you have to figure out whether you are bailing out at the bottom or not. You should be adding to positions. That's why it often makes sense to do something when you are down 15 percent, so you don't have to make that hard decision at when you are down 30 percent."

STRATEGIC NEEDS REBALANCING: WHEN CLIENT CIRCUMSTANCES SHIFT

Strategic needs rebalancing—changing target asset allocations in accordance with some change in the client's needs, goals, or circumstances—is an important component of asset allocation. Ron Carson points out that making a major shift in asset allocations based on changes in a client's life "wouldn't be rebalancing, but would be a total objective change, moving out of one model and into another." Whether a significant change in a client's life creates the need for a new asset allocation or a modified asset allocation that can be accomplished through rebalancing is indeed a difficult line to draw.

In an extreme case, a new client of Raj Sharma's experienced a dramatic change in his financial situation. Shortly after he transferred his modest portfolio to Raj, the client sold his business to a fiber optics company for around two million shares of the acquiring company's stock, which was around $25 a share. The stock later skyrocketed to over $153 (as of this writing it is around $3). Because the client was the founder of his company, nearly 100 percent of his wealth was tied up in the stock, and he was determined to hold onto it indefinitely. To come up with a concentrated stock diversification strategy, Raj asked the client a series of questions: "If you had the value of this holding in cash, would you invest all the money in one stock? How would you feel if this stock dropped by 80 percent?" Then Raj asked him, "Would an increase of 50 percent be more joyful for you than a decrease of 50 percent would hurt?" "Oftentimes the pain of loss is greater than the joy of winning," Raj says. "Our advice essentially was, 'You may own the greatest company in the world but it's very important to preserve the wealth you have created.'"

The client kept 20 percent of his original position, mostly for employee and investor perception. Raj diversified the remaining 80 percent through a variety of strategies: exchange funds, for immediate diversification and to defer taxes indefinitely; a liquidity option contract with a collar, providing downside protection in exchange for a cap on the upside; and hedges on a laddered basis, to preserve the value of the stock. These transactions were executed when the stock was in the '80s and '90s.

"It heartens me," Raj says, "to think that this client has been able to monetize and save so much money for himself and his beneficiaries for generations to come, all because we were thoughtful and asked a few questions. In reality, we were simply taking him through our tried-and-true disciplined process."

Paul Tramontano tells us that as far as he is concerned there is no automatic point at which changes in a client's life need to be reflected in a change of asset allocation. "We don't have set trigger points for rebalancing assets. In other words we don't automatically rebalance if somebody owns 40 percent in stock. It's based on individual client needs. If somebody is in retirement and her income needs are changing and evolving, we will know that because we are spending time with her. Based on that, we will adjust things. When equities become too large a percentage of someone's portfolio during their retirement years, we may rebalance. But we don't have a magic buzzer that goes off and says, 'You have this much in this asset class. Change it.'" For Paul, the real magic comes through regularly keeping in very close contact with his clients and their needs, often by phone:

> It's the most important thing. In those phone calls, you find out that things change. People die, people inherit, people decide they want something different. There are certain inflection points in life when you get ready to talk about estate planning and generational planning. It is imperative that we be supportive during those times. We want to be part of those important decisions. Many of the families we are dealing with wouldn't even think about those kinds of decisions without talking to us.
>
> We are now in the process of helping a woman negotiate a very high-level contract with a new employer. She left a very high-level job at a Fortune 50 company and we've managed her money for a while. She called to talk to us about a couple of career opportunities she was weighing. We might adjust her portfolio based on what she's going to be doing in the future. For example, she might need more income, or she might have more exposure in her new job to a certain sector, and so we will reduce exposure of that sector in her portfolio. We can really help people by being of value in unconventional matters, matters we might not have addressed just a few years ago.

Joe Jacques expects that his clients' needs and goals will likely change over time, so he makes sure to keep up with what's going on in their lives: "Just because you've sat down with your clients once doesn't mean you are done. This is a stepping-stone type of relationship. It's ongoing, and every so often you have to meet again and reevaluate the investment mix you've chosen. You have to make sure it's still current with their goals, and also, that the markets are still in line with their objectives and your investment strategies. With large portfolios we sit down probably semiannually and with medium-sized to smaller portfolios, yearly."

Tim Kneen has a straightforward approach with respect to strategic needs rebalancing: He undertakes it only "if the required rate of return is going to change or if the risk parameters have changed." To verify that there have been no changes, he and his staff check in with his clients "once a quarter. We look at cash flows. We look at requirements. We look at withdrawals that have occurred." Jim McCabe also has a straightforward approach. He typically rebalances annually to return to the original asset allocation targets, but "if there are client changes, if they are becoming uncomfortable, or if there are mitigating circumstances, we'll work with them and reallocate more often."

Michael Johnston explains how asset allocation changes "can be client driven." He points out that "if a client is transitioning from an income-generating job into retirement, all of a sudden the existing portfolio might not be generating enough income. Or clients who were very nervous in 2001 through 2003 might be willing to take some more risk now. So we might be changing portfolio allocations for those reasons."

With respect to rebalancing, Dana Jackson says, "It's more people based. Risk tolerance changes as people get older, and sometimes changes when people go through a bear market. Often you are trying to keep them in the market, but sometimes they can be more aggressive than they should. A lot of people were more aggressive than they should have been in the late '90s, when they thought there wasn't as much risk as there certainly was. I had a client come in this week who is retiring and who has a fair amount of money. He's got some family issues that he's dealing with, and he's basically saying that 'it's most important to spend time with family.' So we are reviewing his asset allocation based on the fact that he's retiring. Changes in circumstances probably tend to be the biggest driver of rebalancing."

John D. Olson discusses his overall rebalancing timetable, as well as the importance of regularly meeting with clients to see if their needs or situations have changed:

> What I've read, generally, is that annual rebalancing is important. We are not going to fine-tune every quarter if we are $1\frac{1}{2}$ percent over in large-cap growth versus value. Our fine-tuning is typically done annually, unless something more tactical happens or something else brings it up.
>
> One of the things we always stress to clients is that asset allocation is a process. We meet with them quarterly, and if something is out of whack, we address it. But, typically, we are not going to do an overall rebalancing quarterly. We do show them their asset allocation. We go over all the performance statistics, and I have a chance to relay what's working and what's not working, overall.
>
> In that meeting, the client also has a chance to say what's changed in his or her life, in goals and needs, and in risk tolerance. We try to have these meetings face to face, but they can't always be, even for local clients.

With respect to new money becoming available, Jon Goldstein says that it's "important to keep the balance with new money coming in as clients periodically sell some stock or their income increases." Jon explains how he handles this: "If one asset class starts to run up a little, you can allocate new money to the areas you think are attractive rather than having to sell one investment to buy another."

Jim Hansberger likes to meet with his clients at least quarterly to assess their personal situations, but rebalancing decisions, if any, are often made at an annual meeting:

> We talk in terms of quarterly meetings, but the reality is that quarters come around a lot faster than people realize. No matter how often we talk to a client, we certainly want to make sure that we have a very serious, lengthy annual meeting. That's when we talk about rebalancing. Obviously, if there's been some extraordinary change in the course of the year—dramatic changes in interest rates or very serious changes of one asset class relative to another—we might make adjustments. Often something dramatically changes with the client. If a client goes from having $10 million to having $50 million in a nine-month period, you don't wait until the end of the year to rebalance. If there's been some odd new thing that's come into his life that causes him to

retrench, you rebalance. But in general, we try to use the annual meeting as that most serious opportunity to focus on where we've been, where we are going, and what the proper percentages are. And, by the way, there's nothing that says you must do any rebalancing at all at the annual meeting. You just focus on it. In the end, you are only dealing with four major asset classes. If you rebalance any more often, I'm not so sure that you aren't just making too many small moves.

Sanford Katz tells us that because of the high-net-worth nature of his clientele, he tries to keep his finger on the pulse of what's going on with his clients and their family members: "Fortunately, because of the small number of clients we work with and the nature of the high-net-worth business, we tend to be more integrated into their daily, or certainly monthly, life with regard to expenses and income. Since we tend to manage the majority of their wealth, if not all of it, we see the events in their life such as cash flows, major purchases, major dispositions of property, and things like that. So usually, what doesn't come up in a periodic meeting comes up in the most basic of telephone conversations, because we ask them what is changing. The dialog we have with clients is frequent enough so that major life changes rarely go unaddressed for any extended period."

Taking this one step even further, Sanford does his best to anticipate changes in a client's situation and especially their risk tolerance—changes that if not anticipated can have substantial detrimental effects on the client, the client's portfolio, and the client-advisor relationship:

> If we get the sense that a client, despite all our due diligence and the client's apparent understanding at the outset of the investment process, is expressing a level of risk tolerance that is lower than what we understood, then we will often make changes. We want to maintain a logical relationship with clients, without whipsawing or trading our allocations in a reactive way, at all the wrong times. We hate to be in the position of having clients wanting to make changes at the absolute worst possible times, which often is human nature. So, we try to anticipate this. We will often makes changes if we sense that there is a misstated level of risk tolerance or a misunderstanding of certain asset classes, subasset classes, hedge funds, or private equity. We might make early changes to ensure that clients stay in line with what they are willing to accept over a two- to five-year time frame.

Jim McCabe describes how the very personal needs and experiences of one client has affected his asset allocation:

> Whether this is a change of this client's strategic asset allocation or just a rebalancing is difficult to say, but it reinforces that the individual needs and circumstances of the client must be the determining factor in the practice of asset allocation.

Whether this is a change of this client's strategic asset allocation or just a rebalancing is difficult to say, but it is clear that, once again, it is the individual needs and circumstances of the client that must be the determinative factor in the practice of asset allocation.

MONITORING FUNDS AND MANAGER PERFORMANCE

Top advisors, whether by themselves or with the help of specialists on their teams, keep close tabs on the performance of individual funds and managers, measuring them against benchmarks, and will rebalance portfolios (on a variety of difference schedules) based on performance. Whether this takes place on a shorter, more tactical basis, or is part of keeping to the longer strategic asset allocation plan, this kind of monitoring can usually be seen as rebalancing within asset classes rather than between asset classes. In other words, without changing strategic asset allocation target percentages, this kind of rebalancing can take place between two (or more) investments that both fall within a particular style box, market sector, or other specific asset class.

Mark Sear integrates an analysis of manager performance into his formal quarterly client reviews: "We look at every week from a sort of macro level standpoint. And then, at the end of every quarter, we sit down with each client and talk to him or her. 'Here's where you are. Here's where the indices are. Here's where the managers are that we selected for you versus their benchmarks. So, which investment manager is doing better than others? Which ones are following their benchmark? Which ones are trailing?'"

Michael Johnston explains how manager performance fits into his overall rebalancing assessment: "We monitor the portfolio on an ongoing quarterly basis, looking at all managers to see how they are doing relative to benchmarks. We are also looking at the overall allocation and whether we should we be overweighting or underweighting asset classes because of changes in market conditions, or because certain asset classes have moved up or moved down more so than others." Michael shares more of the thought process that he and his team take in evaluating managers:

When we go into an investment with a manager, we look at the historical performance of that manager relative to the peer group, and we select one who has done well. But over time, a particular manager might not continue to do well. It's not that we fire every manager who's not doing well, because within a given asset class certain investment strategies are going to be in and out of favor. You have to take into account whether the style of investing is appropriate for this current market condition. If it is appropriate, the manager who is not doing well might be fired for underperformance.

When asked if he rebalances within an asset class from underperformers to outperformers, or whether he moves resources from one asset class to another, Jim McCabe responds, "That's going to vary. The general or simplistic answer is to sell the expensive asset (outperformer) and buy the cheap asset (underperformer). However, it all depends upon the manager, the client, the objectives, and the client's risk tolerance. This evolves over time; it's never simple or universal."

TEAM PROCESSES AND INFORMATION SOURCES

Meg Green, who describes the type of tactical rebalancing that she does as "shifting" and not "market timing," shares in detail how she and her team take in new information in order to reach a group consensus:

In our investment management meetings, we want everyone on the same page when we shift weightings, if there is any shifting to be done. Every Monday morning we have a meeting. We sit down and discuss anything we've read over the weekend and update everything that's going on in the office for everybody, so that we're all on the same page. Then we agree on investment perspectives and asset allocations so that we are all moving forward together.

Different kinds of things come into play in terms of how an asset class is going to be weighted in a portfolio. For example, we'll talk about how much international we think should be in the portfolio and whether emerging markets should be part of that. And why. And who could sit still for it and who couldn't. And whether a shift applies to the whole portfolio, or just to the equities. We'll ask each other, "How do you want to work this one?" We eventually get to a place where we are really comfortable.

Jon Goldstein (Smith Barney) and his team follow a process similar to Meg Green's:

> We are looking at things all the time, from both a strategic and a tactical point of view. All the principals of our group meet weekly. We try to get input from as many sources as we can to develop our own consensus, whether it's TV business channels, news items, reading commentary from our outside managers, newsletters we subscribe to, and even our own firm's research. We pay attention to major issues like the direction of interest rates or the slowing and acceleration of the economy or the direction of the dollar. We are trying to identify long-term secular trends, which influence what we recommend. Then with our clients, we formally discuss the outlook for the markets on a quarterly basis.

As for outside sources of information, Ron Carson tells us that he is a "huge fan of using quantitative software to help make better buys and sells, and to identify which sectors are overweight or underweight." Ron explains that he uses "two separate services independently of each other" and that they provide him with both daily and weekly data. "What I've found," says Ron, "is that if I pay attention to what they say in general terms, they are very good at saying, 'This asset class is really looking good.'" Interestingly, Ron tells us that "I have been a fundamentalist asset allocation philosopher since the early '90s. I did not believe in technical analysis. Now we use these systems to manage a percentage of the entire portfolio. We compare it to what it would have been had we not made the changes. And I've come to the conclusion that technical analysis gives you a great deal of positive or negative information that the market has not yet reacted to."

As an example, Ron says that he "reallocated our energy exposure about three years ago, based on information gleaned from these services. Our relative performance has been great since then, because we've been in sectors that have been performing well. The indices haven't done anything over this time period." When asked if he is ever tempted to day trade with this type of information, Ron admits that sometimes "you get real tempted," but then adds that in fact he has not day traded anyone's portfolio. Instead, he says, "We'll raise cash or sit on cash and not deploy it as quickly if the information services are saying that conditions aren't as optimal as they are going to be later on." Ron adds that overall, since he started receiving this kind of information, his practice has changed somewhat:

> Our activity has gone up. It has not necessarily changed the percentage I'll have in an asset class. But, for example, we completely eliminated the emerging markets position for about three months in 2005. It had gotten way ahead of itself. And the services we use came out and said, "We think the downside outweighs the upside." We recommended an allocation elimination. And later they got us back into the emerging markets—once emerging markets reached a support level, they issued a buy for that asset class, so we moved back in. So far, it's been a great call.
>
> So, yes, activity has increased. I hate to be called a "market timer" because that implies that we are only going to be in the market when it's going up, and all the data says that's impossible to do. But, our experience so far with these services is that they've been right more than they've been wrong. And it's worth the additional activity for our clients, because it has generated more positive returns than a buy-and-hold strategy would have. You know what prospects ask when they come in? They say, "Okay, what's your sell discipline? Anybody I've ever worked with told me how they buy stuff. But how do you know when to sell stuff?" Well, we've got an answer now. We can say, "Here's how our system works. Here's how it polices itself. And here's why we get out of a particular asset class for a time."

For Mark Sear it's a question of always looking for new ideas and new trends, and using that information to "move money slightly at the edge":

> We are always looking for themes that are different from those everybody is talking about. What is are going on in our environment? Well, we're getting higher inflation. You've got a ton of money raised by private equity firms that are looking to put it to work. You've got an aging demographic. There are five or six things like this going on in our economy, and we try to find ways to benefit from them. Given the aging demographic, we are somewhat overweighted on health care; we have a little bit broader of an allocation, and are looking for interesting ways to play it. That's not a different asset class, it's just a weighting.

We're not specifically looking for a new great idea that we haven't thought of; we are paying attention to the different ideas and moving among those asset allocations to try to come up with trends and then move money at the edge from here to there.

Mark and his team meet weekly to discuss asset allocations. He then use the outcomes of these meetings to make sure that his clients are on track and to rebalance portfolios when necessary:

We know what our viewpoints are on different assets and allocations. So every Monday we have a meeting. When the market closes, we sit around as a group, both partners and analysts, and we talk about what happened during the previous week. What are the mathematical changes and values of different small-cap stocks versus large-cap stocks, value stocks versus growth stocks, and bonds versus stocks versus high-yield bonds versus municipal bonds? What happened? How did our clients benefit or how have they been hurt?

For example, the last couple of weeks have been very good for us because we've had a long commodity/short U.S. dollar bias. So, portfolios with fixed income securities would have a higher proportion than normal of nondollar bonds. And we'd have more assets than normal in commodity funds. And we have more exposure to utilities and related investments that would benefit from rising energy prices. We do this so we know that, week after week, we've done a good job.

But let's say the opposite happens. Let's say, for example, there was terrorist activity in Europe and people flocked to the U.S. dollar and so the dollar rallied, gold fell, and all the energy stocks fell because there's been a terrorist event. We would know that what we advised on the margin didn't do so well. So on a week-to-week basis, we kind of know how we are doing, and then we have a comprehensive review every quarter when we do each client's performance report to make sure we understand how the performance is or isn't consistent with what we thought it was going to be based on the weekly meetings.

When seeking for opportunities within equities, Paul Tramontano says that he and his team "look for the weighting in a portfolio versus the asset base. Right now we really like the consumer staples sector. If consumer staples represent about 8 percent of the S&P, we might overweight and get them to 12 or 13 percent of our portfolio. Back in the heyday of tech, certain tech stocks may have represented 75 percent of a typical investor's portfolio while technology and telecom represented only 30 percent of the S&P Index. We would tend to underweight tech during a time like that, just as we would be trying to underweight public real estate holdings in the current environment. We use the S&P as the benchmark and either underweight or overweight against that benchmark."

Brian Pfeifler says that with respect to gathering information and detecting "anomalies," he and his team try to keep even complex events simple. "I try to be as simple as I can in what we do." Brian chooses to focus on plain old hard work and diligence:

> It's coming in every morning and checking all the global markets. A lot of guys come in and check the bond market. Yes, but are you checking global bonds? Are you checking every single bond market around the world, trying to figure out where the yields are? That's the standard we try to achieve every day. We do the same in global equity markets as well as other markets. I think if you do this, not only is it more interesting, but it really tunes you into finding good investment opportunities. In my view, a major responsibility of my role for my clients is to gather information. It's living and breathing with great hedge fund managers, great strategists, and great research people. Then, once the research is done, I present our findings to our clients and help them understand and evaluate the investment opportunity—including potential timing. You can have a great idea, but if you don't have the right timing, it's not worth the effort.

Michael Johnston, in considering asset allocation changes, relies on both reports from his research staff and on keeping a keen eye on market conditions:

> If a research staff member who is following a particular asset class or specific money management firm comes out and says that the business of a money management firm is in jeopardy because the chairman left, or the founders retired, or the portfolio manger responsible for that particular class has moved to another firm, then that might be a reason to exit an investment with that money management firm. Another potential reason is market conditions. In the summer of '03, when the ten-year Treasury bond hit 3.1 percent as a low, that was a catalyst to say, "Maybe it's time to start reducing the exposure of our clients' portfolios to the bond market. What's the likelihood of interest rates continuing to decrease and therefore bond prices continu-

ing to increase?" That was a time period where we started shifting client's bond portfolios to other asset classes or reducing the average maturity of those portfolios to reduce interest rate risk. Those are market condition reasons why we would make a change.

Sanford Katz describes another source of external information—televised media—which, like it or not, has to be taken into account these days: "Another thing that might cause us to make a change in allocations is what we see in the media. We have to be really careful about this, because I think the media these days, particularly televised media, can be very single-subject–oriented to the point of affecting markets. I don't think that's the intention, but I think it's an unavoidable outcome."

On balance, rebalancing is a critical activity that must be diligently undertaken by all advisors practicing asset allocation. As this chapter has shown, however, there are many different ways to actually go about rebalancing—different timetables, different triggering factors, different scales of activity—depending on the skill, experience, and perspective of each advisor, as well as the needs and circumstances of each client.

CHAPTER 9: IRA WALKER: AN INNOVATIVE ADVOCATE OF MANAGING MONEY WITH ETFs

Ira Walker (Morgan Stanley, Red Bank, New Jersey) believes so strongly in ETFs that over the past several years he has built an entire money management practice around them. The remainder of this chapter will take an in-depth look at Ira's views, including why he shifted over from his previous practice, the benefits he finds for himself and his clients, and how he performs asset allocation using ETFs. As will be made clear, Ira elegantly combines a sense of history, an in-depth knowledge of asset allocation and money management, and a willingness to embrace new technologies in the service of his clients.

BUILDING A MONEY MANAGEMENT PLATFORM AROUND ETFs

Ira begins with the big picture, comparing ETFs to mutual funds and money managers, and from there describes how he arrived at his current ETF-centered money management practice:

> From a big picture point of view, I believe that ETFs are going to explode over the next ten or twenty years, like money managers and mutual funds exploded in the '80s and '90s. It's really important, therefore, to understand the benefits of ETFs. Based on this understanding, I was able to formulate the concept of my ETF-based money management practice. ETFs today are a great vehicle to invest in because you can trade them intraday, there are potential tax benefits depending on the scenario, and their internal expense ratios are lower, in many cases, when compared to alternatives that accomplish similar investment goals.
>
> Wanting to build this business for my children, I knew that I needed a scalable platform that could utilize investment vehicles that are suitable for my clients' goals. After assessing the vast array of possible investment vehicles, I determined that ETFs were the most appropriate solution. My ability to implement this strategy was opportune, since my firm developed a software program that can manage ETF portfolios in a scalable fashion.

This allowed me to change my clients' allocations very quickly if market conditions dictated such.

Morgan Stanley added a 100 percent ETF platform to their Custom Portfolio program. The Custom Portfolio program allows me to manage ETF portfolios on a discretionary basis, within the confines of certain program-specific guidelines. Because it is a discretionary program, I was able to implement my client's investment strategies without having to contact them for direction on every trade. The nature of ETFs makes them easy to explain to my clients, and they offer the same flexibility as actively managed and index investment options. Subject to certain program specific limitations, I can control the amount of cash in a client's account. I can be aggressive or defensive. I can easily adjust the style that I want to be in, the capitalization of the investments I want to be in, and the sectors I want to be in.

These capabilities are very recent. In '01 and '02, there were not many ETF investment options, because they were just starting out. In addition, the technology to trade ETFs using a scalable system was relatively new, in terms of available software systems. We didn't have the technology to push a button and change a portfolio. Now, with a wider array of ETF securities, and improved technology, we can manage money in a very efficient way.

RECEPTIVE CLIENTS AWARE OF THE BENEFITS

Ira's move to an ETF-centered money management practice represented a substantial shift for his clients. Nevertheless, Ira found that his clients were very receptive to his new investment philosophy, because they quickly understood the benefits that were being offered.

> Most of my clients were receptive to the change, and it is my impression that once I explained the strategy in detail, they were attuned to the potential benefits of ETFs and their use in a discretionary portfolio, where risk tolerance is matched to a specific asset allocation. Ultimately, I find my clients are very comfortable with ETFs because they are liquid, transparent, and, depending on the circumstance, can be very tax efficient.
>
> My clients also find the model easy to understand. They recognize what ETFs are and how my strategy works. With the advent of new technology over the last couple of years, they can

now look at their accounts online and measure their account against various indices, as well as obtain performance reporting. This is a dream come true for my clients and for myself, because everything is transparent, and that's the way it should be.

But still, there is much to be educated on with respect to ETFs, and many Clients have basic questions. A common question Clients will ask is if I actually understand what's inside the ETF. Clients also want to know about ETFs that are somewhat redundant: "There're four or five different large-cap value ETFs. Why would you use one versus the other?" Despite these questions, in my experience, I believe clients are becoming more educated, since information about ETFs is more readily available through the Internet and my firm's internal research. We have to give it some time, but by 2010, I believe that investing in ETFs will be much more widespread.

GIVING CLIENTS A WAY TO STEADILY
BUILD THEIR WEALTH

Given the needs of his client base, Ira describes how ETFs can support the steady accumulation of additional wealth:

We are not looking to knock down the house. Most of my clients are high-net-worth or ultrahigh-net-worth individuals who have already made their wealth and who don't need us to make their wealth for them. They want to hit a lot of singles and doubles with their money and get a reasonable rate of return. We want them to use the customized portfolio we've designed for them as a core product. At any given time, we have ten to twenty ETFs that will cover all the areas we think we should invest in. Then we fill out the asset allocation model with other vehicles.

After '99, clients realized that they weren't going to make 20 percent a year forever, and they were happy compounding their money at reasonable rates of return with less chance of risk.

My first step is to educate my clients to understand their needs and investment objectives. A client who has an extremely high net worth does not need to take risks. If he wants to take risks, he can go to Atlantic City, he can buy penny stocks with another broker, he can put his money in an extremely risky hedge fund and fool around. I am not looking for that business. If they are willing to listen and let me educate them, and if they are willing to buy into the concept that these models can potentially give them a reasonable rate of return, allowing their money to compound at a reasonable level, then they become clients.

ASSET ALLOCATING FOR A TYPICAL CLIENT

Ira is a firm believer in asset allocation and diversification, and begins by putting each of his clients into one of seven core models.

Let me run you through a typical client such as myself—I have my own money invested in this way. Basically, a client will fill out a basic risk tolerance questionnaire that is straightforward and easy to understand. We can then quickly identify if the client will fit into a certain category. Once the client fits into a category, we have seven different models, developed with both Morgan Stanley's internal research and external research that we match to the client's risk tolerance:

- Conservative
- Moderately conservative
- Moderate
- Moderate plus
- Moderately aggressive
- Aggressive
- All equity (100% invested)

Clients generally don't shift from one core model to another, because that's based on their risk tolerance. But if clients want to be more conservative, they can be moved to a more conservative model. Right now, for instance, we have a lot of cash on the sidelines. In some of the models, we have up to 30 percent in cash, but at the push of a button, I can increase my small-cap growth exposure or my emerging market exposure, or I can add a sector.

Finally, we diversify further within sectors that we think will do well. Sector rotation is very important to us. For example, we may rotate out of oil and REITs, to build up a position in pharmaceuticals and biotechnology and health care.

When key ratios are as high as they are today, you have to really think about managing money from a trading perspective as well as from a buy-and-hold perspective. You have to be nimble, so in addition to the U.S. equity portion, we are also going international. Currently we are buying emerging markets and developed markets all over the world. We are beginning to do some research on Japan, because we think that once Japan corrects, it could be an interesting place.

My team reads both external research and internal Morgan Stanley research, so that when we meet every Monday to talk about investment policy, they are up on what's going on from a technical point of view. We use an eclectic approach: technical analysis and fundamentals analysis, in-house and external. If that means that we have to have 35 percent of their portfolio in T-bills until the market corrects, then we are okay with that.

A SCALABLE AND EVOLVING PLATFORM

Ira was originally attracted to an ETF-centered money management practice in part because of its scalability. "Originally," says Ira, "the whole idea was to get into a state-of-the-art platform that was scalable, because what good would it be if we couldn't produce a scalable entity? ETFs, as it turns out, are very liquid and easily traded. With the press of a button, we can adjust a client's portfolio. We can build enormous positions in these ETFs. The volume is there. I can put sell stops. There are so many different tools at my fingertips, and I can be totally defensive in managing money."

But ETFs are still rapidly evolving, and this will give Ira and other ETF-centered practitioners even more opportunities and capabilities over time:

> ETFs are evolving, of course. So if I have a growth tilt to my portfolio, I can look at an ETF that might have positive earning surprises, which would be very attractive to me. There are other companies that are developing ETF strategies that are favoring dividend plays. However, you have to be very conscious of the expense ratios for ETFs, since many new products are increasing such expenses. It is my opinion that you ideally want to keep the expense ratios in ETFs around 25 basis points for an overall portfolio. Today, many individual ETFs have expense ratios greater than this, so you must be attentive and keep your clients informed.
>
> The kicker that really put this into play was the ability to buy bonds along with ETFs. We can buy Treasuries, and I anticipate that in the next one or two years we will be buying municipal bonds. We can buy a T-bill, and if it's to the advantage of the client, we will still go out and buy an individual Treasury bond. Generally, we are looking for liquidity, so we are not going to put too many individual bonds in a portfolio. We try to get the best rate of return on the client's money given their individual risk tolerances, but we also have to be very conscious of liquidity,

because if we want to get back into the market, we need to be able to liquidate assets quickly.

At this point, ETFs enable us to gain exposure to nearly every type of investment option; from specific asset classes, to individual sectors. Many new and useful ETFs have recently been released. For instance, at certain points in the past, I wanted to buy a pure natural resource fund, and they didn't quite have that. Natural resources were mixed with gold, however, they've since released an ETF that tracks just gold, and others that track just oil. We are getting there very quickly, and I anticipate things will only get better, because new ETFs are coming out every month. We are in the 95th percentile in terms of having instruments that will give us exposure to all areas in which we are interested.

I think the next phase of ETFs will be those that are actively managed. Such vehicles will further enable me to develop more specific and comprehensive asset allocation models.

APPROPRIATE FOR MIDDLE-CLASS INVESTORS AS WELL

Although most of his clients are very wealthy, Ira feels that his ETF-centered money management platform can be suitable for middle class investors as well:

> People have a segmentation concept, where they believe there are certain securities only for ultrahigh net worth, and certain securities only for high net worth, and certain ones only for the little guy. Well, I don't believe that this is true, and I think that my method of money management eliminates those barriers.
>
> I know it takes away from the ultra-high-net-worth cachet, but the fact of the matter is, I can asset allocate a $100,000 account as easily as I can a $25 million account. The scalability of the process that I've developed is phenomenal. That was one of the key criteria when I developed this strategy. I didn't want to have difficulty in managing my client's money. I wanted the concept to be streamlined, and that's what we are doing here. Technology has given us an incredible ability to manage money.

THE FUTURE OF MONEY MANAGEMENT?

Ira concludes with some thoughts as to why other advisors haven't yet embraced ETFs as fully as he has. "As to why other advisors aren't doing this, I don't know. I would venture to say," Ira continues, "that this would be a difficult thing to do without having a deep enough staff. It requires a significant number of people to develop this kind of concept, along with the confidence to understand the markets and transition your business from being a financial advisor to being a money manager. Any type of advice that we give on estate planning or lending or anything like that now comes from somebody else. I'm not going to be involved in those areas, because I'm focused on managing money."

Ira is completely confident that he has embraced the future. "Let's face it," he says, "unless you are sitting in front of this screen all day long and managing your own money yourself, I feel this is the cutting edge way to manage money. If you believe that you can buy a group of blue chip stocks and make comparable returns, I think you are just flat-out wrong. I think this is a much better way. It's spectacular to be able to run a portfolio management system like I do, with tremendous benefits to my clients, my firm, and myself."

CHAPTER 10: TURNKEY ASSET ALLOCATION FUNDS

Turnkey asset allocation funds are a relatively new product designed to help advisors streamline asset allocation for certain clients. Turnkey asset allocation funds provide a single investment that features an asset mix appropriate to either the risk tolerance or the life stage of an investor. Such funds therefore offer a kind of one-stop asset allocation using a variety of investment selections. As described later in this chapter, some *Winner's Circle* Advisors make regular use of turnkey asset allocation funds, especially for smaller "relatives" and other secondary accounts, while others feel these products are less appropriate, especially for their client base.

TWO TYPES OF TURNKEY ASSET ALLOCATION FUNDS

A single provider of turnkey asset allocation funds will typically offer a range of funds from conservative to aggressive, varying the mix of cash, fixed-income vehicles, and stocks accordingly, as well as the mix among small-, mid-, and large-cap stocks; U.S. versus international; and so on—according to the objectives of the portfolio. Importantly, turnkey asset allocation products come in two basic types: lifestyle, or age based, and risk based.

Lifestyle turnkey products generally include a series of portfolios from aggressive to conservative, with an age range associated with each portfolio. Investors are placed into a given portfolio based on years until retirement. Aggressive funds are typically targeted at investors in their 20s and 30s; the more conservative funds are for investors in their 50s, 60s, and into retirement. As the investor ages, the portfolio automatically rolls into the next most conservative portfolio, ending with a "retirement" portfolio—usually a very conservative mix of income-producing bonds and cash vehicles, and sometimes including a certain amount of equities for continued growth of capital.

Age-based products are often used in college savings plans, particularly for parents who don't want to have to closely monitor a separate account for their child's education. The portfolios are structured in terms of "years to college," growing progressively more conservative until the "in college" portfolio, which generally resembles a retirement portfolio—that is, income-producing bonds with some equities and a reasonable allotment to cash products.

Risk-based portfolios are structured according to an investor's risk tolerance, running the gamut from aggressive to very conservative. Advisors choose the appropriate portfolio for their client, and the client remains invested in that same portfolio until his or her financial goals, time horizon, or risk tolerance changes.

Each fund company has its own model portfolios—age-based or risk-based—but the better products are constructed to land as close as possible to various points on the efficient frontier. Most of the products are created as a "fund of funds" structure—a fund company creates models of optimally mixed portfolios for each given risk tolerance. Turnkey products offered by actively managed mutual fund families give the client the benefit of all of their portfolio management skills in one portfolio. In addition, the products are well diversified and provide automatic rebalancing. Some products are rebalanced annually, and some quarterly or even monthly.

ADVANTAGES TO ADVISORS

The sophisticated research process that goes into developing these model portfolios includes an optimization program to determine asset classes and then an investment selection process to actually build the portfolios. The benefit to advisors, obviously, is that they do not have to undertake these same rigorous processes and instead, can simply choose the product that best fits the client's needs. Many advisors find these products attractive for less affluent clients because the minimum investment is typically so low.

A similar product is a fund of funds that offers diversification across a specific asset class, such as international investments. This type of fund allows an advisor to determine a client's appropriate total allocation to a given asset class, and put the entire amount into a fund that is already diversified across that asset class, saving him or her from having to sift through thousands of funds. Again, these types of funds typically offer automatic rebalancing, low minimum investments, and, in the case of actively managed funds, the expertise of a group of managers instead of just one or two.

ASSESSING TURNKEY ASSET ALLOCATION FUNDS

Because turnkey asset allocation funds are already asset allocated for a given risk tolerance, they're designed to be the primary investment in an individual's portfolio. The *Winner's Circle* advisors interviewed for this book typically work with high-net-worth clients who require customized asset allocation plans. As Michael Johnston (Smith Barney) puts it, "I think lifestyle funds are appropriate for the small investor who's trying to get some diversification and trying to minimize the amount of paperwork involved, and wants somebody else to make the decisions for them to create a diversified portfolio. But for the size of clients that we are working with, I feel it's our responsibility to customize their asset allocation for their particular needs and their particular tax rate."

Many *Winner's Circle* advisors add, however, that they will use turnkey asset allocation funds for family members of their main clients who have smaller accounts or for the accounts of children and grandchildren, especially for educational and 529 Plan purposes. Ron Carson (Linsco/Private Ledger), for example, says, "I work with clients who have $5 million or more of investable assets. But I invariably get family members with a $200,000 or $300,000 portfolio. In some of these cases, we will use a turnkey asset allocation fund." Louis Chiavacci (Merrill Lynch), who serves accounts that are typically in the $50-million-and-up category, says that he will use turnkey funds, "but that's usually for a small account, like a child's account or an IRA account where you can't get efficiency across asset classes otherwise." Paul Tramontano (Smith Barney) agrees: "We have some people in these turnkey funds in the 529 plans. For the past two or three years they've done nicely, and I think 529s provide a reasonable way to start investing for college."

Joe Jacques (Jacques Financial) says that while he doesn't use turnkey asset allocation funds for individualized portfolios, he will use them for a client's 401(k) plans. "Most of my clients come to me with their 401(k) plans. If I know somebody who is totally unsophisticated and doesn't really want to hedge their downside risk, I'll recommend against trying to pick a couple of funds that may get out of date within a couple of years. Instead, I'll put them into those lifestyle funds because I know that their proportions are being revalued and reanalyzed on an ongoing basis. So yes, I've been using quite a bit of these in 401(k) plans for my clients." Kathy Tully (Morgan Stanley) echoes this sentiment: "Those are great in 401(k) plans, especially when a person does not have an advisor."

Jim Hansberger (Smith Barney) feels that turnkey asset allocation funds have value for some individuals but that in the long-run most people will be better off with finding a trusted advisor who will customize an asset allocation approach: "Of course there is value because what's the alternative? If someone does not have experience, or if they don't have a trusted advisor who in turn has experience, then they are flying by the seat of their pants. So, of course, a turnkey fund is better than none. But it doesn't compare, in my opinion, to finding a trusted advisor or educating oneself, or some combination of the two."

As for the difference between risk-based and age-based, Dana Jackson (Smith Barney) offers an alternative: "It's more people based. People make changes to their risk tolerance as they get older or go through a bear market. Changes in circumstances tend to have the most influence." Jim Hansberger offers a similar perspective: "It's really about the individual, his asset base, his needs, his plans, his objectives, his family, his interest, and so on. Age doesn't have anything to do with it."

Sanford Katz (UBS) feels that a focus on risk is more useful than a focus on age or time-based factors: "When we look at the time-based approach to asset allocation, how long does it take for asset classes to cycle or correct? How long does it take to generate a return? And how much of a time frame is the client working with? I think you are more apt to get surprises and make mistakes counting on those time-based variables, whereas, you are less apt to be disappointed if you are just taking an intermediate- to long-term view and assume that corrective forces will give you more reliable results over time."

A VALUABLE TOOL

Turnkey products are popular among investors who don't use financial advisors, probably because they give a "set it and forget it" feel. This can amount to a dangerous assumption, however, and both investors and advisors should remember that any change to an investors' financial goals, risk tolerance, or time horizon requires a regular review to ensure that an individual's financial strategy remains on track. Overall, turnkey asset allocation funds can be a great tool, but like any tool, they have to be used in the right place and at the right time, and they have to be properly cared for.

Chapter 11: Some Cautions and Criticisms

From the perspective of most clients, asset allocation is straightforward, makes sense, and works as promised. Moreover, the vast majority of advisors—not just the top advisors interviewed for this book—are ethical, hardworking, intelligent, and committed to serving their clients. Thus we can assume that asset allocation is widely used by today's advisors because it is among the most effective and powerful methodologies at their disposal.

However, even though asset allocation may be almost universally accepted, it has not gone uncriticized. Whether the call is for a "postmodern" portfolio theory or a next-generation asset allocation model such as "asset dedication" (see *Asset Dedication: How To Grow Wealth with the Next Generation of Asset Allocation*, by Huxley and Burns, McGraw-Hill, 2005), it seems that there is almost always a new book, academic paper, or online polemic aimed at knocking asset allocation and modern portfolio theory (MPT) from their high-status perch. Consider, for example, William Jahnke's article "The Asset Allocation Hoax" (*Journal of Financial Planning*, 1997), which takes a dim view of the ultimate value of asset allocation in the context of Gary Brinson's well-known studies. (See Chapter 1 and Appendix B, "A Brief History of Asset Allocation," for a discussion of Gary Brinson's research.)

It may be that asset allocation has attracted criticism simply because it is the pragmatic aspect of Modern Portfolio Theory (MPT) the dominant financial paradigm. Whatever is on top, in any field or endeavor in life, tends to attract criticism. This is not necessarily a bad thing, because it is only through such criticism that an even better paradigm, model, or method may one day arise. (This was a central point of John Stuart Mill's famed essay, "On Liberty," that is, if we quell the voices of dissent, in the long run we only hurt ourselves.) In other words, it is entirely possible that one day, asset allocation and MPT may be supplanted or transcended, just as Einstein's physics has included yet transcended Newton's. (But note that when you are crossing a busy street, you still want to rely mainly on Newton's description of how things work.)

For the most part, the overriding assumption and perspective guiding this book is that asset allocation does indeed have the power and value that it is generally assumed to have. In the interest, however, of one day perhaps finding an even better approach to portfolio and investment management, the following list of asset allocation criticisms, plus brief responses, are gathered together in one place for your consideration. No attempt will be made to finally resolve these criticisms; they are presented to spur constructive dialogue and provide a basis for a more refined and useful approach. Following this list, some additional criticisms brought up by the *Winner's Circle* advisors interviewed for this book will be considered in greater detail.

- *Risk is improperly measured by variance and volatility:* Harry Markowitz (the orginator of asset allocation) and his followers have assumed that risk is best measured by variance and volatility, but there is no real proof that this is what is most important to investors.

  Response: Volatility is indeed important to investors; just ask any advisor or investor who was overly concentrated in technology stocks during the recent bubble and crash.

- *Asset allocation starts with the client's risk tolerance, but there is no precise way to measure this:* The questionnaires that advisors give their clients cannot possibly enable a detailed understanding of the client's risk tolerance, which is subjective and cannot easily be pinned down.

  Response: Questionnaires are only one tool used by advisors, and a helpful one at that. Experienced advisors can rapidly and accurately assess the risk tolerance of clients, even if they spend only an hour or two with them. The questionnaires provide an excellent starting point, and different advisors learn to use them to maximum advantage in their own unique ways.

- *There is no scientific way to determine the asset allocation for a given client even if that client's risk tolerance is known:* A client who goes to three different advisors will end up with three portfolios consisting of three different asset allocations. Asset allocation is therefore not really scientific.

  Response: Indeed, while asset allocation has scientific elements, it is just as much an art, depending on the skill and savvy of the advisor to determine a portfolio that most closely meets a client's overall needs and goals and that is appropriate for the client's risk tolerance and liquidity situation.

- *Asset allocation is mainly about pigeonholing investors in order to sell them more product:* Asset allocation mainly amounts to a marketing and sales tool designed to peg investors at one of several levels (conservative, moderate, aggressive) so that a predetermined mix of investment vehicles set by the firm's home office or central investment committee can be easily sold.

  Response: The notion that asset allocation is primarily a marketing and sales tool is cynical and misses the point that asset allocation reliably enables investors to control risk while building wealth in the long run, thereby adding great value to the lives of investors at all levels of the economic spectrum. Also, as shown in this book, developing asset allocation strategies for clients often leads to deeper relationships and a consultative role for the advisor.

- *"Efficient portfolios" are only known retrospectively:* Portfolios that combine asset classes to maximize return for a given level of risk, or that minimize risk for a given level of return are only determinable with hindsight. Thus, using the efficient frontier to choose asset classes for a portfolio amounts to little more than "picking classes," which, like "picking stocks," is extremely difficult or impossible.

  Response: The long-term behavior of asset classes, including how they covary with each other, is for the most part well-known and fairly stable. The efficient frontier, while only determinable retrospectively, is nonetheless an enormously useful construction and practical tool.

- *Rebalancing—bringing a portfolio back to a desired asset allocation—is a haphazard and often costly process:* Different advisors advocate different rebalancing schedules, varying widely from quarterly (or even weekly, for some advocates of tactical rebalancing) to yearly. Advisors also vary greatly on how far out of alignment with original target percentages a portfolio must be before rebalancing is triggered. The lack of consensus here points to a lack of theoretical understanding and agreement, and the amount of rebalancing that goes on may be related to the transaction fees that some advisors generate through rebalancing and may have unconsidered and substantial tax implications for investors.

  Response: Asset allocation is an art as much as a science, and it is not surprising that different advisors rebalance on different schedules and in accordance with different trigger points that are most in accord with their experience and understanding. For those advisors who work on a transactions basis, rebalancing may result in some charges to the client, but these are necessary to bring the portfolio back to the desired allocation, and in any case, ethical advisors take these charges and any tax implications into consideration before making recommendations.

- *Many investors would be better off just investing in an index fund of all stocks:* Since we know that higher returns come with higher risk, many investors would be better off just choosing an S&P 500 index fund or its equivalent (such as an ETF) and holding on until they are ready to retire.

Response: Investing in all stocks until nearing retirement is too risky for most investors and also ignores and devalues a wide variety of other issues, including, for example, tax considerations and set income needs. Moreover, clients in general, and wealthier clients in particular, have a wide range of wealth management needs that can be addressed much more effectively with the help of a professional financial advisor.

- *Asset allocation may work for institutional investors because of their very long time frame and ability to access a wider range of alternative investments, but it will not work for individuals:* Asset allocation essentially amounts to a "buy-and-hold" strategy, which, over long periods of time, should be able to ride out sharp declines in the market, but individual investors have much shorter time frames than institutional investors and can be hurt by this strategy. Similarly, average investors cannot access many of the alternative investments that provide substantial diversification benefits.

Response: Asset allocation can't turn a down market into an up one and does have some limits. But just as institutions will benefit from the reduction in overall volatility and the intelligent management of risk/reward trade-offs, individual investors will benefit as well. Moreover, as individuals live longer and longer, and have intergenerational concerns and objectives, longer time frames begin to come into play for many people. Also, an ever-widening number of alternative investments and investment vehicles generally (including ETFs) have become available to individuals over time; therefore most of what is available to large institutions is available to wealthy investors and, to some degree, even to smaller investors.

- *Asset allocation is designed for investors who wish to preserve or slowly grow capital, not those who wish to make a "killing" in the market.*

Response: This is really not so much a criticism as it is a statement of fact. Indeed, asset allocation is not designed to double or triple wealth in a short period of time, but is best at preserving capital and growing it in a steady fashion. Importantly, the power of compounding returns benefits those with a sensible asset allocation strategy in place in two ways. First, a properly asset-allocated portfolio, because of its diversified nature and the inclusion of noncorrelated assets, is less likely to suffer major capital drawdowns, allowing the positive effects of compounding to continue relatively unabated. Second, individuals with a properly asset-allocated portfolio are less likely to panic, make bad timing decisions, and leave themselves less than fully invested when markets rebound.

SOME ADDITIONAL CAUTIONS AND CRITICISMS

The advisors interviewed for this book have offered some additional cautions with respect to the practice of asset allocation. As a starting point, Jon Goldstein (Smith Barney) points out that especially from the perspective of an investor, asset allocation should not be treated as a one-time event, like the purchase of a product. Asset allocation involves ongoing monitoring and vigilance, and the investor cannot abdicate his or her active role in this process:

> An asset allocation approach is not a product sale. It's not that you decide on an allocation and you are good to go. You must monitor it diligently, and alter it based on the investor's needs and changing capital market conditions. An investor plays right into our business model when he believes he needs professional help to accomplish that. The world changes constantly. For a client to think that one particular asset allocation or investment program is going to work indefinitely is absurd.

Mark Sear (Merrill Lynch) offers a similar caution and criticism, focusing in detail on a lack of follow-up by many advisors after they create an initial allocation for their clients:

> One of the biggest problems in our business is that people do a great job of attracting new customers. They have a great pitch. They talk about asset allocation. They talk about managers. They talk about all these things. When they acquire the new client, they put them in a static model, and then they go to find new clients. But the key factor in making the process work isn't the

first allocation you do. That's just the first one. The key thing is that it's being reviewed on a quarterly basis. Our theme right now is that bonds, at the time of this interview, are probably not a great place to put a tremendous amount of assets. Stocks seem to be a little bit more fairly valued, and we like high quality versus low quality, and we like commodities and nondollar. Those are our themes.

You have to know what the plan is. You have to know where you should be. If we get a couple of months down the road, or a couple of quarters down the road, and one or two of those themes has either worked or not worked, we may need to adjust the portfolio if we are ahead of plan or behind plan. So, we have a quarterly review process that we go through with clients. This process is critical. While that first allocation is important, it's no more important than the third or the fifth or the sixth or the tenth. And that's the essence of what we try to do.

On the strategic side, it's like anything in life. Bad data on the way in creates bad data on the way out. If somebody says that they are going to spend $200,000 a year and they spend $400,000 a year, that's a big problem, strategically. Because you've built something with a certain mind-set in place and certain variables. If those variables are wrong, then the allocation is worthless. The biggest con there is when you are not being realistic and are not looking back to determine how realistic those variables were.

Suppose I think stocks are going to return 12 percent. I build that into the model, and then I have only a 4 percent return. If the historical average has been 10 percent, and this feels like a period of time when there are going to be lower returns than that, then expecting 12 percent returns for stocks is insanity. Not being realistic is where you get into trouble with the strategic part of the allocation. So, if you are not looking at it on a quarterly and annual basis, it's all worthless.

Again, I think the biggest problem in our industry is that people are very strategic on the front end, and then they don't follow up. They don't follow up on their own results. "How did we do? We said we were going to do X, but we did Y?" It's really hard to go to a client and say, "I was going to do X but I only did 30 percent of X. I'm a knucklehead." You have to follow up. In a business, you wouldn't think twice about it. Clients don't look at their portfolios for five years and then they complain that they have lost money. Well, somebody needs to be on it all the time, and that's the advisor's job.

Mark offers one final caution, which relates to the importance of an advisor having a specific viewpoint so that they can add value to their client's portfolios: "I think we are hired for our viewpoint. You have to have a viewpoint. Our viewpoint could be wrong. And so, at the end of the day, we'll be evaluated by how many times we were right versus how many times we were wrong. People say, 'You can't time the market, you have to just be in the market.' Well, I don't have any interest in trying to time the stock market. But I do think there are times when stocks are expensive relative to bonds. And I think there are times when cash is expensive, relative to something else. I'm not trying to time the stock market. I'm just saying if I can take A or B, I will take a lot of B versus A if B is a better value, and that's really what we try to do from a tactical standpoint. We spend a lot of time looking at the relative value."

Tim Kneen (Citigroup Institutional Consulting) strongly echoes this point, stating that an advisor can't just believe in asset allocation. Instead, he or she has to come to the table with his or her own perspective and themes in order to add maximum value.

All people who think they know about asset allocation have to have some belief in asset allocation beyond just "I believe in asset allocation." Correlation is a prime example of this. Believing in asset allocation is great, but all that really says is, "I won't put all my eggs in one basket." So, "what do you believe about asset allocation?" is the most important question that anybody can ask. What we believe in is asset allocation for risk reduction and using a mean regression or extra output model behind it.

Asset allocation by itself, without a strategy to employ it, is only half the battle. If all I did was asset-allocate for lower risk and just use my correlation studies and stop there, I would really hurt my clients, because where we create much of our excess return is our mean regression model, which is like putting asset allocation on steroids. You will find that over long periods of time—you don't have to go back that far, just 10 or 15 years— there is very little difference between small and large, value and growth, international and domestic. It's the same concept as asset allocation—you try to allocate your assets to those asset classes that have recently underperformed. It's just another form of asset allocation.

A lot of younger people in the business say they believe in asset allocation, but their idea of asset allocation is that they diversify a portfolio and that they understand that all asset classes are not correlated with each other. They get that far. But what do they do after that? If you read The *Winner's Circle* book about the great money managers (*The Winner's Circle: Wall Street's Best Mutual Fund Managers,* Horizon Publishers Group, 2005), you will find that every one of those money managers believes in something. There is something inherent in their process that they believe in and continually repeat. What I see in many people in our business today is a lack of conviction. They understand asset allocation to a limited level, but where is that next level that produces the extra output?

Jim Hansberger (Smith Barney) begins his caution with a theoretical review of the MPT assumption that risk is equivalent to volatility:

> By no means do I automatically buy into all of modern portfolio theory. This isn't asset allocation we are talking about. We are talking about modern portfolio theory, where you measure risk by volatility and create standard deviations. Standard deviation basically measures volatility. But does it really measure risk?
>
> Warren Buffet's standard approach is that if we were drawing a chart right now, and we drew the letter M, then we would see something very low going straight up, then back down, then back up, and then down again. Let's pretend that was a stock chart. It would certainly indicate a lot of volatility in one year, and standard deviation would measure that as high risk. Warren Buffet would say, "Phooey." In fact, that's his exact terminology. Phooey. Why not just have an investment philosophy that causes you to buy at the low points of each of those downward movements?
>
> Just because something has volatility does not mean it's an automatic risk. Risk is the price you pay. The price you pay determines your rate of return. So if you are focused on the outstanding fundamentals, and know the business well rather than the individual stock, the business may not be volatile. The stock is volatile, and you focus on the price you pay, whether it's for a piece of real estate or a common stock or whatever it might be.

Jim then offers a more specific criticism that is reminiscent of something that Yogi Berra once said: "In theory there is no difference between theory and practice. In practice there is." Jim's point is not to forget that asset allocation is part of modern portfolio *theory,* with an emphasis on its theoretical nature. The devil, as always, remains in the details and in the execution, and the skill of the advisor or money manager can never be overlooked.

If we are to apply Modern Portfolio Theory to asset allocation, then that automatically means that we are talking about alpha, which is the term in modern portfolio theory that identifies a return over and above what could reasonably be expected. If we are up 20 percent in one year in our equity portfolio and the vast majority of portfolios are up 10 percent, then we have provided some real value added in the form of 10 percent alpha. And the question mark is whether that is a result from pure science or whether it's all in the art. The devil is in the details.

All you have to do is find a handful of managers who outperform to say, "Well, this is not a science." So, individual manager skill is critical. Think about the whole terminology of Modern Portfolio Theory. The last word there is "theory", not fact. This is a theory about how portfolios should be managed today. As far as diversifying by asset class goes, or recognizing what correlates and what doesn't, what is and isn't a realistic return, what's liquid versus not, I am going to say for the tenth time that I have no problem buying into any of that. But the devil is in the details. It's the execution that matters.

We do have a model that a very brilliant guy inside Citigroup has put together. At any given time it can look at all the different asset classes and spit out some numbers based on projected rates of return and acceptable levels of risk. Oftentimes we'll run through this risk-based model, but it is by no means our guide. He is excellent, and his model is excellent, but I refuse to believe that any formula has ever proven to be the final word. The new paradigm—that everybody needs to be broadly diversified by asset class and that there is a perfect analysis of how to measure risk and that you can arrive at some perfect asset allocation by plugging in numbers—I think that's baloney. It's not scientific.

A related caution, mentioned by several advisors, is that advisors naturally become better at asset allocation over time, and that it's therefore impossible not to make some mistakes along the way. Brian Pfeifler (Morgan Stanley) relates a bit of his experience: "I've been reading what they've been doing at Yale and Harvard with endowments. Morgan Stanley went out and did research on who the best money managers were, and in that process, I learned a lot more about asset classes. Six years ago, I knew what hedge funds were, but I certainly didn't know as much about them as I know now. I certainly know a lot more this year about what's going on in terms of multistrategy investment opportunities than I ever did before. I think you are constantly learning with this job, and that you are growing every single day."

Brian goes on to admit that certain of his picks were more successful than others. "In hindsight, I would change some of my prior recommendations. For example, we've recommended managers who have not outperformed to the extent we had hoped, and we've then thought it wise to recommend pulling that money out earlier than we originally intended. In my view, there will always be decisions that a person would want to change given 20-20 hindsight. But the real question for our clients would be, 'Is my representative doing the best job possible with the information he or she had at hand and have they collected all of the best available analysis and investment/market information?' Clients also need to evaluate whether their representative has recommended an effective asset allocation that will protect them and diversify their portfolios over the long term. We work hard to do well on both accounts."

Mark Curtis (Smith Barney) speaks of the importance of learning and evolving as an advisor and of seeing how academic concepts have their impact in the real world: "I think that in this job, you continue to learn and mature and get better as you go. First of all, you learn on the job the need and benefits of diversification. You can study it in an academic sense, but when you see the real-world benefits you appreciate asset allocation more because you see that it works. There may be periods when diversification disconnects, as it did in the late '90s, but over time it absolutely works. You can't separate the evolution of your experience with asset allocation from your personal evolution as a financial counselor."

Along the same lines, Sanford Katz (UBS) suggests the value of learning about asset allocation by trading with one's own funds:

> My own appreciation of asset allocation evolved through investing my own money, in small amounts early in my career, and in larger amounts later on when the compounding became more meaningful. Having that true-to-life experience makes me more credible when I try to explain it to clients. Trading your own money at an early age, you find out the hard way that asset allocation really is more important and fundamental than you may have realized in a business school classroom.

Sanford then adds that the way he and his team work with clients is always evolving, but at the same time, it's important for them not to overeagerly follow current trends and lose track of what works. "The overall process, the way we work with clients, is always evolving. It's evolving by experience, sometimes the hard way, as to what works and what doesn't. At the same time, like any money manager or manager of managers, we don't want to abandon what has worked. So we spend just as much time trying to stay on the reservation, making sure we don't drift too far when following recent trends."

A final caution comes from Paul Tramontano (Smith Barney), who advises us that while many people are very excited about various automated asset allocation programs and modeling technologies, they will never replace or be as important as the individual relationships the advisor has with his or her clients.

What is asset allocation going to look like in the future? Technology has greatly changed asset allocation, and many people might think that it is becoming a technology-based solution where there are new programs every day. Smith Barney has a bunch of programs, and I know that there are a lot of off-the-shelf programs available for asset allocation. People might think that the future is going there, but I don't. I think the future is right here, when we are sitting across the table from a family and understanding what's important to them.

I might be old-fashioned, but I think the most important part of asset allocation is understanding what a client's needs are and then making sure that they understand what their actual portfolio looks like. And you can't do that with a program. You can't get the innuendo in there. You can't get the body language, and you can't get some ideas of particular interest in there—for example, interest or disinterest in particular sectors. You can't get a lot of those subtle details in there, and I think they are important. The technology might help prove your thesis, but I think the most important thing is going to remain the personal relationship. As I say all the time, I'm not very good at many things, but this I can do. After a couple decades' experience, I'm pretty good at it.

CHAPTER 12: STORIES AND LESSONS: THE TECH BUBBLE, 9/11, AND BEYOND

The technology and telecommunications related "dot.com" stock bubble of the late 1990s reached its peak in March of 2000. (Technically, the Dow Jones peaked in January of 2000, while the NASDAQ peaked in March.) Stocks, especially Internet-related technology and telecommunications stocks, saw a precipitous drop through the rest of 2000 and into 2001. Then, on September 11, 2001, the Twin Towers of the World Trade Center, in the heart of Manhattan's financial district, were destroyed by an act of terror. After the heady late-1990s, with their unprecedented gains in certain stock sectors, these were difficult times.

For those who steadfastly followed it, the asset allocation approach resoundingly proved its merits during this period. Those clients fortunate enough to have an advisor who persuaded, cajoled, or even forced them into sticking with their target asset allocations as tech and associated stocks rose stratospherically, and who later helped them not to panic or make disastrous timing decisions as the markets tumbled, fared far better than those who followed the herd.

Our discussions with *Winner's Circle* advisors revealed that during those boom times they were indeed sticking to their investing disciplines, which included proper asset allocation. Nearly all advisors complained that their relative underperformance was a chief concern among their clients, many insisting that at least part of their portfolios be exposed to the seemingly always rising tech stocks. Many *Winner's Circle* advisors who allowed their clients to invest in these stocks established limits of 4 or 5 percent of portfolios, or set up new accounts that were defined as "play money" accounts, with the understanding that such accounts could be wiped out. Other advisors refused to invest in tech stocks altogether.

These were trying times. Some clients began to lose confidence in their advisors, who were underperforming both the NASDAQ and personal acquaintances who were fully participating in the boom. Many of these clients opted to believe in recommendations from their neighbor, barber, or brother-in-law over those from their advisor. Many advisors lost some clients as a result, and their businesses grew far less than those of other advisors who believed in "the new paradigm" of ever rising tech stock prices.

Once the market began its downturn and started showing no signs of recovering, something remarkable occurred: Many of the clients who had left asked their advisors to take them back, and they told their friends and families about their advisors who remained true to their investing disciplines. Through the down market, clients of these *Winner's Circle* advisors enjoyed limited—or no—loss of capital, instead outperforming their friends and families, sometimes by 70 or 80 percentage points.

This chapter will recap some of the many lessons that were learned, and some of the many stories that are still being told, from this tumultuous period.

PREVENTING PANIC

When clients hear bad news—especially on the level of a natural disaster, a terrorist attack, or a substantial market tumble—it is inevitable that some of them will panic. During such times, it's critical importance that their advisors keep a steady hand on the wheel and a ready hand at the phone. In the months that followed 9/11, we were heartened by the long hours these *Winner's Circle* advisors were working, maintaining constant communication with their clients.

Meg Green (Royal Alliance), for example, describes what she and her team did in reaction to the events of 9/11: "After 9/11, everybody was in a panic. So we actually spent the week calling each and every client, saying 'Let's get together.' We set up meetings. We didn't sell anything to anybody at the time. That wasn't our job. Our job was to keep everybody happy and comfortable. We did a lot of changing around at that point for people who were in panic mode and who just needed to sleep at night. Right or wrong, some really needed to lighten up on their equities. It might not have been the right thing at that time, but as it turned out, it was perfectly fine. And if it hadn't been, they understood the price they might be paying for a good night's sleep."

Sometimes clients panic unnecessarily. For example, Michael Johnston (Smith Barney) had a client call him in an irrationally frightened state. The client eventually came to understand that Michael had done the right thing for him and that he was not nearly as badly off as he expected to be:

> A client who called me the first week of March of 2003 was panicked because we had invested the nonfixed income portion

of his portfolio in late 2000, specifically on November 1 and December 1 of 2000. He was watching the news, and the markets were down maybe 44 percent from the market top. I think the S&P 500 was down about 40 percent in that time period. So, he was in a panic, even though he had an equivalent-sized bond portfolio that we had put together over the two years prior to that and he had finally sold a good bit of his single-stock position by the end of 2000. Well, he was looking at CNBC and watching the local news and seeing that the markets were falling, but not really doing an analysis of his portfolio, where we had him diversify more into small-cap value U.S. stocks and also had him take a large exposure into market-neutral hedge funds.

Wondering why he had panicked, I performed an analysis. As it turned out, from December 1 of 2000 to March 2003, he was down 5 percent in the nonfixed income part of his portfolio. We had provided him with broad diversification, and in 2000, we knew that growth-oriented stocks were overvalued, so we underweighted his investments in growth stocks and over-weighted his investments in value stocks. After we did a return analysis on the nonfixed income portion of his portion, his fears were reduced. He still didn't like it that he was down 5 percent, but things were much better than he imagined. He thought he was going to have to go back to work.

STICKING WITH THE PLAN

From the perspective of Mark Curtis (Smith Barney), it's important for clients to stick with the plan, even when the going gets tough. Importantly, however, sticking with the plan does not necessarily mean making no changes whatsoever. Here, the art of asset allocation involves holding the fine line between making appropriate adaptations and not going too far overboard in any one direction. Mark puts it this way:

> You've got to stick with it in bad times. Now, let me say that everything is fluid. Everything is a process. So by "stick with it," I mean, for example, what did you do post 9/11? Well, we did make changes. For example, we somewhat underweighted growth, overweighted value, and overweighted fixed income. In times like that, you do adjust. But you never go to zero in the major asset classes. Nor do you ever put 100 percent in any one asset class. You never make those kind of all-or-nothing deci-sions. You overweight and underweight. You are constantly

adapting, but at the same time, you are not making big huge bets for or against anything. It is important to note that our clients are not looking to us to make them wealthy. Our role is to advise them so that they can maintain their wealth.

Hank McClarty (Gratus Capital Management) relates how he stuck with his disciplines before the tech bubble burst, and now, having been through it, he is even less willing to "bend" and go with the client's intuition:

> I definitely lost a few prospects in 1999 and 2000 by saying, "I think, based on what our discussions have been, that you need 30, 40, or 50 percent in bonds. And I know it doesn't look attractive right now, but I really feel strongly that's what you should have as part of your allocation. You should expect a real rate of return of 7 percent." They'd respond, "Well, so-and-so down the street said I could get 12 percent and I should be in all equities." There were a lot of advisors out there who were just playing up to their clients' unrealistic expectations, saying, "Oh yes, I can give you 12 percent or 15 percent. That's what you should expect long term." Of course, they had no possibility and, frankly, no intention of doing that.
>
> I was saying this before the bubble burst, but afterward I got a lot of referrals because I stuck to my guns, kept my clients in bonds, and continued to rebalance through that time period. We were selling off stocks and buying bonds when everybody thought we were crazy and saying that "This time things are different. It's not the market of old." Our asset allocations and the annual rebalancing we did definitely saved a lot of people's portfolios.
>
> After the tech market crashed, I got very rigid with my recommendations on bonds and stocks. I've been through it now, and any client who has been through it would listen. Any client who hasn't, or who didn't have money in the market at the time, may still have difficulty agreeing with me. But as advisors, we are here to do a service for them, not to go with their intuition. Otherwise, they wouldn't have come to me in the first place.

Jim McCabe (Wells Fargo Investments) says that most of his clients were not tempted to get caught up in the tech bubble in the first place. This was due to a combination of Wells Fargo's investment style (wealth preservation), the education Jim and his team provide to their clients, and the clients' temperaments: "Most of our clients weren't that involved in tech speculation. During cocktail conversations, they heard about people doubling their money, and they may have witnessed a portfolio manager doing 95 percent in one year. That looked great. Of course, a year later, it was negative 141 percent. Most of our clients were satisfied earning above-average returns with lower risk. They intuitively knew that the speculative return picture was not sustainable. Everybody wanted the return, but most of our client's didn't want the risk. We limited our investments to companies with earnings and revenue, not just speculative returns."

Was Jim ever tempted to move clients into "hotter" securities? "It's tough," he answers. "It would have been easy to do the hot, popular thing at that moment. But in the long run we are all grateful we stuck to our discipline. At Wells Fargo there are also internal governors on what we do that wouldn't allow us to buy some things at that point in time. Our portfolio management team didn't allow us to buy companies that didn't have earnings and revenues. Most of our clients have already accumulated their wealth and their objective is to preserve it. They want to grow their capital as much as possible, but within safe parameters. They are more interested in preserving wealth than they are in doubling it."

STICKING TO THEIR GUNS (REGARDLESS OF THE COST)

During the tech-bubble it was common for clients to demand that their asset allocation strategy be abandoned in favor of purchasing equity investments that seemed likely to rise forever. Advisors who would not "give in" to these demands knew that they might lose some of their clients. Ron Carson (Linsco/Private Ledger) describes one such situation:

> We spent much of our time during the bubble defending asset allocation. Clients would say, "Oh, this tech fund is up 100 percent and these bonds are boring." But we stuck by our guns. I had a couple of clients leave because they said we were way too conservative, but I haven't heard that argument now for about five years.
>
> Very specifically I had one long-time client who had his entire portfolio invested in long-term CDs earning right about 8½ percent. I remember that when he and his wife originally came in they said, "If you can even get close to this amount, we will be very, very happy." Well, we invested his money in a broadly diversified portfolio, and at the beginning of 1999 his portfolio had averaged over 14 percent a year, which was much higher than what he expected.

But during this particular meeting, he was really dissatisfied because he had friends who were earning a lot more money. He said, "Why don't we own this fund? It is up 70 percent. And look, almost any one of these funds in the newspaper have earned more than 14 percent a year." In fact, the equity funds he was referring to were probably all full of tech stocks, and we had a big component of his portfolio—depending upon the time, anywhere from 30 to 40 percent—invested in bonds.

So I said to him, "You know what? I would rather lose you as a client than move you into a growth or an aggressive growth portfolio because I know, I have it right here," and I pulled out his personal financial profile, "that you said to me you cannot stand to lose more than 25 to 30 percent of your portfolio. And if you are invested in growth or aggressive growth, that's exactly what could happen." He ended up transferring his portfolio to someone else. I don't specifically know what happened, but I can only assume that things did not turn out well.

Meg Green has had similar experiences, telling clients that she would not assist them in making what she believed would be a huge mistake. In one case, an unsophisticated wife wanted to trade stocks in her husband's pension plan. When Meg refused to participate, the client and his wife went elsewhere. Disaster ensued, perhaps indefinitely postponing the client's retirement:

> I had a client with a large pension, maybe $1.8 million at the time, and that's all the money he had in the world. He was in his late 60s and he had never saved outside of his pension, so his pension was it. If he was ever going to retire, it had to be from the pension. Well in those days in the late 1990s every grandmother and every stay-at-home mom and every club was buying stocks, and his wife was in an investment club. She was having the best time because she bought Qualcomm and it just went flying.
>
> She wanted to start trading in his pension because they had no other money, so she called me up and said, "I want to buy some stocks in his pension." I said, "I'm so sorry. You are going to have to talk to him about that." So she called him and badgered him, and he called me up and said "You are going to have to let her." I said, "I am not going to let her. This is your money. You can't do this. She can't start trading stocks. What does she know about trading stocks?" He said, "Well, she's been doing well." I said, "If she wants to trade stocks, then tell her to start trading at a

discount house or online." He said, "But we don't have any money there." I said, "Tell me where to send it, and I'll send your money over there."

Well, he took his whole pension out for his wife. She just absolutely creamed it, and he's still working. It's just pathetic. But I wouldn't participate, because I am going to stand firm. I was able to avoid making a huge mistake. And if I had been wrong, well then at least they got to buy whatever they wanted to buy, wherever they are now. I did the right thing. I'm the advisor in this picture. How dare I, if I think it's wrong, do something just because the clients want to?

Meg had another client who wanted to buy stocks using money from his IRA. She refused to assist him, so he left her for another advisor. He eventually came back to Meg after losing good deal of his money:

I had a client whom I had known for a long time. A nervous Nellie I would call him, he was a retired physician and had some illnesses. He was not a happy camper and was focusing way too much on his portfolio. I knew for a fact that he couldn't withstand losses. Our portfolios for him were beautifully done, giving him everything that he should have, an 8 to 10 to 12 and even 14 percent return. But I wasn't giving him 90 percent returns, because I wasn't playing the tech game.

So he came to me at the end of '99. He said, "I want to get out of my value funds, my big old dividend-paying funds, and I want to buy Cisco, Intel, and Microsoft. And I want to invest a lot of money in them." So I said to him, "Well, I'm not doing that with you, because you know what the flip side of that is." He said, "But I really, really want to." So we had a whole discussion about it, and I said, "I hear you, but I am not prepared to sit with you while these things go crashing. And I don't know when they will. They might go up for another year or two. I have no idea. But there is going to be an end and you are not going to know when it is, and neither am I. This is so totally inappropriate for you, especially in your IRA. You can't even take losses."

He said, "It's my money." I said, "Well, you know what? I respect you. You have another broker. How about if we ship the funds that you want to invest in those assets over there. I'll sell what we have here. And then you can go buy it over there." He was very silent. Then he said, "Alright." And I did. And he did. But I have to tell you something: it's been a nightmare for him, because he invested just at the wrong time. Whatever is left of that money is back here now. The other broker took the trade, and never should have. But I refused to. We don't buckle if somebody wants us to do something that we know will turn out badly.

Paul Tramontano (Smith Barney) relates a similar story with a different ending. He and his team would not vary from their disciplines and eventually ended up losing the client for good:

> One client was very aggressive in asking us to buy tech stocks. And we wouldn't do it because we didn't think they were appropriate. And we didn't think that his net worth justified his being overweight in technology. He called every day for six months during 1999 and 2000. If CNBC came on and said that XYZ Semiconductor was going up, the phone would ring and this client would say that we should buy XYZ Semiconductor.
>
> I brought him in several times. I sat him down and explained why this stock wasn't appropriate for him. And I couldn't get through to him. He ended up moving to another firm. I regret that he was upset with me. But I know I did the right thing for him. I don't know what happened after that, but I hope that he didn't find somebody to get him invested. It would have been at exactly the wrong time.

Paul explains the importance of the disciplines that he and his team follow: "There were a lot of people out there howling that we weren't in enough of the names that they wanted to be in. But we just didn't do it. We resisted the temptation. We just didn't get away from our discipline, nor will we ever." Paul concludes that the biggest mistake an advisor can make is having clients' emotions dictate investment decisions:

> Probably the single biggest mistake is getting caught up in the short-term thought process of a couple of clients. Often clients will ask us in to change our direction when their financial picture and risk profile do not support the strategy. The only times we've actually made mistakes is when we've allowed clients to dictate too much as to how their specific investments should be handled. Generally, people say, "'I can take the risk if the market goes down," but often they actually cannot. To protect some investors from themselves, we have allowed them to direct some of their own investments with a small portion of their portfolio.

In most cases these investors have ended up rolling those accounts back into the overall portfolio.

For the most part, people listened to us and we were pretty good throughout the bubble part of the market. On the flip side, we had a similar stampede type mentality in 2002: a lot of people were thinking about throwing in the towel and said, "The market is going to be terrible for the next ten years and we really want out of it." And then lo and behold, 2003 turns out to be a terrific year in the market. So we try not to listen on either side, but if there has been a mistake we've made, it's been allowing our clients to take us away from what we do best.

Shelley Bergman (Bear Stearns) reflects on how he lost up to one-fifth of his accounts during the Internet era when he "wasn't willing to buckle" and give in to the demands of his clients:

In the late '90s and early 2000s, it was quite shocking to see how people just wanted to ride that Internet freight train, which they thought would never end. Twenty-three- or 25-year-old Internet CEOs would come speak to us about managing their money. We would sit down with them and talk about municipal bonds, corporate bonds, and income-producing securities. We would talk about putting some cash aside in Treasuries. But they didn't want to have anything to do with any of that. They were so adamant in their beliefs that technology was the way to go and that the Internet craze would never end. Our clients and prospects were beginning to believe that I was a dinosaur.

I would speak to other successful money managers, hedge fund managers, and my peers on a daily basis and we would say, "Hey, maybe we are missing something." And then we would come down to reality and say, "No, we are not. The world is not changing the way people think. These valuations are absurd. Eventually, it's going to come down." We did own some of the technology stocks in '95 through '99. But when they got up to 30, 40, or 50 times earnings and three or four times revenues, we were ready to sell.

The period of 1999 through 2000 was painful. We probably lost 20 percent of our accounts, because 20 percent growth a year was not enough. Some clients wanted 35 percent, 40 percent, or 50 percent. But I wasn't willing to buckle. We were in situations where accounts that I ran on a discretionary basis, whether for 40-year-olds, 60-year-olds, or 80-year-olds, were calling up, wanting to sell their large blue chips and utility stocks and go with Internet stocks.

We had quite a few accounts leave us. We were getting a lot of pushback from clients who said, "Cisco, iVillage, or eTOYS is the way to go." And for a couple of months and a couple of years, that was the way to go. But I don't know too many people who sold out at the top.

Overall, business was fine, because a huge number of people were calling, buying and selling all of these crazy Internet stocks in their nondiscretionary accounts. But some of the accounts that I managed and oversaw on a discretionary basis were being pulled out from under me. And it did hurt.

Martin Halbfinger (UBS) also experienced losing some assets when he refused to give in to the client "stampede":

As some of our clients got taken with the riches that were being made by their neighbors or their brother-in-law or who-ever, we basically said, "You just can't go there. You are asking for trouble." We were dogmatic about what they should and shouldn't do, and we lost some assets at that point in time. It was like swimming against the tide. Since then some of those who pursued "growthy" paths have wanted to reembrace a less volatile and more diversified strategy.

I can remember during that period spending about half of my time telling people what not to do. There are times when our practice is unexciting, but more often than not we are in the race, and we are always there at the end. That's just who we are, and that's the model that we pursue. When any position or asset class becomes overweighted, we are going to cut it back. When an asset class is very depressed and we think it may have a good run coming in three years or less, we get more interested. Also, I think you have to call an equity an equity and make sure that you put into the equity category all things that behave like equi-ties. Don't have a misguided approach that one equity is safer and another is more speculative or more growth oriented.

ALL FIRED UP

Passions ran so high during the tech bubble period that sometimes clients would fire advisors preemptively so they could do as they pleased. Louis Chiavacci (Merrill Lynch) tells an ironic story: "The last time we lost clients because of performance was in the late '90s.

Two families fired us, and one of the primary reasons was that we had purchased REITs for them. They wanted us to put them in tech or large-cap growth, and they told us they were moving the accounts because we just didn't "get it." They said, "Everybody else in the world realizes that there is a technological revolution going on and are profiting from it, and here you guys have us in shopping centers, and nobody is ever going to go to a shopping center because they are going to buy everything over the Internet." Ironically, five years later, what's been the best performing asset class? REITs."

As the bubble was inflating in 1998, with the S&P returning 28.34 percent, Louis and his team stuck to their value-based disciplines: Their core portfolio trailed by over 13 percentage points; in 1999 the core portfolio returned 22.22 percent, in line with the index. "I was taught to buy low and sell high," Louis says with a chuckle, then points to reports on the table that proves his unwavering faithfulness to his value-based strategy. "At times, we may have felt a bit foolish—often wondering if we were missing something—for not jumping on the bandwagon, but we stuck to our principles. We understand our circle of competence, and not straying from it is an important part of being successful. Our clients are sophisticated individuals who rely on our honest advice and thorough understanding of the markets; one way we earn their trust is by being consistent and sticking to our discipline."

Louis will forever blame himself, however, for not trying harder with one client. In 1998 he earned a referral client who had sold his engineering parts manufacturing business for over $100 million in the 1980s. After the first meeting, the prospect asked Louis to model a $5 million portfolio. Based on the prospect's objectives, Louis's team put together a plan that included an allocation of 26 percent to high-quality, short-term municipal bonds, 10 percent to high-yield corporate bonds, 34 percent to domestic equities, and 10 percent to international equities. Ten percent was appropriated to real estate and 10 percent to futures managers. Louis singled out a dozen portfolio managers, each with a strong long-term performance record, who would be used for these investments. The client was provided with their performance records versus benchmarks, and correlation analyses among the managers and asset classes. Also included in the analyses were complete risk measures, risk-return, and market-line analyses, the proposed portfolio versus its individual components, historical best and worst performances, and more. This plethora of data was then inserted into Monte Carlo simulations to provide a range of expected returns over varying timelines.

The team also provided intensive historical relative-value analyses and economic scenarios for each asset class that justified asset allocations. All in all, the analyses showed that the portfolio would provide far less risk than an all-equity portfolio.

Impressed with this work, in early 1998 the client engaged the team with an initial investment of $35 million. The assets were allocated according to the proposed plan. With almost no exposure to technology stocks, in 1998 and 1999 the diversified portfolio performed according to plan, but behind the technology-laden NASDAQ and S&P 500 indices. In December 1999, only weeks prior to the peak of the tech bubble, the client fired Louis, citing underperformance and an allocation in REITs. "Although we realized we were missing a major move in the market, and even lost a client because of it, we stuck to our principles," Louis says. "To us, it's more important not to lose money than to make money." In early 2000, the client found an advisor who invested most the portfolio in high-growth stocks, only to see a substantial portion of his net worth vanish in the ensuing months.

Louis says, "Losing that client made us a better team. We realized we lost the client not just because of underperformance, but also because of how we communicated our performance to him. We should have done a better job educating him And I shouldn't have let him jump into the market with or without me." At the time Louis made his recommendations, REITs were yielding almost 10 percent and trading at almost a 30 percent discount to net asset value. "We perform extensive relative-value analyses for our clients to determine which sectors are expensive and which are inexpensive," Louis explains. "Thankfully we have built tremendous confidence and trust among our clients; otherwise they may have thought we were crazy at the time."

A relatively common occurrence during the bubble involved clients who felt quite strongly about their own abilities and the money they could make on tech-related stocks. These clients would take a substantial chunk of their portfolio away from their advisor and trade online instead. Often, the final outcomes were not what the clients had hoped they would be, as John D. Olson (Merrill Lynch) describes in this story of a client whose remaining assets eventually came back to him:

> Here's a story about a 15-year client. We met with him, did the portfolio analysis, allocated his investments the way we do it, and went through the whole process. He got a tip in '99 on a

stock that went up just about as much as anything that I've ever seen. The product was something that would speed everything up through the Internet pipeline. The stock kept splitting, literally every month or so. You'd have to look at the charts, but it was unbelievable. On a split-adjusted basis, it went from about 20 cents to about $120. So he bought some at $5, and at $10, and at $20. I kept saying, "Be careful," but then he bought some more at $90. And he kept buying it and he never sold it, because he obviously had it all figured out. Then a friend of his told him about an Internet trading strategy. So he moved a majority of the assets to an E-Trade account where he could do it very cheaply, because he was the one who had all the ideas. It was probably about 80 percent of his financial assets.

I said, "Do a little bit of it if you have to. But don't base your financial future on it. The music is going to stop some day." I don't know, maybe he thought that I had my own interests in trying to keep his assets, but he didn't listen. I never saw his statements, but the stock now is back to about 50 cents. With all of his Internet trading, I'm sure he lost almost everything. He still kept a little with me, though, and now his money has all come back to me.

FIRMLY DIVERSIFYING

Clients associated with companies that were acquired or that went public during the tech-bubble run-up often had substantial amounts of capital to invest. Michael Johnston relates an interesting story where one client initially placed his money with three different advisors in three different firms. Eventually the client brought all his remaining assets back to Michael, since only he had invested conservatively in accordance with the principles of asset allocation, and only he had taken *all* of the client's investments into consideration, including those with other advisors and other firms:

> I have a client whose company had been acquired in 1998. As he was selling out of his stock position in 1999 and 2000, he "diversified." He thought that diversification meant giving me a third of his money, giving his advisor at Firm B a third of his money, and giving his other advisor at Firm C a third of his money. Now, I was the only one of the three advisors who asked the client what he was investing in at the other two firms in order to determine what asset classes I should invest in for him at my firm.

During that time period, technology stocks were hot. large-cap growth was hot. The advisor at Firm B knew that they were in competition with the advisor at Firm C and with me. And the advisor at Firm C knew that they were in competition with the advisor at Firm B and with me, as well. And so, what those two firms did was to put the client's money in those asset classes that were doing the best because they felt that they were in a horse race, trying to compete on performance, based upon this client's stated objective. "Hey, I'm going to split the money out and see who does a better job."

Well, I viewed doing a better job as giving the client the best risk-adjusted return as opposed to who's out there maybe giving the client the best absolute return, independent of risk. What happened? As the tech bubble burst, and as the S&P 500 dropped 44 percent from peak to trough, the client became very upset with the other two firms because they were losing a lot of money relative to my asset allocation. Those particular firms didn't have any alternative investments in their portfolios. They didn't have any small-cap value within their portfolios. They didn't have any bond market exposure. So, in the end, the client consolidated his portfolios from Firm B and Firm C with me. I felt like I was already managing those assets even when they were housed at the other firms, because they were incorporated within my asset allocation, finally I was getting paid on those assets as well.

Another type of portfolio over concentration arose during the tech bubble when one or more stocks would outperform month after month. As Paul Tramontano describes it, "It was an interesting time, and the situation taught us a lot about asset allocation. People were not afraid to have a stock grow to be 10 or 20 or 30 percent of their portfolios. In today's world, of course, this makes no sense, and it probably has only happened a few times over the last hundred years. But each time it happens, people are loath to sell. It makes no sense to them to sell anything. It's a good company and they want to stay with it. Of course, we know now that things change, and you have to have a discipline, and try to stay with your discipline, in all types of markets. That's part of our job."

Paul also feels that it's his job to make sure clients are not just properly asset allocated, but also properly diversified. He explains what he means by this distinction and why it's important:

During the tech bubble we kept saying to anybody who would listen that this is not a new paradigm and that markets do not change. If anything, the tech bubble made us acutely aware of how important asset allocation is, and more importantly, how important diversification is. Many times people came in and said, "Well, I am allocated properly. I own telecom and tech. I don't just own telecom." In their own minds, they thought they were fine, but when you looked at the three mutual funds they owned, their compositions were all the same. So, in addition to understanding that asset allocation was important, the bubble really made people focus on diversification within that asset allocation.

The simple way I would look at it is that asset allocation is the bigger macro look, the big groups, whether it's fixed income, cash, or equities. And diversification is looking within those groups and making sure you are properly diversified there If you have a hedge fund portfolio, don't just have only one or have all event-driven or all arbitrage. If you look at your equity investments, make sure you are diversified in equities. If you look at your fixed income investments, make sure you are laddered and diversified in different kinds of issues and maturities. Its diversification within asset allocation. You can have a perfect asset allocation with 40 percent of your money in fixed income which turns out to be centered in New York Port Authority Bonds, and then a plane flies into a building.

Jon Goldstein (Smith Barney) offers an interesting perspective on why individuals who owned stocks that were doing very well— especially if they played a role in creating the company—had such a hard time diversifying during the tech bubble, as well as a possible solution that takes advantage of the consultative nature of the wealth management approach:

> For a long time, clients were right if they wanted to hold onto their stocks. "Gee, you wanted me to sell at 70 and it's at 120 now." And it goes to 160 or 180, and then it's going up so fast that they want to hold on, they are almost paralyzed. It never rolls over. Then the response gets interesting because it's something like, "Oh, you know, it was just slightly overvalued" as it's gone from 160 down to 120. "It needed to take a breather" as it dips to 70 or 80. "Well, okay, it's a little bit of a correction. I think it's going back to 120." But it's really on its way to 4. And then they are just paralyzed.

Most wealthy people in this country created their wealth through a concentrated equity position, or building a business, or something in that manner. And most of the people we are working with are executives who had a lot to do with building a business. And they know it so well, and have such a comfort level with it, that when you ask them to get out of their "baby" and diversify into other investments, it becomes an emotional decision.

A lot of it is realizing that you have to give clients an understanding of what a diversified portfolio is. How the money is going to be run. How we are going to track it. How we are going to monitor it. And I think that is why the consulting model is a good fit for these people, because they can track things. It's almost like running a company, when they've got their dashboards of everything they are looking at to make sure that sales and manufacturing and all of that lines up. So we provide a report, and we can come to them as their personal CFO and say, "Okay, here's how the portfolio is doing. Here's how it should do going forward. Here's how it has done in the past. Here's how we benchmark it." I think that once they get more comfortable with that, then they can begin to let go of their concentrated position.

Steve Hefter (Morgan Stanley, Riverwoods, Illinois), who works with high and ultra-high-net-worth clients, corporations, and foundations, illustrates the importance of diversification when he describes how a wealthy client was unwilling to diversify his holdings. The client had built a very successful company that merged with another company during the height of the tech boom in 2000. For several years before then, Steve and his partner, Ben Leshem, attempted to educate the client about the advantages of selling some of his stock and diversifying his portfolio, pointing out that founders and executives of many companies sell at least some of their holdings.

But the client refused. "He was getting great accolades on his company," says Steve, "and he felt that nothing could grow in the same way that he could grow the net worth of his company and therefore his own net worth. A diversified portfolio was simply not appealing to him. The bulk of his net worth was in the company stock, and he wouldn't sell or collar any shares." Unfortunately, the merged company failed, and its shares plunged. "He took his shot and went for the gold," says Steve, "and ended up with nothing, basically."

To get his clients to diversify from overconcentrated positions, Sanford Katz (UBS) relates how he would approach them from a rational perspective, asking them to evaluate from a business perspective whether it made sense to have so much of their wealth in one company: "When we had concentrated positions in networking or telecom companies, I would always tell clients that they needed to constantly look at accelerating the diversification process. I grew up working in traditional retail businesses and family ice cream stores and things like that. So I would always tell them to look at the company's income statement, its growth prospects, how competitive the industry is, and what kind of rosy profit margin projections were being made on their products. Keeping in mind that they are losing money, and have never had a profitable quarter, even if they were to achieve their revenue targets, is the stock price justified? In other words, look at this as if it was a shoe store. Would you buy stock in it at this valuation, at an infinite multiple of earnings? Of course not. If you won the lottery, would you put all your money in it? Because that's what you are doing now, predominantly for capital gains reasons."

Sanford describes in more detail his observations about overconcentrated clients, especially those in the technology sector, and how over time he has learned to communicate to them the importance of being diversified:

> The tendency for people in any business is to want to stick with what they know, and that tendency is even greater in the technology business. It's unfortunately a bias that still exists in the Bay Area, and I don't think it will ever go away. I think some hard lessons were learned, not just by financial advisors, but obviously by clients.
>
> We didn't have a crystal ball, but it was just common sense in terms of the necessity to diversify. A client would often come back and say, "I understand all of that, but I know this business" or "I know the semiconductor business" or "I understand Internet Commerce" or whatever it is. I have learned to acknowledge to a client that "Yes, you do, and that's how you made your wealth. And you made your wealth through controlling business interests in that industry. But now that you have been acquired it is passive investing, without perfect information, in a rapidly moving industry. Much more so than industrial or traditional businesses." What I now tell them, almost in their face, is "You may know the business, you may be right about the product's superiority. You may be right about management, you may be right about a lot of things, but you don't have the expertise to parlay that into understanding valuation, or the valuation of that company versus comparable companies, or how that valuation

fluctuates with the slightest change in variables as to revenue or demand or profit margins, and all the things that go into determining a stock's earnings multiple and essentially the price."

Then people start to see the light a little bit. Usually we'll try to give them some room to do that, if they want, and point out to them that surprises occur and those surprises can have a great impact on a single stock position. I think we've gotten well past having clients say, "I only want to hold technology and only five or ten stocks, because I really know these companies." It's a long process, because you are trying to change people's attitudes.

Shelley Bergman (Bear Stearns) describes how one very reluctant client ended being up very happy that he had listened to Shelley's advice:

A client who came to us was the CEO of an Internet company. I sat down with this gentleman and his wife and we discussed how I saw things and what they should be doing. I said to them, "Look, your Internet stock may continue going higher. Your technology private placements may continue to go higher. Your hedge funds, also with a technology bias, may continue to go higher. But let's just take $50 million out of your portfolio (worth about a billion), and put it in municipal bonds. We'll clip coupons at 5 percent. You will get about $2.5 million a year, or roughly $200,000 a month. I'm sure you can live very nicely on that, even if everything else crashes and burns."

It was difficult to get this couple to listen. But they did put approximately $40 million into municipal bonds. And everything else pretty much disappeared. We couldn't do much about it because he was locked up and couldn't sell any more shares. I advised him to sell what he could sell, and he did take some cards off the table.

These clients were very glad that they did what they did, and now they have a very nice lifestyle. Some people tend to count from the top and think that they lost $950 million. Those who don't focus on what they have today.

You heard it all over the street in '99 and 2000. There were many people who had $100 million worth of restricted company stock and were living as if they had $100 million in cash or bonds. They were going out and buying $10 million homes. They were buying planes. They were buying second homes. And when their stocks plummeted from $50 a share to $5, their accounts turned upside down. You read about it. You saw it. You heard about it. And we witnessed it in certain situations.

Mark Sear (Merrill Lynch) describes a situation in which only one of several families that met with him was willing to diversify out of a hot stock. In the end, that one family did much better than the others, and now constitutes one of Mark's biggest and best relationships:

> There was a family that lived in southern California and that sold a private company to a public company for 100 percent stock. This public company was very acquisitive, and it was a hot stock. I probably represented and got in front of five or six families that sold out to the same company, and the stock was between $25 and $35 during the time. When we went to present to these families, in every instance we talked about diversification and selling the stock. We talked about doing collars or prepaid forwards, about doing an exchange fund, and about a number of charitable techniques to diversify and have a charitable benefit. In every instance but this one family, people sold only a small amount of stock or none. Why would they? The stock kept going up. The stock was a monster.
>
> So this one family, through me, sold every share they had. Every single share. They gave half the money to another firm. I don't know what the other firm recommended. But I know what I recommended. We sold every single share of stock that day it came in, and the stock went from a high of $38 to about $3. All I know is that family moved every dollar they had moved to the other firm back over to me, and the value was a lot less than when they first moved it there. Today, they are one of my best accounts, and they've referred a lot of business to me.

SOME SAD STORIES

Unfortunately, many advisors have stories of clients who got caught up in the dot.com hype, who did not listen to their advisors, and who have ended up in a far worse financial position than they ever expected to be in. Jim McCabe tells a story about one of his clients who did not come to a particularly good end:

> We had one client who, unfortunately, no longer qualifies as a client. He's a very smart man and a very good human being. When we met, he had $10 million in money market funds. So he invested $2 million with us.

With a 41 percent average annual return, $2 million turned into $4 million in two years. However, separately he took $2 million and margined and leveraged his investments and they grew to over $20 million. He said, "Why do I need your paltry 41 percent when I did this on my own?" Even though we discussed risk adjusted returns and sector diversification, in early 2000 he directed us to transfer the $4 million in kind to his online account.

He was completely caught up in the market in early 2000. Today, his liquid net worth is less than $400,000. It's a sad story. He certainly would have never had to work again, but now he probably does.

Earlier in this chapter Ron Carson described a situation where he never found out what happened to a client who left him after he and his team stuck to their guns and didn't waiver from their asset allocation disciplines. Ron relates another story, a sad story, where he did find out what happened with a client who left him during the height of the tech bubble:

We managed the 401K for a company, and we handled the finances for a guy who worked for the company. He originally wanted a modest rate of return, and we had done much better for him than the target rate. But then he got a stock tip or two from his golf pro, and the worst thing that could possibly happen, happened: He bought a couple of these stocks on his own, and they did extremely well. Of course, it was the '90s. Everything was going straight up. And when he left the company to retire, he rolled all of his money into an IRA with me. These were all the financial assets he had in the world to live on. He was doing so well with his stock trades that he said, "Ron, I'm going to transfer the account to a discount brokerage firm, and I'm going to just buy and sell. I can do this on my own, basically."

Later, I came to find out that *he had lost every penny he had.* I was at a funeral earlier this year and we were waiting in line, and I saw him and his wife walk in. He came up to me and asked how I was doing. I said, "Good," and then I asked him how he was doing. He said, "Well, you know, I had to go back to work." This guy is about 78 years old. I said I had heard he had some rough times with his portfolio. He said, "Yes, I sure wish I had never left you. I think we all got caught up in the times." Then he added, "I remember giving you a bad time about owning all those bonds. I sure wish we still had those bonds."

SOME HAPPY STORIES

Paul Tramontano describes how by following his instincts in accordance with the principles of asset allocation, he was able to help one family preserve their capital despite the crash of the tech bubble:

> During the bull market, we had a client, a wealthy family, with a really large allocation to equities. And within that allocation to equities, they had large allocations in some of the tech areas. And so, as part of our rebalancing and quarterly reviewing throughout 1999 and 2000, we were trimming those tech holdings and moving money to cash, which we did routinely for a lot of clients. But with this one particular family, we spent a lot of time trimming and moving money to cash because, at the time, they had a full allocation of bonds, and we didn't have other assets that we were investing in.
>
> I can't sit here and tell you we knew tech was going to do what it did for the next couple of years, but we did feel it was overvalued and we took out those pieces of people's portfolios. And so now, five years later, we've been able to preserve an enormous amount of wealth, probably close to $40 million, that came out of those positions for a family that normally, had we not focused on it quarterly, would have found it hard to make the decision to pay a big, big tax on something that had a very low cost basis in order to make that change.

Jon Goldstein and his partner Dana Jackson (Smith Barney) explain how the strategy that they followed was successful in preserving the capital of most of their clients. According to Jon:

> There might have been a small handful of clients who left. But for the most part, we are so consistent in explaining our approach that after several years I think we got through to our clients. They understood what was going on. It was difficult in '99 to sit back and watch tech-oriented funds really sizzle, and some of our growth-oriented managers definitely pursued that momentum. Some were doing quite well, but unfortunately they paid the price on the way down. They didn't recognize that things change.
>
> Fortunately, the bulk of what we do is so defensively oriented that the idea of being balanced was redeemed. The idea of holding bonds is new to most individuals when they accumulate wealth, but it was always a foundation of our capital preservation strategy.

Dana then explains a bit about how they spoke to their clients about their real needs:

> You ask them, "Why? What is your goal here? What are you trying to do? Are you really trying to take the $5 or $10 million that you have and make it $20 million? Won't you do that anyway?" You have to remind people that there's no scoreboard and this is not a race. Around here in Silicon Valley, it's a little bit warped. If you've got $20 million, maybe you are done, and you can take the rest of your money and roll the dice a little bit because you want to be richer than the guy next door. But people got really hurt playing that game. You try to remind them that they've got to take care of their family. A lot of these people worked incredibly hard to make their fortunes. Yes, they were a little lucky. Did all the stars line up in the late '90s? They did. But that doesn't take away from the fact that these guys went out and took a lot of risk, building products in their garage, spending 18 hours a day sleeping at the office. And now it's time to pay their families back, and they really owe it to themselves to sock away the mattress money by making sure a significant portion of their portfolio is safe. Did we get through to everybody? No. Will it be a lot easier next time? Sure.

Jon concludes with a few final observations on human nature and the importance of getting out of overconcentrated positions: "It's about greed and fear. People were looking at returns in a vacuum and they forgot about the other side of the equation, which is risk. But basic mistakes were not made so much in portfolios, as in holding onto concentrated stocks. You get answers like, 'It's going higher,' or 'I don't want to pay the tax.' Sometime you can appeal to them and say, 'Well, how are you going to live any differently if it doubles again?' And the answer, obviously, is they won't. But as Dana mentioned, it became scorekeeping."

For Martin Halbfinger, not only did most of his clients not suffer the downsides of the bear market, many did quite well during that period of time:

> In all honesty, we missed the bubble, and not because we were so smart. It's just that we aren't ever going to be in the most speculative part of the market regardless of how appealing it looks. We never had a lot of exposure to tech because I didn't understand it, so I couldn't be comfortable with it as a large portion of clients' portfolios. So, when things got too pricey, we got very

uncomfortable. But we moved a lot of people into the alternative space in the late '90s. So, where we were very fortunate for our clients is when they were yelling for growth, we were putting them into some low-volatility hedge fund managers with great track records.

For Martin and his clients, "That turned out to be a fantastic way to not experience the bear market. We actually had a very calm period in the bear market. Our business grew substantially when everybody else was not having a good time. We did find a way to participate in equities, but we found it in a much safer vein, where there was real hedging going on in both the long and short side of the market. I am a big believer that that's what you need in the low-growth or nongrowth environment that I think we are now in."

FORGETTING AND REMEMBERING

In the heat of the moment, in the middle of an inflating bubble, it is all too easy for clients (and some advisors) to forget the core tenets of asset allocation. In fact, while the truths behind asset do not change, the receptivity of clients to asset allocation does seem to depend on what's happened recently in the market. As Kathy Tully (Morgan Stanley) puts it, "People have very short-term memories. Now they buy into asset allocation because it was just yesterday that we had this major pullback. I don't see a problem right now, but as time goes forward it will be interesting to see if that awareness and the value of sector rotation changes. I'm sure I will have to do a little bit more educating and reminding, because when times get good, people get a little greedy."

Jon Goldstein relates how he and his partner Dana Jackson have experienced changes in the receptivity of clients to asset allocation over time:

> When Dana and I started, we went to great efforts to build efficient frontier models. It was still in the infancy of these kinds of desktop packages. We invested a lot of time, attention, and money in these client presentations, explaining the asset allocation process and why our consulting approach made a lot more sense than just trying to buy stocks. Clients were really receptive to this. They understood it. It was a revelation in many ways— just basic portfolio theory being explained to them.
>
> And then, as the markets got hotter and hotter in the late '90s, we found a less and less receptive audience to asset allocation,

which almost got a reputation as being a little stodgy; certainly, it was not getting the kind of returns that the NASDAQ was getting. If you didn't own stocks, portfolios weren't performing. Now we've absolutely come full circle. The bear market took out all the big gains that were there, while asset allocation strategies preserved a lot of wealth during that time period. Now, once again, we've got a very receptive audience.

Jon concludes that not only does recent history provide important lessons, it leaves advisors with a certain type of mandate and responsibility: "History is a great provider of lessons. We had a front row seat for both the inflation and the deflation of that bubble. So we share experiences with clients who maybe didn't see things the way we did, and that's always been the basis of our approach to clients. 'Look,' we say, 'this might be your first or even second time in creating wealth. We've lived through this dozens upon dozens of times with clients. And our primary responsibility is to share those experiences with you and help you make better decisions.' So yes, the bubble was a pretty important event for us."

Joe Jacques (Jacques Financial) shares his view of human nature, and his belief that the next time the market starts doing very well, it will be incumbent on advisors to continue educating clients and remind them of what happened back in the year 2000:

> I find that people are basically greedy. We all want the upside without the downside risk. I believe that the real estate market is going to start plateauing, which historically indicates that the stock market is going to start reacting positively, at least over the next five years. And yes, at the end of those five years, when the stock market has started to do very well, we are going to have to be even more diligent about educating our clients, because they will have forgotten the losses of the early 2000s. They are going to come back to me and say, "If you can't guarantee me 15 percent, I am going to deal with somebody else." I know that is going to happen again.

Joe does, however, feel that to a certain degree, fewer individuals will be tempted to "day trade" on their own the next time. "All the do-it-yourselfers, I think, threw up their hands and we've gotten a lot more business since then. The diehard day traders won't give up, but the people who were just trying to buy a stock or two on an ongoing basis with E-Trade and lost their shirts won't want to do that anymore."

John Rafal feels that in the future, when the next red-hot sector emerges, the key is to be forceful with clients and to document the discussions that are had: "Things will eventually get hot. We don't know when or what the next bubble will be, but we know there will be a bubble. I think you have to be very forceful in getting clients to concur with everything that you want them to do. But you also have to document that we had the discussion and what was said and what wasn't said."

Mark Curtis emphasizes that asset allocation did not stop working during the tech bubble; instead, people stopped following the disciplines of asset allocation.

> At the end of the '90s, large-cap growth stocks and technology stocks soared. But the disconnect that happened was not that asset allocation didn't work, but that people's goals and objectives changed. They forgot why they were diversifying their portfolios in the first place. The thing about asset allocation is that you have to be willing to have one part of your portfolio not do well while the other part is doing well, and people simply lost that perspective, that reality check.

Ron Carson similarly feels that people are quite likely to forget many of the lessons learned the next time some sector gets overheated and are especially likely to forget the need to diversify: "It's human nature. Enron originally started here in Omaha. So we had a lot of Enron clients, and we said, 'No more than 5 percent in any single stock, ever, even if it is your company's stock.' We also had a lot of WorldCom stock. Both those companies obviously went broke. Most people diversified, because here in the Midwest we are conservative. But to this day, there are people who run around with 100 percent of their portfolio in UPS stock or 100 percent of their portfolio in Proctor & Gamble. They say, 'That can never happen to this kind of company.' Listen. That's what everyone thought about Enron and WorldCom. As a society, we continue to make the same mistakes over and over. That's why we will always give our clients discipline, and why we will always be there."

Jim McCabe (Wells Fargo Investments) feels that we have already lost some of the lessons from the tech bubble. With respect to the real estate sector and REITs, he says, "Some people have not learned from the past. People are purchasing real estate with 100 percent financing. The real estate bubble could be even more dangerous because people are gambling with their most important asset, their home. When mortgage rates go up, prices will go down, and they could be forced to sell their homes. With tech stocks they lost only their capital. They can lose a lot more than that in a leveraged housing bubble."

OPPORTUNITY GOING FORWARD

Louis Chiavacci (Merrill Lynch) points out that while the crash of the tech bubble was difficult for many, it also created opportunities that fed right into the asset allocation approach going forward: "The other side of the story with the tech bubble is that in the late '90s we had the opportunity to buy certain assets at extraordinarily cheap levels. Value stocks. Specialty small-cap value was at a 15-year aberration in terms of its undervaluation. In 2002, high-yield bonds got to a level of spread to Treasuries that we had not experienced for 10 or 12 years. REITs got to a level of undervaluation in 1999 that had, to my knowledge, never been experienced in their history. So, at the same time that you had large-cap growth stocks, not just tech and telecom, at extraordinarily expensive levels, you also had other opportunities."

In reflecting on the tech bubble, Jim McCabe's focus is on the future. "Many people have pulled back from the equity markets. Some have gone from 100 percent to 0 percent in equities, which is a mistake. Others have held the course. Some people chase markets, and now that there have been a few good years of equity returns, they are back to 100 percent equities. I think we need to help people temper all-or-nothing behavior and look at the long term, not invest with a rearview mirror. Individually and collectively we need to lead and educate our clients and the public at large."

Joe Jacques thinks that many clients learned an important lesson from the tech bubble, and that post 9/11, asset allocation is working better than ever:

> Asset allocation works even better since 9/11. Before that, everything was growing; everybody was willing to take great risk because they didn't think there were really going to be any downside consequences. Everybody was making money. No matter what they touched, people were making money. Clients would tell me technology stocks were doing great and were never going to go down, and that's what they wanted me to put them in. And I just told them to go to somebody else because I was not going to do that. That's not my MO. I have always diversified.
>
> Now clients are coming back to me, saying, "Okay, I don't want to go it alone any more. I want a professional to handle my port-

folio, because I found that I don't want to spend the time, nor am I capable of doing it." People used to come in and demand a guaranteed 15 percent. Now those same people are saying, "If you can get me a 5 percent return, I am happy. And I am willing to give up my upside if you can protect my downside."

THE UNFORTUNATE NECESSITY OF ESTATE PLANNING

As described throughout this book, high-net-worth individuals, especially youthful entrepreneurs, are often susceptible to overconcentrating their portfolios in their own company's stocks, or in high-growth equity issues generally. Unfortunately, life can take sudden and unexpected turns for the worse, and that's why sensible and comprehensive estate planning should be woven into asset allocation strategies and put into practice for everyone.

In the summer of 2001, Raj Sharma (Merrill Lynch) recommended that a new client follow a wealth preservation plan, which included estate planning. The client, a 30-something-year-old founder of a technology company that had gone public replied heedlessly: "I'm too young. I've got all the time in the world." Once Raj and team took the entrepreneur, a non-U.S. citizen, and his family through their multistep wealth management process, Raj's first order of business was estate planning.

Raj recommended a Q-DOT, or qualified domestic trust, which preserves the marital deduction when the surviving spouse is not a citizen. The trust would pay principal and interest to the family for the rest of their lives, which complemented Raj's wealth preservation strategy. Until that point, the client's orientation had still been growth oriented. "They just didn't need to take risk," Raj says. When Raj informed him that in addition to capital gains taxes, 90 percent of his wealth would go to taxes upon his death, he changed his mind and followed Raj's advice.

Three months later the client died when his airplane crashed into Trade Tower Number One. Raj was there to console the family, helping them through an emotionally challenging experience. Fortunately, the last things the wife and two young children had to worry about were their financial affairs; Raj and his team simplified the process for them. And the client's decision to follow Raj's advice saved the family over $80 million in estate taxes.

Raj may appear to have been "lucky" in regard to the timing or in simply having done "what's best for the client" (his client satisfaction ratings are superior and his client-loss ratio is almost nil). In reality, he simply followed a series of processes that he replicates for every single client. He considers every client a "chairman of the board." He has developed his entire team to provide such extraordinary advice and personal service that a client may feel like Raj's only client. Raj asks the right questions. He listens. He leverages his team to offer superior and creative advice. Raj is emphatic about constant communication with clients to ensure not only high-quality service, but also that their investing plans effectively reflect their changing lives. "Building a relationship with a client," says Raj, "is not just a process of ensuring the proper management of their investments. It's really about understanding their psyche, what really concerns them, and what is most important to them."

THE REAL EFFICIENT FRONTIER

Postbubble, where does the real efficient frontier lie? As has been emphasized throughout this book, if asset allocation is an art and a science, it is probably the art, and especially the art of relationship, that is ultimately at its core. Meg Green relates that during a luncheon held to honor prominent women advisors she was asked for the secret of her success. "My answer," she said, "which everybody else agreed was also their answer, was that what makes us so successful is that when we first meet with a new client, we spend 95 percent of our time not talking about investments. We get to know the client, to know what counts for him. The investment end is not as important to the meeting as really understanding who this person is and what makes him tick." To bring this point home, Meg shares a story about one of her clients, a Holocaust survivor with a very different idea of where the real efficient frontier lies:

> The client I saw today, who just came into an amazing amount of wealth, is a Holocaust survivor. We sat down together and she spent the last 45 minutes of the meeting telling us about her escape from prison camp. The money per se means very little to her because, she said, "If you've ever been where I've been, what difference does this money make?" I said, "Maybe the reason you survived is to make a difference. And this money can help you do that."
>
> So we talked about gifting and how she was going to make a big difference in other people's worlds, but not so much about doing 38 percent in bonds, 10 percent in international bonds, just

a smidge in emerging markets, and then the rest mostly in large-cap value. Do you think she would even hear that? Not at all.

I did present her with a beautiful pie chart showing how we were asset allocating for her, which we had already sent to her accountant and her son so she'd be comfortable. But our meeting was all about meeting her granddaughter, whom she brought with her. We also talked about gifts, and she told me she had given her daughter-in-law an $11,000 check. She cried as she described what a wonderful feeling it had been to help her daughter-in-law.

That was our meeting. We did a lot of business, but never once did the words "asset allocation" come up. For my client, the "efficient frontier" was the point when she left the concentration camp and had to run across the snow and avoid the Russians who thought they were Germans. That's her efficient frontier. It's just a whole different way of being. The asset allocation, though, does have to get done. You can't take someone like this and say, "You know what? You've got so much money, I am now going to double it for you." That would not be appropriate. Instead, it's "Let's talk income. Let's talk about what you are going to do with this money, and how much you are going to give away." It's not about the asset allocation per se. It's about life.

CHAPTER 13: THE SINGLE MOST IMPORTANT THING ABOUT ASSET ALLOCATION

If asset allocation were reducible to a single concept or notion, then this book (as well as many other fine books on the subject) would not be necessary. Both as a science and as an art (especially the art of relationship), asset allocation embraces a wide range of details and nuances, and boiling it down to a single statement, concept, or principle that everyone would agree with would be a nearly impossible task. (Michael Johnston's answer in this chapter makes this point quite astutely.)

Instead, this chapter—the last chapter of the book—does the next best thing by presenting the collected wisdom of many of the top advisors we interviewed as to "the single most important thing about asset allocation." The context and meaning of these statements will be clearest if you have read through the rest of this book in order. But even if you start with this chapter, a good deal of what the advisors themselves think is most important about asset allocation will come through.

(Note: the advisors' comments are given in alphabetical order by first name.)

Drew Zager (Morgan Stanley)
A Focus on Themes

"When appropriate and depending upon the market environment, I think it's important to have an allocation to real estate securities, to alternative assets, to private equity, and so on. But I think it's more important to have themes, and some of my biggest clients certainly look at their particular asset allocation strategies in terms of themes.

"In my experience, ultrahigh-net-worth clients don't care if they have a public equity or a private equity, but they do want to know where they can get the best return relative to their risk tolerance. For example, if I'm looking to put money into real estate securities, I may speak with my clients about securities with exposure to real estate outside the United States, regardless of the type of instrument that packages that exposure. I like the theme idea—which focuses on types of exposures rather than types of instruments (i.e., private equity or alternatives as contrasted with publicly traded securities)—better than simply having money in instruments that are broadly labeled 'alternatives' or 'private equity.' "

Jim Hansberger (Smith Barney)
No Substitute For Experience

"Well, I would love to throw out something extraordinarily deep for you. You've done a very good job of covering all the bases. Possibly the only thing I would say here is that I genuinely don't believe there's any substitute for experience. No matter how gifted and how great a salesman, or how knowledgeable, or how perfect an education a younger advisors has, he or she would be well served by marrying up with an experienced colleague for at least a number of years. They would serve their clients better, and create a much longer and more prosperous career for themselves."

Jim McCabe (Wells Fargo Investments)
Returns

"The single most important thing about asset allocation is the consistency of long-term returns. It's simply selling expensive assets and buying cheap assets."

Joe Jacques (Jacques Financial)
Don't Put All Your Eggs ...

"Enron is a good example of why asset allocation is so important. Simply, you should not have all your eggs in one basket."

John Rafal (Essex Financial)
A Tool Leading to the Best Possible Outcome

"Asset allocation is a tool, a measuring device to allow you to ensure that your clients will have a correct, or at least a predictable, outcome. So asset allocation is simply a tool to ensure that the best possible agreed-upon outcome can be achieved. The bottom line is that asset allocation in theory leads to diversification, which in theory leads to safety, which in theory leads to a better result."

Jon Goldstein (Smith Barney)
A Means to an End

"The single most important thing about asset allocation is that it meets clients' needs and objectives. It's not an end unto itself; it is absolutely the means to an end. Without question, it starts and ends with the client."

Kathy Tully (Morgan Stanley)
Clients Really Understanding "Don't Put All Your Eggs ..."

"After 23 years in the business, it sounds silly saying, 'You can't have all your eggs in one basket.' People have heard that, and they've thought they believed it, but only now after living through the past five years are they true believers. Now they understand that 'not having all your eggs in one basket' means asset allocation, and not just having stocks and bonds, but what kind of stock funds and what kind of bonds. The past five years have proved the value and the true meaning of asset allocation. I don't have a difficult time selling the concept at all any more."

Louis Chiavacci (Merrill Lynch)
The Client's Temperament

"The single most important thing is the client's temperament. Trying to get the right portfolio in place and avoiding big mistakes is really our primary objective, and the biggest, most expensive mistakes that we have seen were decisions made under financial stress. As an investor, do not ever underestimate the stress of a prolonged bear market. It is very stressful. Especially your first one."

Mark Curtis (Smith Barney)
Managing Toward Your Real Goals

"The single most important thing about asset allocation is making sure your assets match your liabilities. Money is not a goal in and of itself. The goal is being able to do what you want to do. Flexibility and choice, that's the goal. This should mean that you are managing toward addressing your liabilities. Your asset allocation needs to reflect the reality of your current net worth, whatever you are going to save or inherit, and whatever other cash inflows you anticipate— balanced against your future needs or liabilities. Your asset allocation should not be aimed to make as much money as possible. It should be oriented toward getting you to your financial goal with as little risk as possible."

Mark Sear (Merrill Lynch)
Understanding How It Works and Its Limits

"I think the most important thing about asset allocation is understanding how it works, and understanding which clients it will benefit and which clients it won't. Everybody throws the term around.

Well, it is a cool concept, but you need to understand how it works, and you need to help clients understand how it benefits them."

Meg Green (Royal Alliance)
Clients Must Understand What Having an Asset Allocation Will Be Like

"The single most important thing? I think a very important thing is making sure your client understands that he or she has an asset allocation. They need to expect that there will be times when certain things are doing very well while other things are dragging. You need to let them know that some things are going to be darn boring. Bonds, for example, are sometimes in there just for diversification purposes, not because you really want to own bonds, but because it's inappropriate to have 100 percent equities."

Michael Johnston (Smith Barney)
Be Diversified in Approaching Asset Allocation

"It's hard to take something as complex as asset allocation and boil it down to the single most important thing, because if I named one thing as the single most important, that doesn't mean that the other five or six areas that you have to focus on to get an asset allocation done correctly aren't equally as important. So, just as you should have diversification in an asset allocation, I think in answering this question, you need to be diversified."

Paul Tramontano (Smith Barney)
Asking the Right Questions

"Asking the right questions. I think people in our position generally want to fit families and accounts into a box. The firm says the institutional asset allocation is 55, 40, and 5, and you've got to fit everybody into a box. I don't believe everybody needs to be in a box. I think it's more important to ask enough questions to really understand people. If you just ask the right questions, people will tell you what you need to know, and that's how you get a good asset allocation."

Ron Carson (Linsco/Private Ledger)
Clients Can Stay Invested and Sleep at Night

"Asset allocation allows people to stay invested and participate in the overall return of individual asset classes, but spread their risk over several asset classes. While they can still lose money, the goal is to lessen the effect that any one asset class has on the entire portfolio."

Sanford Katz (UBS)
Be Open-Minded to It and Treat It More as an
Art Than a Science

"The single most important thing about asset allocation is to be open to it. It's a process that's been developed over time and has proven statistically to be beneficial in reducing risk for a given level of return. You have to have an open mind toward learning that, believing it, and embracing it. While you can't control directions or events that influence market value, consider the analogy of driving a car. It's better to have a map and a steering wheel, even if it's not calibrated perfectly, than to let the car randomly run down the road and hope you will end up near your destination.

"I also find it to be more of an art and gut feel than it is a science. Scientific and quantifiable methods don't necessarily trump old-fashioned common sense. Taking a longer-term view that integrates what could go wrong with the model—what could go wrong in virtually every asset class at any time due to unforeseen events—is probably the best way to guard against the pitfalls of a purely quantitative approach."

Shelley Bergman (Bear Stearns)
The Way to Get Super Rich ... And Super Poor

"I am a strong believer in diversification, whether it is in my own account or the accounts of others. People who have more than 25 percent in one asset or one sector of an asset class are asking for trouble. I've often been told that the way to get super rich in America is to have too much in one stock. But the way to get super poor in America is also to have too much in one stock."

Tim Kneen (Citigroup Institutional Consulting)
Getting the Correlations and Inputs Right

"The most important thing about asset allocation is doing the correlation study right and using correct inputs. Asset allocation is not just diversifying for diversification's sake. It's diversifying for the purpose of adding value at the end of the day. There are only two ways to add value. You can diversify for increased returns, but if you believe as I do that all asset classes are created equal, then it is a zero-sum game. The only other thing left is diversification or asset allocation for the purpose of reducing risk. And if that's your goal, as it is mine, then the game is all about the correlations. Further, even if you get the correlations right, if you fail to have the correct expected returns on asset classes, your clients' expectations will be askew. An advisor must be able to understand how expected returns are arrived at and over what time frame they should be correct. If an advisor simply uses historical returns, the asset allocation model will be very biased toward the historical period that is chosen."

Appendix A: Table of Contributing Winner's Circle Advisors

This book would not have been possible without the generosity of time and spirit, and the depth of expertise, of the following financial advisors:

Rick Blosser, Morgan Stanley, Los Angeles, California

Shelley Bergman, Bear Stearns, New York, New York

Ron Carson, Linsco/Private Ledger, Omaha, Nebraska

Louis Chiavacci, Merrill Lynch, Louis Chiavacci & Team, Coral Gables, Florida.

Mark Curtis, Smith Barney, Palo Alto, California

Jon Goldstein, Smith Barney, Menlo Park, California

Meg Green, Royal Alliance, Meg Green & Associates, North Miami Beach, Florida

Martin Halbfinger, UBS, New York, New York

Jim Hansberger, Managing Director—Wealth Management, Smith Barney, The Hansberger Group, Atlanta, Georgia

Steve Hefter, Morgan Stanley, Riverwoods, Illinois

Dana Jackson, Smith Barney, Menlo Park, California

Joe Jacques, Jacques Financial, Rockville, Maryland

Michael Johnston, Smith Barney, Irvine, California

Sanford Katz, UBS, San Francisco, California

Tim Kneen, Citigroup Institutional Consulting, Englewood, Colorado

Jim McCabe, Wells Fargo Investments, Beverly Hills, California

Hank McClarty, Gratus Capital Management, Atlanta, Georgia

John D. Olson, Merrill Lynch, New York, New York

Brian Pfeifler, Morgan Stanley, New York, New York

John Rafal, Essex Financial, Essex, Connecticut

Mark Sear, Merrill Lynch, Los Angeles, California

Raj Sharma, Merrill Lynch, Boston, Massachusetts

Paul Tramontano, Smith Barney, New York, New York

Kathy Tully, Morgan Stanley, Ontario, California

Ira Walker, Morgan Stanley, Red Bank, New Jersey

Drew Zager, Morgan Stanley, Los Angeles, California

Richard Zinman, Smith Barney, New York, New York

Appendix B: A Brief History of Asset Allocation

Asset allocation has existed for less than 60 years as an academic concept, and has been put to widespread practical use for less than 30 years. For those who are interested, the chief value of reviewing its history comes from seeing both how critical ideas and tools can be invented by just one individual and how such ideas and tools can first slowly and then rapidly spread through the greater financial services industry and investment community. By considering the history of asset allocation, we gain perspective on its current importance, its long-term value, and the likelihood that some other theory and approach may eventually add to or transcend it.

If asset allocation is revolutionary, then how did this revolution begin? How did "don't put all your eggs in one basket" become leveraged by academic creativity and prodigious mathematics to the point where it has become the dominant paradigm of modern investment theory and practice? While there had been some previous academic work going back to the beginning of the twentieth century, and a few scattered literary suggestions before that, as Chapter 1 indicated, Modern Portfolio Theory (MPT) and asset allocation can be directly traced to the efforts of one man: Harry Markowitz.

A CHANCE CONVERSATION

Harry Max Markowitz was born in Chicago in 1927, an only child whose parents owned a small grocery store. In the autobiography he wrote in concert with being awarded the 1990 Nobel Prize in Economics, he relates that he always had his own room, had enough to eat, and was never even aware of the Great Depression. He was an ordinary enough kid, playing baseball and touch football, and reading *The Shadow* and other adventure magazines. While he tells us that "becoming an economist was not a childhood dream of mine," in high school Markowitz began to read the works of serious philosophers and scientists including David Hume and Charles Darwin.

While studying economics at the University of Chicago, he says, "When it was time for me to choose a topic for my dissertation, a chance conversation suggested the possibility of applying mathematical methods to the stock market." Encouraged by his professors,

Markowitz was provided a reading list to guide him through the financial theory and practice of the day:

> The basic concepts of portfolio theory came to me one afternoon in the library while reading John Burr Williams's *Theory of Investment Value*. Williams proposed that the value of a stock should equal the present value of its future dividends. Since future dividends are uncertain, I interpreted Williams's proposal to be to value a stock by its expected future dividends. But if the investor were only interested in expected values of securities, he or she would only be interested in the expected value of the portfolio; and to maximize the expected value of a portfolio, one need invest only in a single security. This, I knew, was not the way investors did or should act. Investors diversify because they are concerned with risk as well as return. Variance came to mind as a measure of risk. The fact that portfolio variance depended on security covariances added to the plausibility of the approach. Since there were two criteria, risk, and return, it was natural to assume that investors selected from the set of ... optimal risk-return combinations. [Markowitz, from *Lex Prix Nobel. The Nobel Prizes 1990*, Editor Tore Frängsmyr, Nobel Foundation, Stockholm, 1991]

Did Markowitz's ideas really come out of nowhere? Since he was attending one of the world's finest universities, and was being guided by some of most famous scholars of the day, Sir Isaac Newton's famous statement comes to mind: "If I have seen further it is by standing on the shoulders of giants." Mark Rubinstein in his "Markowitz's 'Portfolio Selection': A Fifty-Year Retrospective" (*Journal of Finance*, 2002), notes that a few writers and academicians had touched on some of the topics Markowitz would elaborate on, including Irving Fisher in *The Nature of Capital and Income* (The Macmillan Company, 1906), Markowitz's own dissertation supervisor, Jacob Marschak, and A. D. Roy ("Safety First and the Holding of Assets," *Econometrica*, 1952).

The mathematician Daniel Bernoulli had written in 1738 that "... it is advisable to divide goods which are exposed to some small danger into several portions rather than to risk them all together." And in *The Merchant of Venice*, William Shakespeare's Antonio says:

> ... I thank my fortune for it,
> My ventures are not in one bottom trusted,
> Nor to one place; nor is my whole estate
> Upon the fortune of the present year ...

As Roger C. Gibson points out in his fine book, *Asset Allocation: Balancing Financial Risk* (McGraw-Hill, 2000), there is an even earlier known source of asset allocation wisdom: the Talmud, which some 2,000 years ago proposed the following formula:

> Let every man divide his money into three parts, and invest a third in land, a third in business, and a third let him keep in reserve.

Gibson praises the unknown author of this formula for having come up with a strategy—investing one-third of a diversified portfolio in real estate, one-third in common stocks, and one-third in cash equivalents and bonds—as an effective diversified investment strategy that has worked well for two millennia!

Notwithstanding some of these earlier forays, it was there in the library, in embryonic form, that the basics of MPT and its practical offspring, asset allocation, sprang all at once from the brow of the then 25-year-old Harry Markowitz. He had recognized the importance of focusing on an entire portfolio, not just the individual stocks in it, and even more importantly, *he saw that investors must focus on balancing the possible rewards of investing with the risks of investing.*

Before Markowitz published his paper, most academic thinking and writing on investing had focused solely on the return side of the equation, giving risk and possible loss only a minimal amount of attention. After Markowitz, the necessity of focusing on and controlling risk came to the forefront, and a means to accomplish this had been made available. While risk could not be entirely eliminated, by focusing on the entire portfolio it could be acceptably controlled without a disproportionately large impact on expected return.

Markowitz published his landmark paper, "Portfolio Selection," in the March 1952 issue of the *Journal of Finance*. In 1959 he greatly elaborated on his ideas in *Portfolio Selection: Efficient Diversification of Investments* (Wiley). Markowitz's ideas received some academic attention in the 1950s and 1960s, and began to be practiced by institutional investors and advisors in the 1970s. According to the previously cited Mark Rubinstein (2002): "Markowitz's approach is now commonplace among institutional portfolio managers both to structure their portfolios and measure their performance. It has been generalized and refined in innumerable ways, and is even being used to manage the portfolios of ordinary investors. Its prescriptive extension has led to increasingly refined theories of the effects of risk on valuation. Indeed, *the ideas in his 1952 paper have become so interwoven into financial economics they can no longer be disentangled."* [Emphasis added.]

Markowitz went on to win the prestigious Von Neumann Prize in 1989 and the even more prestigious 1990 Nobel Prize in economics (along with Merton H. Miller, for his work on capital structure, and William F. Sharpe, for his work on the Capital Asset Pricing Model (CAPM), which is often considered part of MPT). Markowitz, who worked at the RAND Corporation after publishing his 1952 paper, is alive and well and serving as an advisor to fund managers at the time of this writing.

THE SPREAD OF ASSET ALLOCATION AND THE BRINSON STUDY

While the early academic history of asset allocation is widely known and fairly well agreed-upon, there are few records or studies of just how fast—and through what vectors—asset allocation spread to the general investment community and financial services industry. In the beginning, MPT and asset allocation actually took off quite slowly. Roger C. Gibson also tells us in his *Asset Allocation: Balancing Financial Risk* (McGraw-Hill, 2000) that "in the early 1960s the term asset allocation did not exist." What we do know is that it spread first through academia, as important contributions to MPT were made by such individuals as William Sharpe, who (at the encouragement of Markowitz) developed the Capital Asset Pricing Model, which describes how securities are priced based on the relationship between risk and expected return.

Asset allocation and MPT were first used as a practical tool in institutional settings. By the 1970s and early 1980s MPT and asset allocation were deployed in noninstitutional investment contexts, making an impact on the portfolios of the very affluent. This increasing usage was made possible in part because of the wider availability of computers which, through programs called MVOs (mean variance optimizers), made it possible to construct portfolios on the efficient frontier with relative ease. (Such portfolios, of course, were either constructed retrospectively, relying on past performance data, or were merely prospective predictions of where the efficient frontier would probably lie.)

It was in 1986, however, that Gary Brinson, a famed investor and money manager, published a watershed study, "Determinants of Portfolio Performance," in the July/August edition of *Financial Analysts Journal*. This study, which has since been repeated by both

Brinson and other academic researchers, with the same results, is at least partially responsible for catapulting asset allocation into its current position of nearly universal acceptance and usage.

Brinson's study analyzed the difference in returns among 91 large pension funds that had at least 40 quarters of performance history from 1974 to 1983. The managers of the funds had used a variety of different active management strategies, and the funds had experienced a wide range of returns over the time period in question. Brinson and his colleagues concluded that over 90 percent of the return variability between funds was attributable to the way the funds had allocated their investments among different classes of assets and that less than 10 percent of the return variability was due to the market timing and stock picking of the various fund managers. *Put differently, asset allocation was an order of magnitude more important than the combined effects of market timing and stock selection.*

The conclusions and methodology of this and similar studies have been debated ever since. For instance, in the February 1997 issue of the *Journal of Financial Planning*, William Jahnke published a well-known article, "The Asset Allocation Hoax." However, according to William Bernstein in *The Intelligent Asset Allocator* (McGraw-Hill, 2001), controversies over whether the studies got it right— whether it was 90 percent, or really only 50 percent or 30 percent, of the return variability that can be attributed to asset allocation—miss the point. Bernstein writes, "Market timing and security selection are obviously important. The only problem is that nobody achieves long-term success in the former, almost nobody in the latter. *Asset allocation is the only factor affecting your investments that you can actually influence."*

Appendix C: Checklists: Are You Really Practicing Asset Allocation?

The following checklists can help you rapidly determine whether you are fully and correctly practicing asset allocation as described in this book. While not a substitute for reading the book itself, the checklists will help point you in the right direction by bringing up relevant questions and ideas.

Note that these checklists are meant to be indicative and evocative, but not definitive, for not every single advisor who does a good or even great job in practicing the art and science of asset allocation will follow every single point in each checklist. Asset allocation is too broad and too diverse, and evolves too quickly, for any set of checklists to hope to definitively capture its fullness. Also note that while the checklists are crafted specifically from the perspective of an advisor serving individual and not institutional or organizational clients, most of the points apply regardless of the type or size of client in question.

1. ❏ **As a financial advisor, are you sufficiently knowledgeable about asset allocation to correctly practice it both as an art and as a science?**

    ❏ Are you sufficiently familiar with the basic principles of asset allocation, including but not limited to risk/return trade-off, correlation, the benefits of portfolio diversification, the efficient frontier, and the necessity of rebalancing?

    ❏ Do you understand how asset allocation is part of and functions as the "practical wing" of Modern Portfolio Theory (MPT)?

    ❏ Do you understand not only asset allocation, but also why it has become the dominant modern money management paradigm?

    ❏ Have you received a thorough education as to asset allocation either as an undergraduate, in business school, through your firm, or on your own?

    ❏ Have you spent sufficient time reading and learning about asset allocation?

❏ Have you kept up with your knowledge over time, that is, have you continued to upgrade both your knowledge and your practice of asset allocation over time?

❏ Have you discussed asset allocation with other members of your team and other financial advisors?

❏ Is each of your team members 100 percent behind the practice of asset allocation for appropriate clients?

❏ Do you understand how asset allocation dovetails with the notion of a client-centric wealth management approach, and do you follow such an approach?

❏ Do you understand why asset allocation is both an art and a science, and do you practice it from both perspectives as appropriate?

2. ❏ **Is your client suitable for an asset allocation approach?**

❏ Does your client have sufficient assets for you to be able to fully practice asset allocation on his or her behalf?

❏ If not, do you have an alternative advisor or other recommendations, such as turnkey asset allocation funds or index funds, for your client?

❏ Have you explained the basics of asset allocation to your client?

❏ Did your client understand these when you explained them?

❏ In particular, is your client clear about the benefits and the possible detriments of the asset allocation approach?

❏ Is your client interested either in preserving his or her capital, or growing it steadily over time, as opposed to attempting to rapidly grow it?

❏ Does your client have a reasonably long time horizon, sufficient to reap the benefits of asset allocation?

❏ Does your client have the general temperament to fully cooperate with you in an asset allocation approach to managing his or her portfolio?

❏ Does your client understand that as some parts of his or her asset-allocated portfolio are going up, other parts will necessarily be going down or will remain steady?

❏ Is your client prepared to hold steady with an agreed-to asset allocation plan whether the market is experiencing a bubble or hot sector growth or is experiencing a sudden or ongoing downturn?

❏ Have you explained the basics of rebalancing to your client, and is your client willing to fully cooperate as you rebalance on a regular schedule or on an ad hoc basis when necessary?

❏ Does your client have a realistic expectation of the long-term portfolio returns that an asset allocation approach is likely to generate?

3. ❏ **Have you correctly understood and determined your client's "inner" or subjective needs, i.e., his or her goals, dreams, hopes, and risk tolerance?**

❏ Are you fully determined to follow the wealth management approach and put the needs, goals, and dreams of your client first and foremost?

❏ Have you spent sufficient personal time with your client to get to know him or her well personally?

❏ Have you used questionnaires, personal interviews, or some other means to develop a deep understanding of the subjective components of your clients needs?

❏ Do you have a good sense of your client's psychological risk tolerance as well as how loss averse he or she is?

❏ Do you know how "bothered" your client will be if his or her portfolio or components of it underperform compared to specific indices?

❏ Do you have a good sense of your client's goals, dreams, and hopes for the future?

❏ Do you correctly understand who all the members of your client's family are and how they fit into your client's life?

❏ Do you have a good sense of your client's family needs and situation, including likely future liabilities such as college funding, taking care of elderly parents, buying cars or homes for family members, etc.?

❏ Do you have a good sense of your client's retirement needs and estate planning preferences?

❏ Do you have a good sense of your client's philanthropic desires, if any?

❏ Do you know what kind of general asset allocation approach—very conservative, conservative, moderate, aggressive, very aggressive—will be necessary for your client (and for you) to sleep at night?

❏ Do you have a thorough understanding of your client's psychological liquidity needs for the immediate future and the likely long run?

❏ Have you made certain to find out whether there is anything else about your client's unique situation that should or will play a role in his or her asset allocation?

4. ❏ **Have you correctly gathered and understood all necessary objective information about your client's current financial and legal status?**

❏ If necessary, have you helped your client to organize and bring order to his or her financial and legal situation, including obtaining, sorting through, and organizing all necessary and relevant documents?

❏ Have you gathered all objective financial information relating to your client, including brokerage accounts and statements, bank account information, retirement accounts and pensions, cash and cash equivalents, outside business ownership, consolidated financial balance sheets, etc.?

❏ Have you made sure to inquire about assets held with other financial advisors or firms so that you can take those into account as you craft recommendations for your client's asset allocation?

❏ Have you gathered all objective legal information relating to your client, such as wills, grants, trusts, deeds and titles to real and personal property, contracts, family partnerships documents, etc.?

❏ Have you gathered a list of, and do you understand the history and value of, all of your client's real property holdings?

❏ Have you gathered a list of, and do you understand the value of, all of your client's substantial nonfinancial assets, such as precious metals, jewelry, antiques, titled collectibles, etc.?

❏ Have you made sure your client has an estate plan, and if your client does not have one, are you facilitating the creation of one as soon as possible?

❏ Assuming your client does have an estate plan, do you have a copy of it, and if so, have you read it, understood it, and checked to see (or had someone with legal knowledge check to see) that it is up-to-date, sensible, and enforceable?

❏ Do you have a thorough understanding of your client's actual cash flow situation and liquidity needs for the immediate future and the likely long run?

❏ Do you have a thorough understanding of your client's current and likely future tax situation?

5. ❏ **Have you recommended and executed an appropriate asset allocation for your client's portfolio?**

❏ Have you taken all the subjective and objective information about your client, from the financial and legal to the personal and idiosyncratic, into consideration?

❏ Have you taken all of your client's assets into consideration?

❏ Have you specifically worked backward from your client's liquidity needs?

❏ Have you specifically taken your client's actual and psychological risk tolerance, as well as their degree of loss aversion, into account?

❏ Have you specifically taken your client's current and likely future tax situation into account?

❏ Have you turned to high-quality research, either from within or from outside your firm, to choose asset classes and specific investments that are appropriate for your client's needs and desired return?

❏ Are there any specific macrolevel, strategic, or long-term themes that you are following with respect to the recommendations you are making?

❏ Have you recommended asset classes and specific investments that are both substantially diversified and reasonably non-highly correlated with each other?

❏ Are you familiar with a wide range of asset classes or subclasses, and have you considered an appropriate number of these in making your recommendations?

❏ Do you believe in style box diversification, and, if so, have you taken this into account in making your recommendations?

❏ Have you excluded any asset classes simply because you do not like them or are not comfortable with them, and, if so, is this truly in the client's best interest?

❏ Are your recommendations likely to provide your client with the desired return at an acceptable level of risk?

❏ Are your recommendations likely to provide your client with the necessary return at the lowest possible level of risk?

❏ Have you determined whether the portfolio mix you are recommending is at least retrospectively located at the efficient frontier?

❏ Have you used all software, programs, or outside information sources at your disposal to help you make the best possible asset allocation recommendations to your client?

❏ Have you recommended that your client move out of any overconcentrated stock positions and have you facilitated at least the start of that process?

❏ Before actually buying and selling any necessary securities, have you fully communicated your recommendations to your client?

❏ Is your client in full agreement as to, and completely comfortable with, your asset allocation recommendations, or are additional iterations and the refinement of your recommendations necessary?

❏ Have you received a clear go-ahead from your client?

❏ Having received the go-ahead from your client, have you executed the necessary transactions in as timely, efficient, and effective a manner as possible?

❏ Have you created an asset allocation policy statement or other record of your recommendations that you can later share with your client if he or she is tempted to make unwise or untimely decisions?

6. ❏ **Do you understand the importance of rebalancing, and do you follow a sensible rebalancing schedule?**

❏ Do you understand the importance and benefits of regular rebalancing?

❏ Do you understand the difference between "Return to Target Allocation" rebalancing, "Strategic Needs" rebalancing,

"Strategic Outlook" rebalancing, and "Tactical" rebalancing, as described in Chapter 8?

❏ Are you clear about which of these four types of rebalancing you are or will be engaging in?

❏ Have you explained the benefits of rebalancing (and in particular "Return to Target Allocation" rebalancing) to your client, and does your client understand these benefits?

❏ Do you understand the disadvantages associated with rebalancing, including potential expense and tax implications for the client, as well as the overall effort on your part that will be required?

❏ Does your client understand these disadvantages?

❏ Do you regularly monitor each of your clients' portfolios to see if any rebalancing is necessary or called for?

❏ Do you regularly monitor and stay apprised of the personal situation (e.g., changes in financial situation, liquidity needs, money in motion) of each of your clients to see if any strategic needs rebalancing is called for?

❏ Do you regularly monitor the performance of funds and managers to see if any rebalancing within asset classes is called for?

❏ Do you meet with your clients on a regular basis to discuss their portfolio generally and to specifically consider their asset allocation and whether any rebalancing is necessary or called for?

❏ Do you have any type of automated warning or triggering system that alerts you when a portfolio has wandered too far from its target asset allocation percentages?

7. ❏ **Have you learned the necessary lessons from the dot.com bubble era?**

❏ Are you prepared to avert panic during the next major market downturn by regularly checking in with your clients, holding their hands, and doing whatever is necessary to stay the course?

❏ During the next bubble, whenever it happens and whatever its focus is, are you willing to "stick to your guns" and not listen to your clients' desires to abandon their asset allocation for overheated sectors, asset classes, or subasset classes?

❏ Are you willing to "stick to your guns" even at the risk of losing clients or assets under management?

❏ Have you insisted that your clients move out of overconcentrated stock positions and then facilitated that movement?

❏ Have you regularly rebalanced to move your client out of his or her best performing assets, regardless of how "hot" they are, to effectuate a "sell high, buy low" strategy?

❏ Are you prepared for your clients to forget everything that they learned during the dot.com bubble the next time there is a sudden or prolonged market upturn?

❏ Are you prepared to take advantage of whatever opportunities arise the next time there is a bubble that crashes or a market upturn that suddenly ends?